Medieval Arms & Armour: A Sourcebook

Armour and Weapons

ISSN 1746-9449

Series Editors

Kelly DeVries
Robert W. Jones
Robert C. Woosnam-Savage

Throughout history armour and weapons have been not merely the preserve of the warrior in battles and warfare, but potent symbols in their own right (the sword of chivalry, the heraldic shield) representing the hunt and hall as well as the battlefield. This series aims to provide a forum for critical studies of all aspects of arms and armour and their technologies, from the end of the Roman Empire to the dawn of the modern world; both new research and works of synthesis are encouraged.

New proposals for the series are welcomed; they should be sent to the publisher at the address below.

Boydell & Brewer Limited
PO Box 9
Woodbridge, Suffolk, IP12 3DF
editorial@boydell.co.uk

*Previously published titles in the series
are listed at the back of this volume*

Medieval Arms & Armour: A Sourcebook

Volume III: 1450–1500

Ralph Moffat

THE BOYDELL PRESS

First published 2024
The Boydell Press, Woodbridge

ISBN 978 1 83765 196 2

The Boydell Press is an imprint of Boydell & Brewer Ltd
PO Box 9, Woodbridge, Suffolk IP12 3DF, UK
and of Boydell & Brewer Inc.
668 Mt Hope Avenue, Rochester, NY 14620–2731, USA
website: www.boydellandbrewer.com

The publisher has no responsibility for the continued existence or accuracy of URLs for
external or third-party internet websites referred to in this book, and does not guarantee
that any content on such websites is, or will remain, accurate or appropriate

A CIP catalogue record for this book is available
from the British Library

For Mr Robert C. Woosnam-Savage –
a fellow of infinite wisdom, generosity, and (of course) jest.

Contents

List of Illustrations

The illustrations are reproduced with the generous assistance of the A. V. B. Norman Research Trust.

List of Documents

Preface

> Bien parece [Sancho] – respondió don Quijote – que no estás cursado en esto de las aventuras: ellos son gigantes; y si tienes miedo, quítate de ahí, y ponte en oración en el espacio que yo voy a entrar con ellos en fiera y desigual batalla.

> 'Well doth it appear [Sancho],' – answered Don Quixote – 'that thou be'st unstudièd in these quests: they *are* giants; and *if* thou be'st afear'd, flee hence, and pray that I shall enter this place with them in fierce and disadvantagèd battle!'

> —Don Quixote.[1]

Meanings change with the passage of time. The eccentric Don's giants are not arrayed at the far end of a tiltyard, nor are his *lanza* and *adarga antigua* the type of lance and shield used in the joust. Only with the introduction of the tilt barrier was the concomitant verb employed. Yet 'tilting at windmills' has become part of the lexicon of everyday speech. Such is the case with medieval arms and armour. It is only by returning to original primary sources that we can gain a better comprehension of the subject. The purpose of this book is to make such sources as accessible as possible to the widest readership. From living history practitioners and crafters to curators and academics there will be *something* of interest. It is inevitable that, just as the deluded Knight of La Mancha mistook windmills for giants, I too have undoubtedly done likewise with some of my interpretations.

---

[1] Miguel de Cervantes Saavedra, *El ingenioso hidalgo Don Quijote de la Mancha* (Madrid, 1605), Book 1, Chap. 8.

Acknowledgments

I would like to thank Profs Stephen Bowd (especially for sharing **72**), Rosalind Brown-Grant, Francesco Guidi Bruscoli, Wendy Childs, Kelly DeVries, Noel Fallows, Drs Tobias Capwell, Mario Damen, Jacob Henry Deacon, Evan Jones, Robert W. Jones, Mario Scalini, Dan Spencer, Mark Tizzoni (especially for translation assistance with **18**, **38**, **56**, and **70**), Iason-Eleftherios Tzouriadis, Mrs Anne Norman, Caroline Moffat, Ms Gemma Andrews, Laura Bennetts, Lucinda Byatt (especially for translation assistance with **34** and **55**), Polly Cancro, Margherita Chiolo, Margaret Condon (especially for generously sharing **48**), Julia Cook, Samantha Gilchrist, Géraldine Glover, Véronique Gorczynski, Lydiane Gueit-Montchal, Deirdre Jackson, Kathryn Jones, Kaitlyn Krieg, Becky Loughead, Caroline Palmer, Iona Shepherd, Sandrine Verreaux, Karen Watts, Amanda Williams, Anna Wreyford, Messers Alan Broadfoot, Nick Clark, Benedetto Luigi Compagnoni, Enzo di Cosmo, Keith Dowen (especially for generously sharing **74**), Andrew Gray, Stuart Ivinson, Philip Lankester, Simon Metcalf, Matthias Millon, Stuart Pyhrr, Helmut Selzer, Jean-Jacques Vandewalle, my colleagues at Glasgow Museums, the Royal Armouries, and the universities of Edinburgh, Glasgow, and Leeds, the team at Boydell, and my family.

Using the Sourcebook

This sourcebook can be used simply as a glossary to quickly check meanings. The documents are printed in chronological order. Each is numbered. When referred to in this section and the illustrated glossary the document number is in bold font in parenthesis, e.g. (**37**). In addition, the volume is furnished with a comprehensive index. The work can, however, be used at a more advanced level in order for the reader to build up their own better understanding of the subject. I provide here one case-study, concerning a Milanese armourer in France, to demonstrate how this can be achieved.

In his letter to the Duke of Milan (**55**), the Milanese Jacomino Ayroldo, armourer to Louis XI of France, makes mention of armourers 'who were sent to the Glorious Dauphin, who returned to Milan when the work was completed' ('quilli fureno madati al glorioso dalphino che complito el lavore retornareno a Millano'). But Jacomino writes this to placate the recipient. Our sources reveal that not all of these men returned. The 'Glorious Dauphin' was Louis' father Charles VII. In a letter of 1455 from the Duke of Milan to Charles (**7**), he requests that the King:

> grant and concede licence to Balzarino da Trezzo, armourer of this Our city, to bring from this Our city to France […] 20 bales of steel for the use of the Most Serene Majesty the King

> voy debiati dare facoltà et concedere licenzia a Balzarino da Trezo armorero de questa nostra cita, de conducere de questa nostra cita, in Franza […] vinti baloni de azale per uso de la Serenissima Maestà del Re

However, he also requests that His Majesty should deign to:

> annul and revoke the assurance that the said Balzarino gave to not bring any workers of his craft outwith Our jurisdiction, although his workers shall always remain bound [to Us] in the event that he wrongfully threatens or brings workers there against Our orders.

> annullare et reuocare la segurtade quale dicto Balzarino havea data de non condure alcuni lavoratori de l'arte sua fuora della nostra jurisdictione, remanendo però sempre obligati li suoi in casu ch'el contrafacese in menare o condure li lavoratori contro l' ordini nostri.

Despite this request, the Duke's ship had well and truly sailed. Two brothers described as 'Our well beloved friends Gasparin and Balsarin de Trez, merchants, natives of the town of Milan' ('noz bien amez gasparin & balsarin de trez marchans natifz de la ville de milan') had been granted royal *lettres de naturalité* in March 1449 (probably old style).[2] The King acknowledged 'the good and agreeable services that the said supplicants have given Us in times past in the sale of harness, We wishing to attract it to Our realm' ('des bons et aggreables seruices que lesd' supplians nous on faiz le temps passe oud' fait de marchandise de harnoiz et voulans Iceulx atraire en n[ost] red' Royaume'). Furthermore, an undated document grants royal permission to 'n[ost]re bien ame balsarin de trez n[ost]re armurier' to transport all the 'marchandise darmures et brigandines' from his household ('mesnaige') at Tours to Bourges.[3] One of the signatories is Jacques Coeur.

It is the record of the dealings of this merchant prince (**14**) that provides so much detail as to the business of the Da Trezzo brothers. Three of the King's bean-counters (his *procureur général*, *sécretaire*, and a treasurer) are sent to conduct a thorough audit. They make a visit to 'Balzarino's workshops, forges, lodgings, and the harness mill in this town of Bourges' ('les asteliers forges hostilz et le moulin a harnoiz de balsarin estant en ceste ville de bourges') and find his accounts in disarray – even ordering him to put them 'en ordre & bon Langaige'. In winding up the accounts, in which substantial sums are recorded, there is mentioned the 'white harness and brigandines which are made in the workshop built and overseen in the town of Bourges by the said brothers' ('harnoiz blanc et de briguandines que on fait de la boutique levee et decree en la ville de Bourges par lesdiz freres').

Using our sources to chart the brothers' progress throws up many questions. What would a warrior from any part of Christendom consider to be a 'harness of Milan' (e.g. **36**, **44**, **65**)? Was this purely based on makers' marks? A merchant's agent in London complained that his 'harneyse complete of the touche of Milleyn' had been stolen by revolting peasants.[4] Another merchant there had traded twenty-one 'harneys of melentouche clene and complete' for nineteen butts of sweet wine.[5] But did such a harness have to be made in the city of Milan itself or its environs? René, duke of Anjou, lavished funds on members of his household so that they could buy armour in the city (**10**) and Henrich – a Swabian imperial governor – contracted armourers there to make horse armour (**7**). Could a harness be made from parts – either roughed-out forms or finished components – exported then assembled elsewhere? Would one made by a Milanese craftsman based in another realm still be considered a 'harness of Milan'? For example, an armourer based in Bruges writes a letter (in heavily Italian-inflected French) promising a bespoke harness for a wealthy English merchant (**43**). And what about differing styles? A Brescian noble purchased a French-style sallet ('vna celada ala franciza') (**72**) and ten new complete armours in the French style ('10

2   Paris, Archives nationales, JJ//180, fol. 42r.
3   Paris, Bibliothèque nationale de France, MS fr. 5727, fol. 115v.
4   *Paston Letters and Papers of the Fifteenth Century*, ed. N. Davis, vol. 2 (Oxford, 1976), p. 314.
5   *Calendar of Plea and Memoranda Rolls of the City of London, 1458–82*, ed. P. E. Jones (1961), p. 12.

armature complete nuove alla foggia francese') were produced by Milanese craftsmen (7). What category would these fall under?

The fact that the field of arms and armour study is one where questions vastly outnumber answers should be viewed in a positive light. That there remains so much yet to be explained is our challenge: a gauntlet thrown down that we must take up.

English Pronunciation

Here I offer a simple guide by the use of rhyme and homophones:

- armet as *are met*, as in: we *are met* in such a place
- basinet as *bass* (fish) *in it*
- bevor with *Trevor*
- couter as *cow ter* (the *ter* in *terror*)
- cuirass – the first syllable can be pronounced *queer* or *cure* (as in *to heal*)
- cuir bouilli as *queer bully*
- cuisse with *quiche* but the initial *qu* sound as in *quack*
- gorget as *gorge it*
- grapper with *trapper*
- pallet as in *colour palette*
- pauldron as *(a)ppalled Ron*
- pisan as *peas Anne*
- poleyn as *Paul ain* (the *ain* in *pain*)
- pollaxe with *doll axe*
- *sallet* with *mallet*

Part I

Introduction to the Source-Types

I

Textual Source-Types

The written sources can be split into two general categories: official documents and prose. By 'official' I mean those of a legally-binding type such as wills, inventories, acts of parliament, legal dealings, craft statutes, and mercantile sources. The 'prose' category includes chroniclers' accounts, fictional stories, personal correspondence, and the advice of experts.

Official Source-Types

Wills, Inventories and Household Accounts, and Legal Documents

The legally-binding nature of these document-types necessitates a certain precision of language by their producers. We have in them, therefore, an invaluable resource for our study.

In his will, a Lincolnshire knight ensures his kinsmen are well provided with 'hole harnas of plate' and axes; and his servants with jacks, sallets, and bows (**3**). Amongst the bequests of two citizens of Douai are a crossbow affectionately named 'Little Bell' and a mail shirt of the type hidden beneath civilian clothing (**39, 64**).

An inventory of Winchester College armoury (**1**) shows it to be well provided with body armour and weapons and a barrel for cleaning mail. There are, among the possessions of four citizens of Douai (**13, 23, 30,** and **52**), such oddities as hounskulls, *huvettes*, and plançons. A Lombardy-made basinet would have been a treasured possession. Precious to our study is a very rare instance of the term *tonlet* which is discussed in detail in the illustrated glossary. A Breton nobleman is in possession of two spears of a distinct type – one for hunting the other for single combat, and a silver-decorated sallet (**27**). A man-at-arms (**35**) in the service of the *Sénéchal* of Santoigne has fine plumes to adorn his horse's shaffron.

Items of note in the Tower of London (**19**) in 1455 are training swords with blunted blades (wasters) and a little gilt harness. The Tower's 'remain' of 1492 (**67**) lists many different sorts of gun.

Whilst Reims (**50**) has an adequate supply of 'Habillemens de guerre' for its defence, it is the awesome might of the English war machine that is made plain in the victualling of the encincture of fortresses defending the Calais Pale (**45, 47, 49, 53, 57, 60, 61, 63, 65, 68**). These sources are crucial to tracing the development of the terminology of gunpowder weapons – as is an inventory of the Château of Montbeton (**70**) which lists falcons and arquebuses. The longbow was still a trusted weapon and we find various arrow-lengths recorded in inches (**53**).

The wily old veteran Sir John Fastolf paid for the construction of his castle with ill-gotten gains from the wars in France. The inventory (**25**) lists much fine armour and weapons as well as revealing his penchant for hunting-themed tapestries. That of William Catesby (**59**) explains to us the changing terminology of plate defences for the arms and shoulders (see the illustrated glossary under *Bumbards*).

We are presented with a curious kind of museum at the Château of Amboise (**89**). There appear to be labels explaining each object allowing us to gawp at such exhibits as Lancelot of the Lake's sword, the harness of the Maid of Orléans (Joan of Arc), and the black-velvet-covered armour of John, Lord Talbot – a man lionised as a paragon of chivalry by *both* sides in the Hundred Years War (see **21**).

Household Accounts

These are a veritable treasure trove of information. They too are legally-binding documents and are most often compiled by professionals who must be accurate in their use of terminology.

The Hostiller of Durham Priory (**12**) makes payment for 'Scowrynge' mail and oil for its protection from rust. René, duke of Anjou, invests in some secret jousting equipment. The pig fat and olive oil purchased for the care of his harness was no doubt the finest from his beloved Provence (**10**).

Guillaume, the Prince-Bishop of Toul (**16**), was evidently not a man who took needless risks. He had his torso-defences proofed by crossbow-shot under the watchful eye of trusted members of his household. A French-style sallet and two more that have been broken by crossbows appear in the accounts of a Brescian noble family (**71**).

Other Legal Documents

In records of lawbreaking, we gain insight into the efficacy of weapons: the widow of a murder victim (**6**) blames a bloodthirsty gang 'arraied in fourme of werre' armed with 'unmerciable forbodon wepons'; one of Nottingham's City Watch is assaulted with a langue de boeuf, a type of wide-bladed staff weapon (**15**).

The *Journal* of Maître Jehan Dauvet (**14**) is an audit of the business affairs of the merchant prince Jacques Coeur. It provides a great deal of information about the setup at Bourges and Tours of the Milanese Da Trezzo brothers, as investigated in the Using the Sourcebook section above. It is in the latter city that a harness mill (**28**) is sold by a father to his son – both of them armourers.

Court Pothof (**17**) can certainly be identified as the Conrad Putholf who paid tax on his imports to London in the late 1440s.[1] A bill of debt lists stock, including very

---

[1]   R. Moffat, *Medieval Arms and Armour: A Sourcebook. Volume II: 1400–1450* (Woodbridge, 2024), doc. 103.

poor-quality armour, at Southwark; some of it barely worth more than the roll of parchment on which it is recorded.

Two sources provide useful information about the common soldier. The first is a muster roll of the townsmen of Bridport (**24**). A few have complete harnesses or brigandines – one even has a gun – but most have jacks, sallets, knives, and bows and sheaves of arrows. Interestingly, there are women's names recorded. Due to their social standing, it is more likely that they are providing the equipment for others rather than fighting themselves.

The second is an act of the Scottish Parliament (**66**). It stipulates the battlegear, and concomitant fines for the lack thereof, that must be provided by able-bodied men of the kingdom between the ages of sixteen and sixty at the 'wapynschawing' held four times a year. There is also the threat of a stiff penalty for time wasted playing football, golf, and suchlike 'vnproffitable' sports, this time being better spent training for the defence of the realm.

Royal Decrees, Payments, and Correspondence

The fatal consequences of an altercation in a tavern are reported in a letter of remission (**37**). This provides us with an early instance of the partisan in a French context.

A key member of the English royal household is the master of the high-status boys raised therein (**42**). Not only is he to teach them how armour is borne and jousting skills but also proficiency in languages and musicianship.

English royal payments include those made for bows and gunners (**26**) and for equipment for the garrison at Calais (**44**). One (**32**) covers the wages of the servants who bring 200 jousting spears for May jousts. After all the action they must scour the lists to collect all the reusable metal fittings of the shattered spear-shafts. Henry VI orders the sergeant of his armoury to oversee the proofing of his brigandines (**20**) and to cover the best in purple velvet. The King is very tardy in payment to the craftsman who made them.

Due to the content of the remainder of the English royal correspondence it is discussed in the Mercantile Sources section below.

Craft Statutes and Related Documents

There is an air of desperation in the language of the statutes of the armourers of both London (**4**) and Paris (**11**). The Londoners refer to the privileges established in their statute of 1347 for the inspection of all armour put up for sale. This matter also concerns the Parisians. It is in this source that we have a clear explanation of how plate armour must be proofed and marked accordingly.

If the second half of our century witnessed the fortunes of these two capitals' armourers wane, then truly there waxed those of another city along with its environs. We are most fortunate to have so many sources concerning Milanese armourers (**7**). Just two examples are the production of plate armour for horses and the sum spent on fine fabrics for a cuirass for Duke Francesco's eight-year-old son. In a legal agreement between the armourers and armour-furbishers (**18**) the minimum rates for the refurbishment of individual pieces of plate armour are set and business contracts restricted so that they may only be made between recognised masters of the craft. A master from this city contracts an armourer (**38**) for piecework making plate armour, some of it in various foreign styles. The contractor's prospect of having to share his bed with *two* fellow workers at the end of a hard day's toil cannot have been an enticing one.

Other craft-types are also to be found. That it was deemed necessary to commission new punches to mark armour with the coat of arms of the City of Tours (**41**) shows that the old ones must have worn out through extensive use. The detailed instructions (**2**) for the construction of a tomb effigy (Figure 1) of an illustrious English nobleman ensure that the brass-founder works from the patterns provided.

Mercantile Sources

The products made by the craftsmen in the sources discussed in the section above required an extensive network of merchants to supply the demand from their clientele across Europe. Arms and armour were shipped with various other goods in the capacious carracks owned by such well-connected mercantile houses as the Genoese Grimaldi, Venetian Giustinian, and Florentine Bardi. These were berthed at the English ports of Southampton (**9**) and Sandwich (**29, 31, 46, 58**).

Edward IV is provided with gear for his own person (**36**) from the celebrated Missaglia firm of armourers-cum-merchants. Significant to our study is the fact that this document contains the earliest, as yet known, reference in English to a horse bard – although it is made of cuir bouilli (hardened animal hide) not of plate. Richard III ensures that the 168 good-quality complete harnesses landed at Sandwich are delivered directly to the Tower (**58**). Olivier de La Marche was an urbane Burgundian courtier and insightful chronicler. A royal decree (**40**) proves he was also a peddler of run-of-the-mill military equipment to a war-torn English realm.

Lastly, the haubergeons and basinets shipped from Bristol to Ireland befit many of that island's warriors' manner of fighting (**48**).

Prose Source-Types

Personal Correspondence

Three well-known letters are here printed and translated in full. Each serves to hammer home the importance of the correct fit of a good harness. A Bruges-based armourer, Martin Rondelle (**43**), tactfully discerns if his client has put on weight since his measurements were last taken and enquires as to the fashion desired. There is a decidedly sniffy tone to the Milanese ambassador's missive to his patron (**34**). A skilled master armourer is permitted, even encouraged, to spend a great deal of time with the French King studying his delicate frame – even in the royal bedchamber! This same king's own armourer points out to the Duke of Milan (**55**) that it is preferable for His Majesty and His courtiers to be studied in person rather than sending measurements and harness back and forth. It is for this reason that a small group of craftsmen should be granted permission to travel.

In a fourth source of this type, René, duke of Anjou, expresses his life-long passion for shooting the crossbow, gifting his finest to a friend in a touching, if somewhat boastful, letter scrawled in his own hand (**51**).

Narratives, Descriptions, and Two Tall Tales

Both the courtier-chronicler, Olivier de La Marche, and an anonymous writer pen vivid narratives of the combat at the *Pas d'armes* of the Fountain of Tears (**5**). Although the drama and pageantry of such ostentatious events was inspired by chivalric romance, the combats themselves – and the injuries sustained – were all too real.

For a well-travelled French herald, the Bavarians are fine crossbowmen (**8**).[2] Their choice of bows of composite construction is due to the fact that these are perfectly suited to withstand the great fluctuations in seasonal temperatures.

The Paris-based scholar from Rome, Domenico Mancini, takes the time to include in his report from England a description of its soldiers and their gear (**56**). The archers have hands and arms of iron. Moreover, he is astonished that even women know how to draw a bow.[3]

Of the two short stories from *Les cent nouvelles nouvelles* (**21**) one is a little *risqué* and the other is very humorous. Both give us a valuable insight into the arms and armour in use by men from different levels of society at the time of their composition.

Expert Writers

René, duke of Anjou, humbly referred to his extraordinary work (**22**) on how to hold the perfect tournament as a 'petit traictie'.[4] It is undeniably much, much, more than this. In this extract we receive his meticulous instructions for arming both man and mount complimented by detailed illustrations (Figure 12i. to Figure 12ix.).

Jehan de Bueil, author of *Le Jouvencel*, was a hard fighting man who had spent a lifetime in arms. In this passage (**33**) he indirectly instructs us – through the character of an observant grizzled greybeard – on how best to protect the head with an armet in mounted combat.

---

2 Victor Gay, in his *Glossaire archéologique du Moyen Âge et de la Renaissance*, vol. 1 (Paris, 1887), p. 50, dates this passage to 1455. One of the reviewers kindly raised this point. The original manuscript, however, is not dated precisely to this year.

3 One of the reviewers has generously drawn my attention to a recent edition of this source in its entirety. Domenico Mancini, *De occupatione regni Anglie*, ed. and trans., with intro. and historical notes, A. Carson (Horstead, Sussex, 2021).

4 Paris, Bibliothèque nationale de France, MS fr. 2695, fol. 1r. For an in-depth study that includes some discussion of the arms and armour depicted, see J. Sturgeon, *Text and Image in René d'Anjou's Livre des Tournois: Constructing Authority and Identity in Fifteenth-Century Court Culture* (Woodbridge, 2022).

In a short extract from his comprehensive instructional work on military matters the Milan-based Iberian fightmaster, Pietro Monte, opines on the quality of iron and steel for armour and the different tempering techniques (**69**).

The English manuscript produced at the behest of Sir John Astley (**62**) must rank as one of the sources most celebrated by our discipline's disciples. In the first extract, an anonymous writer (or writers) draws us to the lists to be spectators of a joust of peace. The specialised equipment that was well developed by this time is itemised in detail. The second extract, with its remarkable illustration (Figure 26), provides step-by-step instructions for arming for foot combat. The reader must bear in mind that these serve only one specific purpose. The writer refers to the 'day that the Pelaunt and the defendaunt shall' fighte' – here employing the long-established legal terminology of the trial by combat.

Intriguing recipes and – somewhat foul-smelling – recommendations for the care of armour (**73**) were scribbled by a London merchant in his commonplace book at the start of the sixteenth century. Due to the nature of the other contents, such as fourteenth-century poetry, it can be confidently asserted that these texts are very likely much older.

Note on Transcription and Translation

Transcription

> I found at times scraps of parchment that had drifted down from the scriptorium and the library and had survived like treasures buried in the earth.
>
> —Adso of Melk.[5]

The fictional image of an aged monk scavenging fragments from an ancient monastery utterly destroyed in a conflagration captures vividly my attempts to salvage some of what has been lost. Quite a few of our documents have only just endured the ravages of time. In many cases the parchment or paper is in very poor condition, sometimes little but damaged fragments, the ink faded and only visible under ultraviolet light. Some transcriptions have been made from old photographs or microfilms (or even photocopies of these) of lost originals. Others are transcribed from early scholars' copies of manuscripts which have subsequently been lost to us. By including detailed references, I hope that doubters will check my transcriptions for themselves. The availability of full manuscripts online has proliferated exponentially since the beginnings of the research undertaken for my studies. Such institutions as the French Bibliothèque nationale and British Library have made a great many freely accessible.

Wherever possible, I have endeavoured to provide my own interpretation of the most probable meaning. There is no standardised spelling, capitalisation, or punctuation in any of these documents. I only include the bracketed corrective [*sic*] if the

---

5   U. Eco, *The Name of the Rose*, trans. W. Weaver (London, 1983), pp. 491–2.

spelling, proper noun, or word order drastically affects the meaning. For example: the two 'bordes of Curyboyli' imported for the use of Edward IV are undoubtedly horse bards of cuir bouilli (**36**).

In order to be true to the original script, where recognisable contemporary scribes' signs (*notae communes*) are used they are expanded in square brackets: e.g., p[ro], p[ar], q[ue], p[re]d[ic]to[rum]. For word endings, abbreviations, and contractions that do not have specific scribal signs – an example being a single macron penned over a word – I use a single inverted comma: thus cu' for *cum* (Lat. with), London' (Lat. *Londinensis, -dinium*), Reg' R' (Lat. king's reign). Thankfully, this neatly avoids the need to provide what might be considered 'correct' declensions in Latin. It should be strongly argued that, as many of these words are neologisms and originate in vernacular tongues (e.g., breastplate, haubergeon), they cannot be declined at all.[6] One exception to this general rule is that some English (and Scots) sources have had some words such as [t]he, i[n], and i[s] expanded for better comprehension.

A great many of the documents are written in the form of lists with only one entry per line. In this sourcebook they have been condensed into single paragraphs to reduce their length without compromising their meaning. I have expunged such terms as 'item' and *eidem* (Lat. 'to the same' person) commonly employed by the compilers of inventories, household accounts, and legally-binding documents. Superfluous elaborate honorary titles such as mon dit seigneur (Fr. my said lord) have also, wherever possible, been removed. So numerous are the lacunae in the paper and vellum that these gaps are represented by bracketed ellipses: […] only if the meaning is substantially affected.

Translation

> si le franceis ne soit pas bon, jeo doie estre escusee, pur ceo qe jeo sui engleis et n'ai pas muelt hauntee le franceis.
>
> If the French be no good, I ought to be excused because I'm English and I don't often use French.
>
> —Henry, duke of Lancaster.[7]

Although his self-deprecation proves to be false modesty, Duke Henry encapsulates a concern held by – or one that ought to be held by – Anglophones. To best allow the reader to engage with these primary sources I have presented the original text in as clear a form as possible. Therefore, it is not necessary to be completely reliant on my translation. It is highly likely that, by looking again, better interpretations will be suggested and more useful insight gained.

---

6   See their entries in the illustrated glossary of R. Moffat, *Medieval Arms and Armour: A Sourcebook. Volume I: The Fourteenth Century* (Woodbridge, 2022).

7   *Le Livre de Seyntz Medicines: The Devotional Treatise of Henry of Lancaster*, ed. E. J. Arnould (Oxford, 1940), p. 239.

Since the publication of my first two volumes my un-ashamedness to translate into English has been in no way dulled. My challenge to colleagues with expertise in different dialects and languages to make sources accessible will always be there to be taken up.

There is not space in this volume for a detailed etymological examination of new words. A brief explanation is given if it is beneficial to understanding, for example the derivation of tasset from a French word for a type of pouch hung from the belt.

In a letter of 1590, Sir Henry Lee, Master of the Royal Armoury at Greenwich, writes that he had the armourers forge two breastplates: one of a 'certayne metell w[hic]h grewe or was made in Sropshere or ther abouts' the other of the high-quality imported steel used as standard in the workshop. He was ordered 'to make a trail of them bothe w[it]h all indyfference' and informs the recipient:

> I chose a good and stronge pystolle, I took very good powder and weighed it, so I dyde the bulletes and w[it]h equall charge I tryed fyrste the one and then the other; that made in the Offyce and of the mettell of Hungere held out and more than a littell dent of the pellet nothinge perced, the other clene shotte thereowe [...]. Thus muche for this Yenglyshe mettell.[8]

In such a spirit do I encourage the reader to level their (critical thinking) pieces at my translations of the sources and interpretations thereof.

---

8   The letter is printed in Viscount Dillon, 'A Letter of Sir Henry Lee, 1590, on the Trail of Iron for Armour', *Archaeologia* 51 (1888), pp. 167–72 (at pp. 171–2).

Material Source-Types

Choice of Images

As Curator of European Arms and Armour at Glasgow Museums I have selected some from the remarkable collection generously bequeathed to the people of the City of Glasgow by R. L. Scott in 1939, as well as from that of Sir William and Lady Burrell which was gifted to the people of the same city between 1944 and 1958.

Armour and Weapons

Three types of helmet are illustrated. The sallet (Figure 8 and Figure 13) was the head defence *par excellence* of the century and they have a good survival rate from its second half. The armet (Figure 17), and the fitting of its visor, is the subject of a passage from Jehan de Bueil's *Le Jouvencel* (**33**). The barbute (Figure 18) is referred to in an armourer's letter to an English merchant (**43**).

This pauldron (Figure 20) was made by a Milanese working in France such as those referred to in a letter (**55**). Its distinctive fluting (linear ridges) and scalloped-edged 'batwing' form is a very good example of the 'German' style armour these Lombards were capable of crafting (**38**). The earliest surviving plate armour for a horse – known as a bard (Figure 29) – is of the type to be supplied in a contract signed between a Swabian customer and a Milanese maker (**7**).

The crossbow (Figure 3), now known as a 'composite' type, serves to explain a herald's description (**8**). A fine sword hilt (Figure 28) has a heart-shaped pommel (**73**), as described by the compiler of an inventory of a French château. A combination of object and artwork works to demonstrate the sword and buckler play so beloved of England's youth (Figures 21, 22, and 23), as reported by Domenico Mancini (**56**). A fine hunting sword (Figure 6) is worthy of an extremely wealthy nobleman (**10**). Staff weapons are represented by a halberd and a partisan (Figures 31 and 32), and the increasing use of firearms by an early handgun (Figure 30).

Artworks

Paintings and Book and Manuscript Illustrations

Lucas Cranach (Figure 15) paints a servant spanning a crossbow with a cranequin in the type of hunting scene that would have appeared on a wall hanging adorning the chambers of an English castle (**25**). The Master of Moulins' 'Saint with Donor' (Figure 24) gives an excellent impression of the lance-rest of the sort affixed to the breastplate of a French duke's fine armour (**59**).

An allegorical work on rulership, *Der Weisskunig*, forms part of the literary output of Emperor Maximilian I's court at the very outset of the sixteenth century. Two woodcuts have been selected (Figure 4 and Figure 27): the first to demonstrate the use of the crossbow in freezing conditions as described by a herald (**8**); the second for a very detailed illustration of armourers in their workshop at Innsbruck as discussed by Pietro Monte (**69**).

Two vibrant miniatures (Figure 9 and Figure 11) depicting the farcical incidents recounted in *Les cent nouvelles nouvelles* (**21**) are from a unique fifteenth-century manuscript version in the care of Glasgow University. The exquisite instructional diagrams from René, duke of Anjou's Tournament Treatise (**22**) (Figure 12i. to Figure 12v.) are from R. L. Scott's own copy of this work. These, and the splendid miniature (Figure 26) that accompanies the text on arming for single combat on foot from Sir John Astley's manuscript, are discussed in the Expert Writers section above (**62**).

Tomb Effigies and an Alabaster

The first tomb effigy (Figure 1), that of the Earl of Warwick, is the product of the detailed instructions provided for its manufacture (**1**). The second is included to illustrate arming points (Figure 10). These functional laces turn out to be the props central to the conceit of a jocular story (**21**).

An English alabasterman has carved common soldiers surrounding Christ's tomb (Figure 14) with great delicacy. His inspiration came from observing his contemporaries such as townsmen of the sort mustered at Bridport (**24**). The point must also be stressed here that there are, at present, no complete harnesses from England from our period.

Stained Glass and Tapestry

Stained glass is an invaluable visual source. The artists' brushes capture the finest of details: a mail gorget (Figure 2) of the kind borne by a competitor in an arranged combat (**5**); a jousting helm with its flamboyant crest of fine feathers (Figure 5), as mentioned in the household payments of a duke with a passion for the pastime verging on fanaticism (**10**); and (Figure 25) an Englishman's 'grete shaft w[i]t[h] a brode Arowe hed' (**60**).

Of the three tapestries, two are products of the skilled makers of the Burgundian Netherlands. In their imagining of Hercules as judge of the Olympic Games (Figure 7) they have armed him in the sort of sumptuously-decorated (and well-proofed) brigandine owned by the Prince-Bishop of Toul (**16**). Indeed, this potentate commissioned his from Charles the Bold's own personal craftsman. The second (Figure 16), with its *denouement* of a boar hunt, would definitely not be out of place amongst Sir John Fastolf's wall hangings (**25**). The third (Figure 19) was woven in France not long after the demise of René, duke of Anjou, author of a letter with which a dear friend receives one of his finest crossbows (**51**). Even the smallest of targets was not safe from those practiced with such well-made weapons. Note that the tapicers have included blunt-tipped bolts tucked through the shooter's belt. These are for killing little birds without turning them to mince.

Part II

The Documents

1

Winchester, Winchester College Library, Liber Albus, Item 22992, fol. 44r

Inventory of Winchester College Armoury, Mid-Fifteenth Century

Armaria

xlvj de Basnett' & Palett' xxxiij ventall' ij par' de plates integ' coop[er]t' cu' blod' veluett' quor' j cu' Frenge de Serico vij Brestplat' iiij Pusiones viij par' Rerebrases & ij p[ro] j arm' viij vambrases iiij par' de legharneys & j leg' cu' Cusshu' ij par' de Sabaturez vj par' cirothecar' xv lorice xiij Pollaxes vn' xij de vna & ead[e]m secta xij archus noui iiij shefes Sagittar' j Gesarme j Barell' p[ro] loric' purgandis

> The Armoury
>
> 46 basinets and pallets, 33 aventails, two complete pairs of plates covered in blue velvet – one of which has silk fringes, seven breastplates, four pisans, eight pairs of rerebraces and two for one arm, eight vambraces, four pairs of legharness and one leg (defence) with cuisse, two pairs of sabatons, six pairs of gauntlets, 15 hauberks, 13 pollaxes – 12 of which are of one sort and one of another, 12 new bows, three sheaves of arrows, one gisarme, one barrel for cleaning hauberks

2

Now-Lost Document recording the Instructions for the Construction of the Tomb Effigy of Richard, Earl of Warwick, at Saint Mary's Church, Warwick, 11 February 1450. Printed in E. Blore, *Monumental Remains of Noble and Eminent Persons, Comprising the Sepulchral Antiquities of Great Britain* (London, 1826), p. 14

The said Will[iam] Austen [citizen and founder of London] [...], doth covenant to cast and make an image of a man armed, of fine latten, garnished with certain ornaments, viz. with sword and dagger; with a garter; with a helme and crest under his head, and at his feet a bear musled, and a griffon, perfectly made of the finest latten, according to patterns; all which to be brought to Warwick, and layd on the tombe, at the perill of the said Austen: the said executors paying for the image, perfectly made and laid, and all the ornaments, in good order, besides the cost of the said workmen to Warwick, and working there to lay the image, and besides the cost of the carriages, all which are to be born by the said executors, in totall, xl *li.*

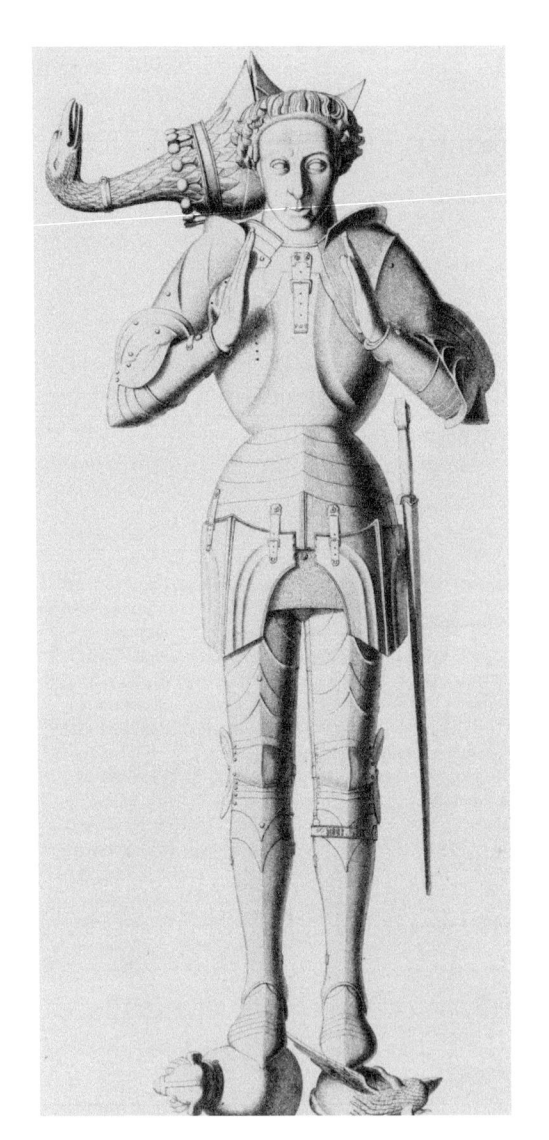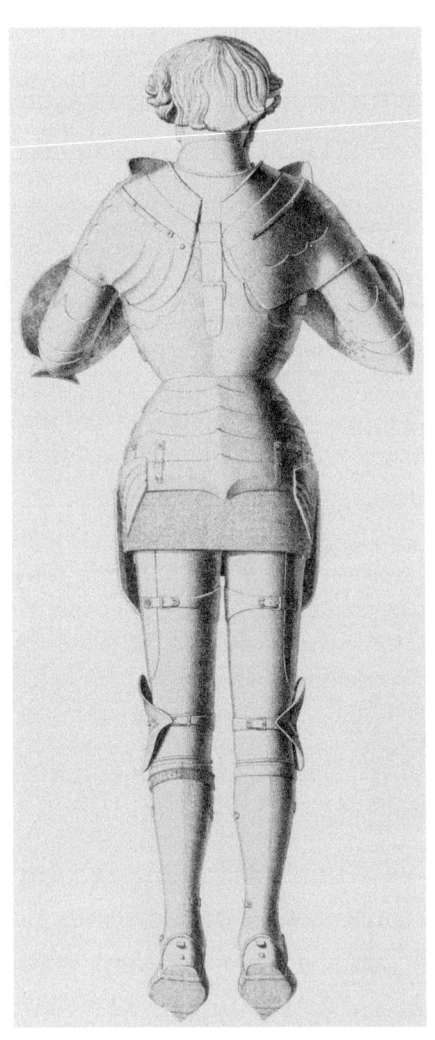

Figure 1. Etching of the tomb effigy of Richard, Earl of Warwick (1382–1439), Saint Mary's Church, Warwick.

3

Lincoln, Lincolnshire Archives, DIOC/REG/19, fol. 43v–fol. 45r
Will of Sir Thomas Cumberworth, Somerby juxta Bigby, Lincolnshire, 15 February 1450

to ou[r]e blissyd lady & hir colage at lincoln [various luxurious fabrics including] my best cote of armes [i.e., coat armour] my Nevew Robert Constabull' the best and hole armyng harnas þat j hafe & my beste axe for werre Williӡam Constabull' j hole harnas of plate best next the Baslard' harnast þ[a]t j boght' gilt my newew hugh' Percy the baslard' that his fadre withid [bequeathed] me my newew his sone a hole harnas of plate & a nax of were hew cresse þe fadyr my bor spere [cristo]fer' cresse a hole harnoiz of plate & my Swirde his brodyr hugh' Cresse a haburion' þe best Prikyng hate pisern [i.e., pisan] þ[er]to & my dagar Stevyn chamberlayn' & Joh[a]n hobson' Joh[a]n Greye harr' harde hafe ilkyn' of þam a Jak' & a salad & a bow & xij Aros Richard' & hys Brodyr Joh[a]n Thymolby Richard' Sargant' haue ilkon' of þam A jak' & a salad' & a Swerde & a baslard' or a dagar all odyr yemen' of my howsald' & the gromes of the wardrope' & of the Bakhows haue ilkon' of þa[m] a bow & Aras wilӡam telby a nax for wer w[i]t[h] the hede and a hande of yrne

4

London Metropolitan Archives, London Letter-Book K, fol. 251r
Petition of the Armourers of London to the Mayor and Aldermen of the City, 3 August 1450

Vn to the full' honourables lord' the mair' aldermen' and Cominalte of the Citee of London'

Besecheth' vnto your' grete wisdome the maister and the wardeins of the craft of armorers of the said Citee tenderly to considre that where it was ordeyned for the grete profitte and wele of the kyng and of his liege people and enrolled in the Chaumber of the yeldhall' of the forsaid Citee in the xxj yeer' of the reign' of kyng Edward the iijde as in the [London letter] book of F' the Cxlij leef more pleinly is contened[1] that hewmerie and other armure that is forged wyth the hamur brought' from beyonde the see or other place to be solde wythin' the said Citee shuld not from that tyme foreward' in no man[er] wise be putte to sale prevy nor appert till' they were couenably assayed by the wardeyns of the said craft and m[ar]ked wyth' [t]her' m[ar]ke on' peyn to forfete the hewmerie and armure so otherwise put to sale The contrie of which' article nowe dayly is laboured and done vnto the grete hurt of

---

[1] For the statute of 1347, see Moffat, *Medieval Arms and Armour: A Sourcebook. Volume I*, pp. 102–3.

the kyng and his liege people and grete disclaundre vnto the said craft of armorers That it please your' grete wisdome the p[re]misses tenderly considered to provide and ordeyne that the said maister and wardeins of the said craft of armorers that nowe been' and here after shall' be may haue the serche and assaye of all' man[er]e [of] hewmerie and armure that is forged wyth' the hamur accordyng to the article aforesaid and as they ben' sworn' eu[er]y yeer' afore the mair' for to doo

5

The anonymous author of the *Livre des faits de Jacques de Lalaing* (Paris, Bibliothèque nationale de France, MS fr. 16830, fol. 139v– fol. 140v), and Olivier de La Marche, *Mémoire sur la maison de Bourgogne*, ed. J. A. C. Buchon (Paris, 1836), pp. 445–7

Two Narratives of an Arranged Combat at the Pas d'armes of the Fountain of Tears, Chalon-sur-Saône, Duchy of Burgundy, October 1450

> *Sir Jacques de Lalaing (1421–53) was a Hainaulter in the service of Philip, Duke of Burgundy. He was well renowned throughout Christendom for his fighting skills – especially in single combat. Sir Olivier de La Marche (1425–52) was a Burgundian poet, chronicler, and historian at the court of Duke Philip and his son Charles.*

The anonymous author
[The foot combat with axes]

Et estoit le cheuallier du pas ainsi armez et habilliez que to[us] Jours auoit este au parauant excepte que Il auoit la gambe destr[e] desarmee Et sy ne portoit point de gauntelet en sa droitte main. Et ledit dauanchier combatty en sallade et gorgerin de forte maille […] et lui print sa hace dune main Lors le cheualier au pas tost et viuement print Icelui dauancier par le gorgerin en le tirant a lui trois ou quatre pas Et en ce faisant fist perdre audit dauancier sa hace de toutes les deux mai[n]s et tant quelle chert a terre Et lors le Juge getta le baston

> The knight of the *Pas* (Sir Jacques) was armed and arrayed as he had been before (in complete harness), save that he had his left leg disarmed. And wore no gauntlet on his right hand. And d'Avanchy fought in a sallet and gorget of strong mail […] and he took his axe in one hand. Then the knight of the *Pas* quickly and briskly took this d'Avanchy by the gorget pulling him towards him three or four paces and, in so doing, d'Avanchy lost his axe from both hands and was forced to the ground. And then the judge cast (down) the baton

Figure 2. Detail of a stained glass panel depicting the Agony in the Garden, Boppard-on-Rhine, c. 1440 (Glasgow Museums, Burrell Collection, 45.485.1.a).

The anonymous author
[The foot combat with swords]

Le cheualier du pas Issit hors de son pauillon le bacinet en teste et tant bien arme que belle chose estoit a le veoir Et Icellui escuier sauuoyen estoit toit arme dun armet en teste Mais ledit sauuoyen ne veoit pas bien en son armet Et pour tant ne se bouga oncques du lieu ou premierement Il se mist Et la attendoit le cheualier du pas chascun cop quil faisoit ses desmarces Lesqueles desmarces fist toujours belles et grandes Et puis alloit assir sur le dit sauuoyen Lequel co[m]me dit est ne se bouga oncques Lors le Juge veant les sept cops acomplis Jetta le baston

> The knight of the *Pas* sallied forth from his pavilion, basinet on head and so well armed that it was a fair thing to see. Now this Savoyard squire (d'Avanchy) was completely armed with an armet on his head, but the Savoyard could not see very well in his armet and thus he did not move from the place he had started (i.e., failed to advance). And there the knight of the *Pas* struck, forcing him back with each blow, every one of these pushbacks was fine and great. And then he set about the Savoyard who – as is said – did not move at all. Then the judge, seeing the accomplishment of the seven blows (as agreed beforehand in the *chapitres*: prearranged rules), threw (down) the batton

The anonymous author
[The mounted combat with lances]

Et auoit demande Icelui dauancier le nombre de xxv courses Mais Ilz nen coururent que six Ausquelles six courses lescuier sauuoyen rompit deux lances et le cheualier du pas en rompit vne De laquelle Il attaindit Icelui sauuoyen en la teste vn tresrude cop duquel cop Il sembla estre greue et vn peu estourdy et rechanga nouuel armet Auquel armet Il ne veoit pas bien Pourquoy le Juge veant quil estoit mal armez enuoya deuers lui en lui remonstrant quil nestoit pas bien armez de la teste en lui priant q[ue] Il se voulsist deporter de plus en faire

> Now this d'Avanchy had demanded that twenty-five courses (be run) but they ran only six, in which six courses the Savoyard squire broke two lances and the knight of *Pas* broke one, from which he struck this Savoyard a very rough blow on the head. He seemed to be injured and a little stunned by this blow and changed into a new armet. He could not see very well from this armet. Therefore, the judge – seeing him to be badly armed – sent to him pointing out that his head was not well armed and entreated that he should wish to do no more

Olivier de La Marche
[The foot combat with axes]

saillit l'escuyer de son pavillon, la cotte-d'armes au dos et de sa teste il fut armé d'une salade à visière et avoit le col couvert et armé d'un gorgerin de mailles seulement et avoit le visage tout découvert et, quant à messire Jacques de Lalaing, il estoit armé à la manière acoustumee réservé qu'il n'avoit point de gantelet en sa dextre main et au regard des haches que fit présenter l'entrepreneur, elles furent fortes, et pointuees dessus et dessous et, depuis les armes precedents du luy et du seigneur d'Espiry, il fit toujours présenter haces, a dague dessous. Ce qu'il n'avoit pas fait devant comme dicte est.

Ainsi marchèrent les deux champions les haches empoignees, l'un contre l'autre et l'escuyer (qui fut homme menu, et petit personnage) assembla courageusement et du premier coup ferit du maillet de la hache, apres la main senestre de son compaignon mais le chevalier le rabatit foridement et, du second coup, l'escuyer recouvra du haut des bras, pour cuider plus haut atteindre et le chevalier rabatit de la queue de la hace, du plus-grande force tellement qu'il fit tourner l'escuyer ainsi qu'à demy et de ce coup le chevalier recouvra de la dague de dessous, et l'atteindit au fort du gorgerin, tellement qu'il fit démarcher l'escuer, plus de deux pas loing de luy et, quand l'escuyer (qui fut aspre, et asseuré) se vit au danger du batton du chevalier, et congnut que, tant qu'il estoit plus loing, moins lu estoit le faix du batton soustenable, il s'aventura et marcha, la hache au poing, jusques à messire Jacques et de la main droitte prit la hache du chevalier et prestement recouvra, de la senestre main et abandonna la sienne, pour tenir plus fort celle de son compaignon et me souvient que la hache dudict escuyer demoura appuyee contre messire Jacques mais le chevalier demarcha deux ou trois graps pas, en tirant apres luy, de toute sa force, l'escuyer, qui tenoit sa hache et par celle demarche cheut la hache de l'escuyer au sablon mais l'escuyer ne perdit point sa prise et quand le juge vit l'escuyer desembattonné, il getta le batton

the squire sallied forth from his pavilion, coat armour on his back, his head was armed with a visored sallet and his neck was covered and armed with only a mail gorget, and his face was totally uncovered. Sir Jacques de Lalaing was armed in the customary manner – save that he had no gauntlet on his right hand. Now as regards the axes the *entrepreneur* (defender of the *Pas*, i.e., Sir Jacques) had presented, they were strong and fitted with spikes above and below (the head), and prior to the (feat of) arms against the Lord of Espiry (the challenger before d'Avanchy), he had always presented axes with a spike *below* (the head). This (i.e., two spikes) he had never done before, as is said.

Thus, the two champions advanced against each other with axes in hand and clashed courageously. Now the squire – who might be described as being of medium build – struck near his companion's left hand with the axe-hammer with the first blow but the knight calmly deflected it. With the second blow the squire thrust with arms held high (i.e., from a high guard), intending to strike higher, but the knight deflected it with the axe's *queue* (spike at the end of the haft) with very great force, so much so that he made the squire turn halfway round. With this blow the knight thrust with the underside spike and struck his gorget strongly, so much so it forced the squire backwards more than two paces further from him, and when the squire – who was violent and confident – saw he was in danger of the knight's weapon, and knowing that he would not long be able to sustain the weapon's blows, took a risk and advanced, axe in hand, on Sir Jacques. He grasped the knight's axe with his right hand and swiftly thrust with his left hand and loosened (his grip on) it (his axe) to grasp his companion more forcefully. Now I recall that the squire's axe remained caught on Sir Jacques but the knight took a good two or three paces backwards, dragging the squire, who held his (Jacques') axe, after him with all his force. And with this backward move he knocked the squire's axe down to the sand. The squire, however, did not lose his grip, and when the judge saw the squire disarmed of his weapon he cast (down) the baton

Olivier de La Marche
[The foot combat with swords]

Jacques d'Avanchies, lequel saillit hors de son pavillon, armé de toutes armes, la cotte-darmes au dos, et l'éspée (que l'on dict estoc d'armes) empoignée et tenoit la main senestre renversée, et couvert de la rondelle de l'estoc; et estoit armé, de la teste, d'un armet à la façon d'Italie, armé de sa grande bavière. [...] et messire Jacques marcha baudement, et celuy coup ateindit l'escuyer, entre l'espaule sensestre et le bord de la bavière de l'armet, un moult grand coup et l'escuyer ateindit messire Jacques sur le flanc senestre. Si se mirent les escoutes, ordonnees, entre deux et furent recules trois pas, comme il estoit dict par les chapitres et pour la seconde fois marcha ledict messire Jacques sur son compaignon mais l'escuyer s'afferma en sa marche, comme devant, et mit la pointe de l'estoc au devant du coup et le chevalier, marchant pour la seconde fois, atteindit assez pres de la premiere atteinte, tresdurement mais l'escuyer soustint froidement, et sagement n'onques n'en demarcha. Le chevalier (qui moult estoit asseure en ses affaires) ne fit autre poursuite mais de luy mesme demarcha les pas ordonnes et revint pour la tierce fois et, pour abreger mon recit, tant continua le chevalier sa poursuite, et les demarches ordonnees, que les onze coups d'espee furent ferus par le chevalier, et soustenus par l'escuyer, par la premiere forme, qui dicte est, sans ce que l'escuyer fust demarche de sa premiere place prise at ainsi les fit le juge departir et se retrait chacun en son pavillon et s'en alerent les champions desarmer, et rearmer de nouveau, pour faire les armes de cheval

Jacques d'Avanchy sallied forth from his pavilion armed with all his arms, coat armour on his back, and sword – which is called an arming *estoc* – in hand; and he kept his left hand behind and covered by the rondel of the *estoc*. His head was armed with an armet in the Italian fashion armed with its large bevor (i.e., wrapper). [...] Now Sir Jacques advanced fearlessly, and with his blow struck the squire between the left shoulder and the edge of the armet's bevor a very great blow, and the squire struck Sir Jacques on the left flank. This was seen by the appointed guards who separated the pair and had them take three paces back, as stipulated in the *chapitres*, and for the second time Jacques advanced on his opponent but the squire was firm in his advance, as before, and thrust the point of the *estoc* (towards the same place) as the previous blow whilst the knight, advancing for the second time, struck very hard quite close to (the place of) the first blow, but the squire took it calmly and cannily without being forced backwards. The knight – who knew exactly what he was doing – did not make another attack, but took the regulated step backwards and came back for the third time, and – to abridge my account – the knight continued his attack, and the regulated step-backs, until the eleven blows were struck by the knight and sustained by the squire in the said same way, save that the squire was forced back from his starting point. So, the judge had them withdraw and each returned to his pavilion where the champions were disarmed and then rearmed to (undertake) the mounted feats of arms

Olivier de La Marche
[The mounted combat with lances]

A la nuefième et dernière course d'icelles armes, le chevalier atteindit sur le bord de la croisée de l'armet de l'escuyer et fut l'atteinte si grande que ladicte coiffe fut enfoncée jusques à la teste et si le coup fust descendu aussi bien qu'il monta, certainement l'escuyer eust eu la teste faussée mais la pointe glissa en amont, et ne fut point l'escuyer blécé mais il fut tellement endommagé de son armet qu'il fut conseillé de soy déporter de plus-avant poursuyvre, ne parfaire icelles armes

On the ninth and last course of these (feats of) arms, the knight struck the edge of the cross of the squire's armet (i.e., T-shaped face opening usually covered by the visor) and the blow was so great that the 'coiffe' (i.e., helmet skull) was caved in as far as the head. Now had the blow been any lower and better than (the spot) where it struck, it would have certainly injured the squire's head. However, the point (of the lance) skyted over the top and the squire was not harmed at all, but his armet was so damaged that he was advised that he should do no more, nor complete these (feats of) arms

6

The Parliament Rolls of Medieval England, 1275–1504, ed. C. Given-Wilson and others, digital edn (Leicester, 2005), v-212, membr. 2

Petition presented in Parliament by Isabel, Widow of William Tresham, November 1450

The Alleged Crime took place at Thorpelands Close, Milton, Nottinghamshire, 23 September

[the ten accused] gadered and assembled with theym dyvers mysdoers and murderers of men, to the nombre of an .clx. personnes or moo, arraied in fourme of werre, with jakkes, salettez, longe swerdes, longdebeofs, boresperes, and all other unmerciable forbodon wepons, [and] logged them under a longe hegge adjoynyng to the high wey, [they] issued out uppon the seid William Tresham, and the seid Evane [Aprice] thenne and there with a launcegay, smote the seid William Tresham thorough the body a fote and more, wherof he died, and other dyvers persones of the seid mysdoers above named, gafe hym many and grete dedely woundes and kutte his throte, of every of the which woundes and kuttyng of throte he shuld have died, if he had not died of the wounde which the said Evane gaf hym

7

Unlocated Entries from the Registers of the Dukes of Milan concerning Milanese Armourers, 31 December 1450–1 August 1470, printed in: F. Fossati, 'Per il commercio delle armature e i Missaglia', *Archivio Storico Lombardo*, 6th Ser., 59 (1932), pp. 279–97; J. Gelli and G. Moretti, *Gli armaroli milanesi. I Missaglia e la loro casa* (Milan, 1903); and E. Motta, 'Armaiuoli milanesi nel periodo Visconteo-Sforzesco', *Archivio Storico Lombardo*, 5th Ser., 41 (1914), pp. 187–232

Issued at Milan, 31 December 1450

I 'datiarii datii rippe mercantie et additionis eiusdem civitatis Mediolani anni presentis MCCCCL' chiedono la somma loro dovuta per le merci entrate o uscite senza pagare il dazio, 'quod solvi non debebat, secundum datum dicte datii': tra l'altro 'pro armaturis tribus integris conductis extra dictam civitatem per quendam Stefaninum teutonicum familiarem Ill. Domini Ducis Alberti Austrie, vigore unius bulletini signati Antonius, Johannespetrus, Cristoforus sub die XI maii, lib. III, ss. VII, d. VI.'

> The 'excisemen for (river) navigation duties on merchandise and extra things of the same City of Milan in the present year 1450' demand the sum due to them for goods imported or exported without the payment of duty, 'which ought not have been paid, according to (the letter/*datum* of) the said duties': among other items, 'for three complete armours brought from the said city by a certain Stephan, German, servant of the Illustrious Lord Duke Albert of Austria, by authority of a bill signed Antonio, Giovanni Petro, Christoforo [prob. Missaglia] on 11 May, 3 *lire* 7 *soldi* 6 *denari* [*imperiale*]'

From the Duke to Giovanni de Landriano, Milan, 22 April 1452

'Volimo et cossì te commettino che daghi a Fran.co Magiolino' L. 21, s. 13 'per braza tre de zetonino raxo cremoxilo et per terze doe de veluto piano cremoxile et per braza cinque de doppiono d'oro et per dinari 20 de setta de grana che sono tolte da Ant.o del Missaglia per la coraza del conte Galeazo Maria nostro figliolo. Anchora volimo che dagi a Leonardo magistri *(sic)* de tessuti' L. 40 'che sono per onz. 13½ de tessuti d'oro et de cremoxile tolti per lo soprascripto Ant.o per fornimento de dicta coraza, che sono in tutto libre 61, ss. 13.'

> 'We wish and thus commission you to give to Francesco Magiolino' 21*l.* 13*s.* 'for three *braza* (measurement akin to an ell) of crimson-red satin and for ⅔ of soft crimson

velvet, and for five *braza* of double-woven cloth-of-gold, and for 20*d.* of grained silk which was taken by Antonio da Missaglia for the cuirass of Count Galeazzo Maria, Our little son. Furthermore, We wish that you give 40*l.* to Leonardo, master of fabrics, for 13½oz of gold and crimson fabrics taken by the above-written Antonio for fitting the said cuirass, which makes in total 61*l.* 13*s.*'

From the Duke to his envoys in Genoa: Giovanni de Alessandria and Antonio Guidobono, Milan, 28 April 1452

Havimo molto honorato accarezato et etiam apresentato questo M.co ambassatore del Serenissimo Re de Barbaria, in modo che, secondo el nostro iudicio, se parte molto bene contento e satisfacto da noy, et havimo facto vestire li suoy, et ulterius facto dare alcune armature belle, astori bellissimi, drappi, fornimenti da uselli et altre de belle cose de qua per presentare all May.tà del Re. Et certe remanimo troppo contenti de l'honore glí havimo facto.

> We have most honourably treated as well as presented (i.e., he had been received at court) this Marco, ambassador of the Most Serene King of Bavaria, in such a manner that, in Our opinion, he departs well content and satisfied by Us, and We have had his followers finely dressed, and furthermore have given (him) some fine armours, the most beautiful hawks, draperies and falconry accessories, and other beautiful things from here (i.e., Milan) to present to His Majesty the King. And certainly, We were very happy for the honour We showed him.

From the Duke to Francesco di Ser Antonio, Lodi Vecchio, 18 May 1452

Diray al Pisanello subito che vada a trovare Zohan Coyro [*sic*] et lo compag.o de magistro Nicolò armarolo et chel sappia da loro quando haverano fornite le noste coraze et che el ce ne avisi presto.

> Say to Pisanello that he should go immediately to find Zoan (Giovanni) Corio and the companion of Master Nicolò the armourer and find out from them when they will provide Our cuirasses and tell him to let Us know soon.

From Angelo Simonetta to the Duke, Milan, 13 September 1452

Illustrissimo Signore. Ho havuto le lettere de la S. V. circha quello ve ha scritto el S. Messer Alixandro [*sic*] dicendo non essere spagiato de le armature et che non poseno spagiare più che quatro homini d'armi el dí, de la quale cossa la S. V. se ne duole assay etc … Sichè, Signore, aciò intendiate se questo è vero, facio avisato la S. V. che già sono deci giorni passati che fece assignare tute le armature a Ser Andrea con tale ordine, che qualuncha venesse se dovesse spagiare, et cussi non havendo io altro a fare cercha questo perchè me pariva non fasse altra difficultà, se non in li cavali, che se ne trovava pochi, et vedendo luy se excusa in questo, ho fatto veniri da mi tri armaroli che banno a dare dicte arme et Ser Michele et Ser Bartolameo [*sic*] cancelleri del prefato signore Messer Alixandro per sapere a que modo possa essere sequito tale manchamento, li quali tuti affirmeno non essere vero questo se dice, imo che loro haveriano spazati quanto ne fosseno venuti, et dichono che sono stati tali tri dì et quatro che non ce sono venati alchuni homini d'arme, et che loro havveno [sic] lo modo e habilita de spagiare fin a deceocto homini d'armi el giorno, cioè sey per caduno de loro tri armaroli. Et in questo modo la S. V. vede et intende se'l dice lo vero. Et cussi di dirrecto ne scrivo al prefato S. Messer Alixandro et chel mandi tuti quelli che resteno ad essere spazati, che li farò forniri in uno gionro e mezo, che si li havese mandati en cinqui dì seriano spazati tutti …

> Most Illustrious Lord, I have had your Lordship's letters concerning that which Lord Messer Alessandro (poss. the Duke's illegitimate half-brother) has written to you saying that he was not sent the armour and that they could send no more than four men-at-arms a day, which was to your Lordship's considerable displeasure etc. … So, my Lord, in order for you to know the truth of the matter, your Lordship should be aware that ten days have already passed since I assigned all the armours to Ser Andrea and ordered that, whatever happened, it should be dispatched, and therefore, not having anything further to do with it, because I thought there were no other difficulties – except for the horses, of which few could be found – and seeing that he excused himself in this, I asked three armourers to come (to me) to give the said arms (to) both Ser Michele and Ser Bartolameo [sic], chamberlains to the aforesaid Lord Messer Alessandro, in order to know how this shortfall can be remedied. All (i.e., the three armourers) affirm that what he says is untrue, and that they had dispatched those that came, and they say that for three or four days no men-at-arms have come, and that they had the means and ability to send up to eighteen men-at-arms a day, namely six for each of the three armourers. In this way your Lordship can see and understand whether […] is telling the truth. And thus, I will write directly to the said Lord Messer Alessandro and ask him to send all those that are still to be dispatched, that I will arrange for them to be supplied in a day and a half, and if he had sent them in five days, they would all be dispatched …

From the Duke to Francesco di Ser Antonio to instruct the Masters of the Treasury, 23 June 1453, Camp near Seniga

Fartiti dare da Ant.o del [sic] Missaglia ad Ser Andrea da Foligono nostro canc.o una panzera, una cellata, uno paro de guanti et uno gorzarino belli per la persona soa, et per uno suo tam.o tute l'arme de uno galuppo. Et non manchi.

> You should request Antonio da Missaglia to give to Ser Andrea da Foligono, Our chamberlain, one mail shirt, one sallet, one pair of gauntlets, and one (mail) gorget – all fine quality – for his person, and the complete arms for a horseman for one of his familiars – and make sure you do this.

From the Duke to Charles VII of France, Milan, 15 April 1455

a contemplatione de la Serenissima Maestà del Re de Franza siamo contenti et volimo che voy debiati dare facoltà et concedere licenzia a Balzarino da Trezo armorero de questa nostra cita, de conducere de questa nostra cita, in Franza due some, videlicet vinti baloni de azale per uso de la Serenissima Maestà del Re [...] Volemo etiandio che voy debiati annullare et reuocare la segurtade quale dicto Balzarino havea data de non condure alcuni lavoratori de l'arte sua fuora della nostra jurisdictione, remanendo però sempre obligati li suoi in casu ch'el contrafacese in menare o condure li lavoratori contro l' ordini nostri.

> In response to the Most Serene Majesty the King of France, We are content and We wish that You grant and concede licence to Balzarino da Trezzo, armourer of this Our city, to bring from this Our city to France two loads, viz.: 20 bales of steel for the use of the Most Serene Majesty the King [...] Furthermore, We wish that You annul and revoke the assurance that the said Balzarino gave to not bring any workers of his craft outwith Our jurisdiction, although his workers shall always remain bound [to Us] in the event that he wrongfully threatens or brings workers there against Our orders.

From Cicco Simonetta, on the Duke's behalf, to the Masters of the Treasury, 16 April 1457

[The Duke] vuole si lasci portar fuori di Milano senza pagamento di dazio, 'nomine M.ci Comitis de Virtimbergo Alamani' certa roba, tra cui: Coraze VIII vel corsit. Par. IV de arnexe Celatas VI cum vixera Para VI de brazali Para IV de guanti Para doy de spalaci Secrete VI Barbat. [sic] VII La porto fuori Iacobus de Almania, 'fecti ligare in ball. IV e fagolat. I'

> (The Duke) wishes that there be taken out of Milan, without payment of duty, 'in the name of the Lord Count of Württemberg, in Germany' certain things, including: eight cuirasses or corsets, four pairs of (leg) harness, six sallets with visors, six pairs of bracers (plate arm defences), four pairs of gauntlets, two (pairs of) pauldrons, six secrets (mail shirts borne beneath civilian clothing), seven *barbutti* (mail neck defences). To be carried by Iacobus of Germany 'bound in six bales and one basket'

17 June 1458

Pietro Innocenzo de Facino [sic, recte Faerno] fil. d. Giovanni, a S. Maria Beltrade, promette a nome suo e del padre suo Giovanni, a d. Pietro Beaqua, a S. Maria alla Porta, di consegnargli dentro la festa d'Ognisanti 10 armature complete nuove alla foggia francese, e a Natale altre 2 armature consimili, a ragione di lire 32 per armatura.

Pietro Innocenzo di Faerno, son of Master Giovanni, in (the Parish of) Santa Maria Beltrade (Milan), promises in his own name and his father Giovanni's to Master Pietro Beaqua, in (the Parish of) Santa Maria alla Porta (Milan), to deliver by the Feast of All Saints (1 November) 10 new complete armours in the French style, and at Christmas another 2 similar armours, at the rate of 32 *lire* per armour.

Issued at Milan, 24 July 1460

Milano lettere di passo a favore di Giovanni Stadler di Ulma per condurre in Germania diverse armature che Bernardo di Winsternach, cameriere ducale, mada al genitore suo, nobile Ulrico di Winsternach. '[…] testeriam unam equi.'

> Letter granting permission to Johannus Stadler of Ulm to take to Germany divers armour which Bernard of Winsternach, Ducal Chamberlain, ordered for his father, the Noble Ulrich of Winsternach, (including) 'one horse tester (i.e., shaffron).'

Probably Milan, 22 February 1462

Patti tra Enrico Vogt di Kempten e il maestro d'armi Pietro Innocenzo di Faerno, [filius] del q[uan]d[u]m d. Giovanni, in Santa Maria Beltrade, per l'acquisto d'armi. Il Faerno consegnava, dentro la metà quaresima, ed al più tardi per Pasqua 'payra duo bardarum ab equo azalis, unus quorum sit e esse debeat a millite et alter a schuderio, et pro uno que payro dare debeat unum coll[ar]um et unam testeram, et ultra predicta dare debeat duas testeras et payrum unum spallaziorum que fiunt e fatiunt in summa duas croperas et duo pectorales et duos coll[ar]os et quatuor testeras et payros VI spallaziorum.' Il tedesco tenuto a pagare lire 100 imp., cioè in ogni settimana lire 4 'usque quo erant complete dicte res, et quando erant complete teneatur dare id, quod restaverit usque ad completam solutionem dictorum libr. 100 imp.'

> Agreement between Henrich, *Vogt* (Imperial Governor) of Kempten (Swabia), and the master armourer Pietro Innocenzo di Faerno, (son) of the late Master Giovanni, in (the Parish of) Santa Maria Beltrade (Milan), for the purchase of arms. Faerno will deliver, by the middle of Lent or, at the latest, by Easter (30 March) 'two pairs of steel horse bards – one for a knight and the other for a squire – and one pair shall be provided with one collar and one tester (i.e., crinet and shaffron), and in addition to the above, there will be made two testers and one pair of shoulder defences, which will be in sum two cruppers and two peytrals and two collars and four testers and six pairs of shoulder defences.' The German is obliged to pay 100 *lire imperiale*, at 4*l.* a week 'until the said things are complete, and when they are complete, must pay the remainder to make complete payment of the said 100*l. i.*'

No place of issue, 18 May 1462

Il duca di Milano conferma i patti e le convenzioni seguite tra Antonio Missaglia e

Filippino d'Erba con la communità di Canzo 'pro azali et aliis metallis' dei loro forni e magli in pieve di Incino.

> The Duke of Milan confirms the agreements and contracts made between Antonio Missaglia and Filippino d'Erba with the Commune of Canzo (near Lake Como) 'for steel and other metals' of their furnaces and hammers (i.e., heavy hammer-works) in Pieve di Incino.

No place of issue, 1 August 1470

Patti dei carbonai Giuseppe detto Zambono di Vallenera, in Lesmo e Bornino Pedrazzoli di Val Camonica, abitant nel monastero di Basiano, pieve di Pontirolo, per la manutenzione de carbone al forno della ferriera di Filippo d'Erba e Damiano Negroni-Missaglia, sitauto in Canzo.

> Contract between the charcoal-burners Giuseppe, called 'Zambono' of Vallenera, in (the Commune of) Lesmo, and Bornino Pedrazzoli of Val Camonica, living in the Monastery of Basiano, Pieve di Pontirolo, for the provision of charcoal for the iron forges of Filippo d'Erba and Damiano Negroni, called 'Missaglia', situated in Canzo.

8

Paris, Bibliothèque national de France, MS fr. 5873, fol. 46r
A French Royal Herald's Description of the Bavarians, after 1451

> *Gilles le Bouvier was Berry Herald from 1420 and Roi d'armes des Français from 1451. His travels as an ambassador took him all across Christendom and beyond.*

Ces gens sont bons arbalestiers a cheual et a pie et tirent darballestres de corne ou de nerfs qui sont bonnes seures et fortes Car ilz ne romperit point Et les arbalestres de bois et les arcs sont aultres car elles rompent quant elles sont gellees et pour ce les font de cornes ou de nerfs car pour le froit elles ne rompent point et plus fait froit et plus sont fortes

> These (Bavarian) men are good crossbowmen, both on horseback and on foot, and shoot crossbows of horn or sinew which are good, secure, and strong for they do not break at all. And other crossbows and bows break when they are frozen, it is for this (reason) they are made of horn or sinew for the cold does not break them at all and the colder it gets the stronger they are.

Figure 3. Composite crossbow, German, mid-fifteenth century
(Glasgow Museums, R. L. Scott bequest, E.1939.65.sz).

9

Petty Custom Books of the Port of Southampton, 25 January 1451–8 October 1458 (Extracts)

Southampton Archives, SC 5/4/7
Petty Custom Book of the Port of Southampton, 25 January–20 December 1451

[25 January] ij C bowstavis Cust' vi li' […] Carraka de Grillo vnde Alisaunder Grille e' patro' […] iij [3 October] Galias de Negr' xij basket' de briganders [con]t' xlviij payer' cust' […] G' de Negr' viij ballez Briganders [con]t' iiijxx xvj valor' pec' xxvjs viijd s[um]ma Cxxviij li' […] G' de Negr' xlviijo briganders valor' lxiiij li' [8 November] xij payr' briganders […] Ciiij xx s Swerdebladis valor' ix li' v s' [21 October *sic*] x Chist' de briganders [con]t' iiij xx iiij brigander' valoris […] s[um]ma Cxxj li' […] xxx payr' bryganders valor' xl li' [20 December] vj C xx bowstavis […] ix payr' briganders valor' xli iij s' iij d' […] iiij C bowstavis […] iiij C bowstavis

Figure 4. Woodcut from *Der Weisskunig*, early-sixteenth century.

Southampton Archives, SC 5/4/8
Petty Custom Book of the Port of Southampton, 8 November 1454–17 July 1455

[8 November] C Bowstavis Cust' ij d [6 January] C d' bowstavis […] [6 March] viij C Bowstavis – cus' j d [12 April] vj C bowstavys – Cu' vj d' [2 June] C bowstavis […] C Bowstavis [19 August] iiijC Bowstavys cust' xvj d [19 July] ij C bowstavys […] cust' viij d [26 August] ij C Bowstavis […] – Cust' viij d [1 October] j bale de bregandins' cont' v peyre val' p[er] peyre xx s [6 January] v […] bowstavis Intru[eru]nt' cust' iiij d […] xx iij C Bowstavis xviijo Cust' ix s iij d [13 January] ij C Bowstavis – Cust' x d […] C d[imid]i bowstavis – cust' vj d [17 February] Bowstavis v m[i]l' iiij C iiij xx – cust' xxij s ix d [15 March] j C bowstavis cust' iiij d […] V C bowstavis Cust' v s [24 March] iij C xl bowstavis cust' xiij d [26 March] mC iiij xx Bowstavis Cust' iij s ix d […] ij d' Bowstavis cust' ix d [23 March] mC bowstavis – cust' iiij s ij d […] j m' bowstavis cust' iij s iiij d [30 March] ijd bowstavis cust' viij d [7 July] j peyre bregandynys val' x s – Cust' j d ob […] j peyre bregandynys val' xx s cust' iij d [17 July] j peyre bregandinys val' xx s cust' iij d

Southampton Archives, SC 5/4/10
Petty Custom Book of the Port of Southampton, 23 October 1455–16 January 1456

[23 October] iij payr' Bregandyn'z iij dobelett' de mayle valor' iiij Li Cust' xij d [9 January] [various?] Arc' Baston' [bow-staves] [16 January] j m[i]l' Baston pur arc' – cust' iiij s ij d […] iiij Baston' pur arc' cust' xx d […] v d'??? Baculij arciu' cust' d' ij s jd

Southampton Archives, SC 5/4/11
Petty Custom Book of the Port of Southampton, 27 March 1457–8 October 1458

[27 March] iiijC Bowstavis Cust' xvj d [12 April] x Salatt' val' p[er] pece iij s iiij d Cust' v d [14 May] C Bowstavis – cust' iiij d [8 August] C Bowstavys – cust' viij d [18 August] ij C Bowstavys – cust' viij d [30 August] iij C Bowstavys – cust' xij d [19 September] Cd' bowstavis – cust' vj d [3 April] d[imid]j C Bowstavis – cust' ij d [28 August] j barrell [con]t' j dozen' Salatt' val' iij li' [12 September] V C Bowstavys cust' xx d [26 September] ix C d' xv Bowstavis Cust' ij s ix d […] m[i]l' vij c xxviij Bowstavys [10 October] ij m[i]l' Bowstavys – cust' xx d [8 October] xv Saladys val' xxxvij s vj d

10

Marseille, Archives départementales des Bouches-du-Rhône, B 2479
Household Accounts of René, Duke of Anjou, 13 March 1451–1 January 1452

Unless otherwise stated, all purchases are for the Duke himself and all gifts are from him.
[13 March] A Maistre fremin coutelier dauignon Quarante deux liures cinq solz t' pour xxxiij bosettes dacier xxvij solz vj d' xij petites bosettes ij s' vj d' trois grandes boucles pour le heaulme & vne petite pour la targe x s' la boucle de lespee v s' pour achatter or fin pour dorer la dicte espee la croix & le poumeau dicelle le harnois dudit heaulme Cestassauoir les arrestes les bossettes dess[u]sd' la boucle le morda[n]t les cloux dune aultre espee & la pate dudit heaulme pour tous ce xxij l' po[u]r sa peine dauoir pourtrait a grandes l[ettr]es anciennes vng heaulme pour tournoier vne espee la croisee & le poumeau la boucle le bout dicelle xiiij clouz pour mectre sur la Renge pour auoir forge le harnois dudit heaulme qui est sur la visiere et po[u]r auoir dore les bossettes dess[us]d' ou Il a vacque luj & son s[er]uite[u]r par espace de trois sepmaines pour eaues fortes vif arg' et autres estoffes pour ce neccessaires xviij l' [19 March] Maistre pierre du billant brodeur Saixante & dix solz t' pour cinq on' de soye blanche violee entires es tresses du heaulme enuoie a mons' de la tour dauuergne lxij s' vj d' et pour sa peine dauoir fait lesd' tresses vij s' vj d', Guill[aum]e le lieure sellier dangiers [...] pour achat dune auln & demie de bla[n]c [prob. cuir] pour doubler le heaulme & fourreau de Jaueline enuoiee au Roy xx s' pour lestuy de cuir dud' heaulme & deux fourreux pour la dicte Jaueline et pour la facon xxvij s' vj d' Thomassin de baigneux armeurier pour deux dozaines de bossettes oultre autre bossettes qui o[n]t este mises en la targe enuoiee au vj s' viij [d'] pour auoir fourbj quatre fers de Jaueline x s' fourbj & garnj lespee doree quj fut a claux que led' s' a voulu auoir xv s' fourbj & garnj vne autre espee doree a boucles dacier pour enuoier aud' s' de la tour xx s' fourbj & garnj vne autre espee garnie dor pour led' s' & pour la fra[n]ge xx s' fourbj les veues de heaulme q' maistre fremin a dore v s' pour le viij donne aux s[er]uite[ur]s dechies huguet larmeur' qui ont fait led' heaulme xiij s' iiij d' [6 March] guillon Lenoix C x escuz cent cinqua[n]te & vne liures cinq solz t' pour achat de deux heaulmes de Jouste qui Il a fait faire a milan pour led' s' xxiiij escuz xxxiij l' achat dun harnois donne a mons' le conte de saint paoul xxxvj escuz xl ix l' v s' t' vng autre harnois tout double donne par a phelippe de leno[n]court son escuier descuierie xl ecuz lv l' apportaige desdiz harnois & heaulmes de milan Jucques a lyon sur le Rosne pour ce en x escuz xiij l' xv s' Jehan de vacincourt tresorier de la Royne de Sicile vjo de fil dor pour la gibeciere & garniture du fourreau de larc turquois enuoie au Roy vj escuz viij l' v s' ixo & quart de soye verde blanche & violee pour faire les floz & cordons de la targette dacier enuoiee au Roy C xv s' vij d' deux on' de fil dor pour franger lad' targe l v s' [19 March] Claux de bellemont tailleur demie aulne & demj q[ua]rtier de veluy cramoisi que ledit s' a fait bailler a maistre pietre le

brodeur pour faire vng fourreau darc dacier vj l' xvij s' vj d' vne auln' de satin cramoisi baillee aud' maistre pietre par ordonnan' dud' s' vne gibbeciere a mettre Jallez pour le Roy C x s' demie auln' de damas bleu pour faire vne doubleure dun heaulme l v s' Phelippe de lenonco[u]rt escuier descu[ier]ie dud' s' vj escuz huit liures cinq solz pour bailler a Jacob paintre du Roy pour vng heaulme dore pour tournoier et pour vng bicoquet ad ce necc[essai]re [18 April] Jehan nicollas orfeure pour or facon & esmailleure dun bout de dague pesant vng escu xlj s' iii d' facon esmailleure & dechiet de viij fers dor pes' ijo la targe dacier donn' au Roy Iceulx tailler & esmailler dun coste a Roses blanches et de lautre a champ de Rose cler vj l' xvij s' vj d' facon dechiet & esmailleure de la garnison dor dune espee pesant Icelle garnison iijo vij g[r]o' & de[m] j esmaillee a grosses gouttes de noir viij escuz xj l' [6 May] Maistre Pietre du billant brodeur dudit seigneur pour achat de cinq auln' & demie de taffetas achatte [a] angiers pour faire xx cornettes de lances a souleiz dor pour les ho[m]mes darmes de mons' de calabre oultre & pardesus xl autres cornettes qui fure[n]t faictes parauant po[u]r les ho[m]mes darmes dudit s' [le] Roy et aussi pour faire deux guictons a ses armes v escuz vj f' xvij s' vj d' vng tiers daulne de frange vermeille pesant ijo pour mettre a la lance dud' s' xxvij s' vj d' facon de lxxij ba[n]neroll' pour mettre sur les sallades des arch[ie]rs & cranequiniers esta[n]s en la compaignie dudit s' vj l' facon dune cornette de damas gris hachee dor pour la sallade dudit s' en iij escuz iiij l' ij s' vj d' [26 May] Gerart le noir sellier dangiers deux grosses c[am]pa[n]nes de laton souldees dargent pour mettre au coul des destriers qui Jousterent au pas de Saumur xl s' deux paires de garderaz de laton pour po[n]it les heaulmes sur les espaulles xxx s' vne poire de laton pour mettre soubz lescu xv s' pour auoir mis a point vng escu de cornes de serf lequel fut Rompu contre mons' de florigny xl s' [6 June] Gilles de maille escuier [du] s' de bresze cinquante liures pour luy aider a soy armer & mettre en point pour aco[m]paigner ledit s' ou voyage quil entend p[rese]nteme[n]t faire en guienne deuers le Roy[2] [21 June [sic]] Pierre de chedeuille trompette quatre liures dix solz pour achatter vng arc et vne trousse de flesches [6 June [sic]] Jehan Nicollas orfeure dudit seigneur ijC escuz deux cens saixante & quinze liur' […] pes' ijM vjo v g[r]o' dor pour garnir vng bicoquet vne sallade vng chappeau de montaulban & vne espee Jehan nicollas quatre vings dix sept liures doze solz six den' pour vng marc dor pour ce quil nen auoit pas assez pour garnir les habilleme[n]s de teste [19 June] Guillemin Theroude plumacier de Tours huit escuz vnze liures pour trois plumes blanches & violees pour vng chanfrain & pour vne grosse poume desd' plumes pour la salade dudit s' et pour vne plume noire pour messire bertan & aussi pour desdoumager ledit theroude de c[er]taines plumes dautruce quil a cuide faire teindre en tanne Thomassin de baigneux armeurier dudit s' pour cuir noir pour couurir pa[n]niers xxv s' pour la peine de celluj qui a couuert lesd' pa[n]niers xx s' pour les ferrerures boucles & crochez diceulx pa[n]niers xxij s' vj d' achat de iiij couroyees pour port' lesd' pa[n]niers xv s' auoir fourbj le bicoquet vij s' vj d' fourbj la sallade vij s' vj d' Roolle les maill' dudit s' xv s' fourbj & garny lespee xv s' les estoffes de la sallade du bicoquet & des gorgerettes vij s' vj d' fourbj larbaleste x s' trois g[a]rnitures de cuir housse pour

---

2   There are payments of 50*l.* to 24 other squires for the same purpose.

les habilleme[n]s de teste v s' clouz pour mettre audit bicoquet iij s' iiij d' vne
gorgerette pour anthoine du tillay lv s' Maistre pietre du billant Brodeur pour estoffes
& facon de xl cornettes faictes a souliez dor pour mettre aux lances des hommes
darmes xl f' Jehan de bonnes armeurier dudit s' pour vng corset que ledit de bonnes
a apporte aud' s' de Rouen xxij l' vng h[ar]nois de Jambes & vne sallade deliurez a
antoine du tillay par commandem[en]t dudit s' xiij l' xvj s' vng h[ar]noix de teste
estrange viij l' v s' auoir couppe & fait vng bort neuf & Recloue vng corset donne
aud' seigneur par ferrj mons' [de Lorraine] xxvij s' vj d' vne haulce sur griesue aux
cuissoz du harnois de Jambes x s' Guill[aum]e le lieure Sellier dangiers pour vne selle
darmes pour le destrier garnie dacier C x s' quatre chappellez & quatre bourses garnies
de couroyes et quatre arrestz pour porter la lance xv s' [20 June] Jehan nicollas orfeure
[…] xxxiij escuz & demj Quarante six liures vng sols trois deniers t' pour ouuraige de
iiijM je on' et demie dor mis en euure tant en la garniture dune sallade dun bicoquet
dun Chappeau de montaulban que dune espee Antoine du tillay vingt sept solz six
den' pour achatter plumes dautruce pour mettre sur la sallade huguet landeny doze
solz six den' pour achat dune once de soyes blanches & violees pour les franges de la
lance [27 June] thomassin de baigneux armeurier dud' s' sept liures quinze solz pour
achat dune harnois de Jambes donne A Jehan de prie escuier [30 June] Maistre pietre
du billant brodeur quatre liures dix solz tant pour soyes blanches & violees pour faire
franges pour vne targe & pour vng vosge [et] facon dicelles q' pour deux plumes
dautruce po[u]r mettre sur le chappeau de montaulban [20 July] Jehan quinnesoit
voicturier vingt & sept solz six den' tant po[u]r le sallaire q' po[u]r despen' de luy &
louaige dun ch[eu]al par trois Jours ven' dangiers a champigny et sen Retourn' pour
apporter trois heaulmes de Jouste q' led' s' a voulu auoir Jehan de bonnes armeurier
dudit s' cinqua[n]te & cinq solz pour la despen' deluj & de son cheual allant de
champigny A angiers pour faire la venir c[er]tain harnois estant en larmeurie dudit' s'
[8 August] Jehan de bonnes armeurier dud' s' vingt sept solz six den' quil a baillez a
vng ho[m]me qui a amene les heaulmes auecques aultres harnois de cha[m]pigne
Jucques a Saumur [14 August] Maistre fremin coutelier cinquante cinq solz pour vne
espee de chase [31 August] Jehan nicollas orfeure six liures dix sept solz six den' pour
vne garniture darg' pesant vne on' vj g[r]o' pour vne espee donnee A bernart mons'
[de Baviere] esmaillee a champ de violet & fleurs de pensees parmy pour esmaill'
facon [1 September] Thomassin de baigneux armeurier pour achat dune espee donn'
a bernart mons' lx s' pour lauoir garnie de fourreau de franges & de couroyes x s'
fourby & garny aussi de fourreau & decouroyees vne autre espee qui est a la
turquesque xx s' pour vne alumelle despee xxvij s' vj d' [1 October] Jehan de Xaintonge
varlet de [la] gardeRobe quatorze solz deux den' pour appareil de larbalestre &
mataraz pour Icelle & pour enuoier querir a launay vne autre arbalestre dudit s' [8
October] Phelippe de lenoncourt escuier descu[er]ie vingt sept liures dix solz tant
pour vng ch[eu]al pour porter le harnois donne a mons' de saint pol [et] po[u]r achat
de deux panniers de clice que aussi po[u]r lauoir Rachatte de guill[aum]e Roux
armeurier dangiers [11 October] Balthazar hirtanhaus [allemant [et] secretaire de la
Royne] xx escuz vingt sept liures dix solz en deduct[i]on de ce q' puet estre deu pour
vng harnois de Jouste que fait faire ledit s' [16 October] Maistre fremin coultelier pour

auoir pourtrait a l[ett]res morisques deux espees pour led' s' dont lune est dud' fremin
& lautre est dicelluj s' xl s' facon dune aultre espee doree le poumeau & la croix iiij l'
x s' [26 October] Ph[ilipp]e de lenoncout xx escuz vingt sept liures dix solz a luj
ordonnez estre bailler en deduct[i]on & Rabaix de ce que puet estre deu pour
c[er]tains h[ar]nois de Jouste que fait faire ledit s' oult' xx ault[re]s escuz baill' [27
October] Jehan Nicollas orfeure pour auoir Rabille les bossettes du corset darmes et
pour auoir Riue leschaples & les morda[n]s xxvij s' vj d' [20 November] Pierre
bouchard de villiers orfeure [et culleurinier] x escuz xiij l' xv s' pour achat de deux
culleurines de metal lune a vj boestes & lautre a xij [2 January] Gerardin de vausaillon
iiij escuz cent dix solz pour vne arbalestre dacier prinse de luy [7 January] Thomassin
de baigneux armeurier dud' s' cent dix solz a lui deuz tant pour bois & facon de xxxiij
bourdons tourn' pour ledit s' & ses seruiteurs allant en sa compaignie a n[ost]re dame
de clerj que pour les virolles & pointes dicelux qui est a Raison de iij s' iiij d' pour
ch[asc]un bourdon [1 February] Jehan de baudrecourt escuier vij escuz seize liures dix
solz [for various saddlery and] pour vne selle de guerre & po[u]r certaines harnois de
ch[eua]lx [5 February] Nicollas grenot trapicier dud' s' ij escuz cinquante & cinq solz
pour le louaige de cinquante auln' de toille pour faire les lices dauant casenoue en
attendant celles de bois a faire [23 March] Geffroy barrel esperonnier dang[er]s cent
dix solz tant pour vne piece douuraige q' Il a faicte de son mestier & baillee A lescuier
descuierie de bernart mons' de baui[er]e par ordonnan' de balthasar de hirtenhaus
pour le harnois de Jouste dud' s' apres son allee a n[ost]re dame de clery ou quel
ouuraige a plusieurs pieces Cestassauoir vne targette vne boueste a deux tuyaulx &
plus[ier]s aultres choses secrettes qon ne vieult pas nommer vng auantaige pour larrest
dud' harnois q' pour vne aultre boeste en laquelle a sembl[abl]ement plus[ier]s secretz
[4 April] Thomassin de baigneux armeurier dud' s' Trante deux solz six den' pour vng
cheuallet de bois mis in larmeurie et aussi pour auoir fait taindre vne plume dautruche
en noir pour mettre sur le heaulme de bernart mons' aux Joustes faictes dauant case
noue [2 May] Jehan de bonnes armeurier dud' s' Quatre liures cinq deniers t' pour
auoir fait faire estuy de boys a mettre vne grosse houppe garnie dor vij s' vj d' auoir
fait faire vng aut' estuy de bois long pour mettre espees & vne hache xij s' ix d' achat
dune pippe a mettre le harnois dud' s' quil fait mener par eaue en prouuen' vj s' viij
d' appareil dun escu de Jouste x s' auoir fait Relier lad' pippe & Renfoncer xx d' pour
paille a mettre auecq[ue]s ledit harnois ij s' vj d' huille dolliue cire & sain de porc
pour gresser led' harnoix ij s' vj d' achat dune aultre pippe a mettre aultre harnoix x
s' x d' auoir paie au charrestier qui a mene lesd' bessongnes du chasteau Jucques a la
Riuiere par deux voiages v s' auoir fait faire vne couuerte de cuir doublee de blanchet
a lespee de parement dud' s' ce xv s' [3 May] Audit Jehan de bonnes armeurier Trante
trois liures pour ses gaiges des mois de Januier feur' mars & Auril derr' passez qui est
A Raison de vj escuz par ch[asc]un mois Ph[ilipp]e de lenoncour escuier descuierie
en v escuz baillez a tours po[u]r achatter vng gorgery de mailles pour led' s' vj l' xvij
s' xj d' Bertran de la haie s' de mallelieure escuier descui[eri]e xij l' xv s' A lui
ordonnez estre baillez pour son voiage allant en bretaigne deuers le duc pour le fait
des xx lances Collas marchais artilleur dang' quatorze liures pour iiij arcs & deux
trousses de flesches donn' a loys painbleu & guill[aum]e de lesnaie sergens armes dud'

s' [7 May] Thomassin de baigneux armeurier dud' s' vingt & huit liures dix solz a lui deuz tant de ses gaiges des mois de Juin Juillet & aoust m iiijc lj A Raison de C v s' par mois comme pour aultres choses quil a faictes de son mestier Jehan truon trante & trois liures quinze solz pour xv paires de coulteaulx de chace garniz de poinczons & de fousilz Jehan Nicollas orfeure dud' s' pour la facon & pour lesmailleure dun bout dor fait po[u]r vne dague x s' la facon & pour le dechiet & lesmailleure dune garnison dor faicte pour vne espee viij f' v s' la facon & pour lesmailleure dun bout dor fait pour vne dague x s' la facon & po[u]r le dechiet de la garnison dor faicte pour vng grant coulteau de chasse lxviij s' ix d' [9 May] Pierre de lettres clerc Quarante & vne liures cinq solz po[u]r achat & paiement dun harnois complet par luy achatte par ordonnance dud' s' & donne A mess[ir]e bertran de beauuau le Jeune comme pour achat & paiement dun gorgery de mailles aussi par luy achatte pour le Roy de Sicile [10 May] Colinet de fontaines sellier dang[er]s Trante & sept solz six den' pour sa peine dauoir affis le velux & satin dessus vne targe de boys que led' s' fait porter auecques luy et les crampons pour la porter po[u]r ce x s' pour vng estuy de cuir garny de blanc pour le couurir xxvij s' vj d' [29 May] Maistre Jehan fremin coulter[ie]r six liures dix solz sur ce quil luy est deu po[u]r estoffes & facon de deux espiez [26 June] Jehan nicollas orfeure dud' s' pour auoir esmaille de neuf la garnison du bicoquet a visiere que aussi pour lauoir Riue viij escuz auoir fait la garniture de lespee en facon de larmes q' pour deux gros dor quil a mis plus que Receu viij escuz facon des garnitures du bicoquet & aussi de larmet qui poisent ensemble ij m' vjo & ij g[r]o' xxviij escuz auoir fait esmaillez la garnison dune espee L escu pour satin & cuir pour mettre dedens les couroyees pour le bicoquet que pour lauoir fait fourby L escu pour or quil a mis pour la garnison du gorgeri[n] que pour sa peine dauoir fait lad' garnison ij escuz & d[em]j pour or & facon de liiij fers daguillettes a armer pes' xij escuz xv escuz pour or & facon du xiiij aultres fers daguillettes a armer pesant trois escuz & de[m]j v escuz [27 September] Mess[ir]e bertran de beauuau le Jeune vij ducaz Treize florins deux gros cinq pataz q' le Roy lui a do[n]nez pour avoir vnes bardes Stephano de la mane marchant de millan pour vne Journee A armer pour Icellui s' & pour led' mess[ir]e bertran LJ f[l]o' Joulques dagolt s' de mison dix huit florins diz g[r]o' cinq pataz pour vng corset a milan [28 September] [Sureon] Spinolla [de spinollis mastr' dostel] dix huit florins dix gros cinq pataz pour vng aultre corset a armer Jehan de bonnes armeu[rie]r dud' s' vingt deux florins huit gros A Jehan de bonnes armeu[rie] r dud' s' vingt deux florins huit gros pour les baillez pour le vin aux varletz de misaille larmeurier Jehan de baudrecourt escuier cinquante & six florins huit gros pour luy aider a soy armer & mett' en point ypolide de housenen escuier cent quatre vings huit florins dix gros cinq pataz ta[n]t pour ses gaiges de homme darmes pour les mois de Juillet & Aoust derr' passez q' pour luy aider a soy armer & mettre en point Loys de fouleux eschancon dud' s' Trante & six flor' huit gros pour soy aider a mettre en point & a armer a millan Charles de la grant escuier homme darmes de la compaignie du s' de mallelieure C escus cent quatre vings trois florins quatre gros tant pour luy aider a auoir vng cheual pour consideraction du sien qui lui fut tue par les gens du s' guill[aum]e daua[n]t alixandre que aussi pour soy armer & mettre en point [29 September] Jehan du plesseis dit le begue [escuier descu[ier]ie dud' s'] pour deux bardes pour les ch[euau]lx du corps dud' s' xxix f[l]o' ix g[r]o' ij p' trois selles neufues pour trois ch[euau]lx de lescui[eri]e xvij f[l]o' deux chanfrains pour deux ch[euau]lx de lad' escuierie v f[l]o' viij g[r]o' pour le penaquier qui a faiz deux plumailz noirs pour led' s' xiiij f[l]o' ij g[r]o' v p[a]t[a]z Audit le begue cent cinquante ducatz pour les baill[e]r a missaille armeu[rie]r de millan en deduct[i]on & Rabaix de la so[m]me de iijC ducatz en quoy led' s' luy est tenu tant pour harnoix pour sa personne q' pour plus[ier]s gentilz hommes & aut[re]s de son hostel Jacques bastard de la tremoille Quatre vings quatorze flor' v gros deux pataz & de[m]j pour soy aider a armer & mettre en point a millan [30 September] Mess[ir]e Bertan de beauuau ch[eua]l[ie]r trante sept florins neuf gros deux pataz pour soy aider a armer & mettre en point aud' lieu de millan [2 October] Guill[aum]e de lesnaie & Loys painbleu s[er]gens darmes sept florins huit gros cinq pataz pour les estuis de leurs massez Jehan de bonnes vng florin deux gros pour achat de deux fers de lance Jehan de bonnes vng florin dix gros quatre pataz pour achat dun espee pour led' s' audit lieu de millan [17 November] Jehanin Cabut de Rebes & andre bobert [pelletier & varlet de chambre dud' s'] iiij ducatz & xvj parpilloll' de millan A Rais' de xxij g[r]o' iiij p' pour [vng?] ducat huit florins quatre gros cinq pataz pour partie de la voiture des brigandines q' a fait venir daniel Arrigi de gennes en ce pais de lombardie pour ce viij f[l]o' iiij g[r]o' v p' [20 November] Jehanim [sic] de maslines poursuiuant vnze florins trois gros pour supportacion de sa despen' allant dudit lieu de gabion a florence porter l[ett]res de par ledit s' a mons' de masseille & Jehan cossa s' de g[ri]mault est la pour les affaires dud' s' [both there and return], [1 January] Jehan de amans armeurier cinq florins six gros pour support' sa despen' allant en prouuen' Surleon spinola vingt & six florins dix gros pour [various merchandise including] vne pansiere de mailles dacier quil a baillees au begue escuier claux [de bellemont] iij aulnes & demie de noir pour doubler vne Jacquette a armer et vne Journade de veloux noir ix f[l]o iiij g[r]o'

[13 March] To Master Fremin, cutler of Avignon, 42 *livres 5 sous tournois* for 33 little steel bosses 27s. 6d., 12 little bosses 2s. 6d., three large buckles for the helm and one little one for the targe 10s., the sword-buckle 5s., the purchase of fine gold to gild the said sword – its cross and pommel – the fittings of the said helm, that is to say: the *arrêtes* (stop of some sort), the aforesaid little bosses, the buckle, the mordant (tongue), the nails of another sword, and the *pate* (i.e., crown plate) of the said helm 22l., for his efforts for having painted large ancient letters on a tourneying helm, one sword – the cross and pommel and the buckle [and] its end (this is most likely the metal tip at the scabbard's end, known in Eng. as the chape), 14 nails for fixing on the (affixing) ring, for having forged the harness (i.e., fittings) of the said helm which is on the visor and for having gilded the aforesaid little bosses, for his and his servant's wages for three months for strong spirits, coin, and other necessary equipment 18l., [19 March] Master Pierre du Billant, embroiderer 70s. t. for 5oz of white and violet silk for the tresses of the helm sent to my Lord of La Tour d'Auvergne 62s. 6d. and for his efforts for having made the said tresses 7s. 6d., Guillaume Le Lievre, saddler of Angers, for the purchase of 1½ ells of white (prob. leather) for lining the helm and javelin-sheath sent to the King 20s., for the helm's leather case and two sheaths for the said javelin and for their making 27s. 6d., Thomassin de Baigneux, armourer, for two dozen little bosses – in addition to the other little bosses which have been fitted to the targe sent to the King 6s. 8d., for having furbished four javelin-heads 10s., furbished and equipped the gilt sword which was at Claux [poss. Saint-Claude, Jura] that the lord wished to have 15s., furbished and equipped another gilt sword with steel buckles to send to the said lord of La Tour (d'Auvergne) 20s., furbished and equipped another sword garnished with gold for the lord and for the (decorative) fringe 20s., furbished the sights of the helm which Master Fremin has gilded 5s., for the 8 [sous?] given to the servants of the deceased Huguet the armourer who made the said helm 8s. 4d. [sic], Guillon Lenoix 110 écus, 151l. 5s. t. for the purchase of two jousting helms that he had made in Milan for the lord 24 écus 33l., purchase of a harness given to my lord the Count of Saint-Pol 36 écus 49l. 5s. t., another harness with all the double-pieces (i.e., reinforcing plates) given to Philippe de Lenoncourt, his squire of the écuyerie, 40 écus 55l., portage of the said harness and helms from Milan to Lyon-on-the-Rhône 10 écus 13l. 15s., Jehan de Vacincourt, treasurer of the Queen of Sicily, 6oz of gold thread for the belt-hanger and fittings for the sheath of the turkish bow sent to the King 6 écus 8l. 5s., 9¼oz of green, white, and violet silk for making the straps and little cords of the little steel targe sent to the King 115s. 7d., 2oz. of gold thread for fringing the said targe 2 écus 55s., Claux [i.e., Claude] de Bellemont, the lord's tailor, a half-ell and a half-quarter of crimson velvet which the lord granted to Master Pietre the embroiderer to make a sheath for a steel bow 6l. 27s. 6d., one ell of crimson satin granted to the said Master Pietre by the lord's command for a belt-pouch to place pellets for the King 110l., a half-ell of blue damask to make a lining for a helm 55s., Philippe de Lenoncourt, the lord's squire of the écuyerie, 6 écus 8l. 5s. to give to Jacob, the King's painter, for a gilt tourneying helm and for a bicoquet necessary for it, Jehan Nicollas, goldsmith, for gold, making, and enamelling a chape of a dagger weighing one écu – 40s. 3d., making, enamelling, and for material wastage for eight gold metal fittings (fers: poss. reinforcing bands for the sheath) weighing 2oz, a steel targe given to the King – fitting and enamelling it on one side with white roses and on the other with a field of plain roses 6l. 17s. 6d., making, material wastage, and enamelling of the gilt fittings of one sword – these fittings weighing 3oz 7½ gross of gold enamelled with large black drops for this 8 écus 11l., Master Pietre du Billant, the lord's embroiderer, for the purchase 5½ ells of taffeta in Angers to make two cornettes (decorations) for lances with gold suns for my Lord of Calabria's men-at-arms above and beyond the 40 other cornettes which were made before for the Lord King's men-at-arms and also for making two gitons (banners) of his (heraldic) arms 5 écus 6l. 17s. 6d., a ⅓ ell of vermillion fringe weighing 2oz. to place on the lord's lance 2s. 6d., making 72 banderoles (ornamental streamers) to place on the sallets of the lord's company of archers and crossbowmen 6l., making a cornette of grey damask hatched with gold for the lord's sallet 3 écus 4l. 2s. 6d., Gerart Le Noir, saddler of Angers, two large latten bells soldered with silver to place on the necks of the destriers that jousted at the Pas [d'armes] of

Saumur 40s., two pairs of latten *gardebras*[3] to keep the helms [*sic*] on the shoulders 30s., one latten pear to place under (i.e., behind) the shield[4] 15s., for having set up for use one stag-horn shield which was broken (jousting against) my lord of Florigny for 40s., [6 June] Gilles de Maille, the lord of Brézé's squire, 50l. given to him to assist him to arm and equip himself to accompany the lord in the voyage he intends to make presently to Guyenne before the King[5] [21 June] Pierre de Chedeville, trumpeter, 4l. 10s. to buy a bow and a quiver of arrows [6 June [*sic*]] Jehan Nicollas, the lord's goldsmith, 200 *écus* 275l. […] weighing 2 marks 6oz. 5 *gross* of gold to garnish one bicoquet, one sallet, one chapeau de Montauban, and one sword, Jehan Nicollas 97l. 12s. 6d. for one gold mark because he did not have enough to garnish the headwear, [19 June] Guillemin Theroude, feather-seller of Tours, 8 *écus* 11l. for three white and violet feathers for a shaffron and for one great plume of feathers for the lord's sallet and one black plume for the Sir Bertran and also for compensating the said Theroude for certain ostrich feathers which he wished to dye tawny, Thomassin de Baigneux, the lord's armourer, for black leather to cover panniers 25s., for the efforts of he who covered the said panniers 20s., for the locks, buckles, and hooks of these panniers 22s. 6d., purchase of four straps for carrying the panniers 15s., having furbished the bicoquet 7s. 6d., furbished the sallet 7s. 6d., rolled the lord's mail (armour, i.e., in a barrel) 15s., furbished and equipped the lord's sword 15s., stuffings (i.e., padded linings) of the sallet, bicoquet, and the gorgets 7s. 6d., furbished the crossbow 10s., three garnitures of padded leather for the lord's headwear (i.e., bespoke helmet-stands) 5s., for nails to place on the bicoquet 3s. 4d., a gorget for Antoine du Tillay 55s., Master Pietre du Billant, embroiderer, for materials and making of 40 *cornettes* made as gold suns to place on the men-at-arms' lances 40fr., Jehan de Bonnes, the lord's armourer, for one corset which the said De Bonnes has carried to the lord from Rouen 22l., one (pair of) legharness and a sallet delivered to Antoine du Tillay by the lord's command 13l. 16s., one foreign head defence 8l. 5s., having cut down and made a new edge and re-nailed a corset given to the lord by Ferry Monseigneur [de Lorraine] 27s. 6d., one reinforce over the greaves to [*sic, recte* and] the cuisses of the legharness 10s., Guillaume le Lievre, saddler of Angers for an arming saddle for the destrier equipped with steel 110s., for four chaplets and four pouches fitted with straps and four *arrests* for carrying the lance [prob. a fewter rather than a lance-rest] 15s., [20 June] Jehan Nicollas, the lord's goldsmith, 33½ *écus* 46l. 1s. 3d. t. for the use of 4 *marcs* 1½oz of gold used in crafting both the fittings of one sallet, one bicoquet, one chapeau de Montauban as well as one sword, Antoine du Tillay 27s. 6d. for the purchase of ostrich feathers to place on the sallet, Huguet Landeny 12s. 6d. for the purchase of an ounce of white and violet silk for the fringes of the lance, [27 June] Thomassin de Baigneux, the lord's armourer, 7l. 15s. for the purchase of one (pair of) legharness given to Jehan de Prie, squire, [30 June] Master Pietre du Billant,

---

3   In this instance they are more likely to be arm guards rather than pauldrons.
4   See Moffat, *Medieval Arms and Armour: A Sourcebook. Volume II*, doc. 100.
5   Payments of 50l. are made to 24 other squires for the same purpose.

Figure 5. Stained glass panel, Swiss, early sixteenth century
(Glasgow Museums, Burrell Collection, 45.508).

embroiderer, 4*l.* 10*s.* both for white and violet silk to make fringes for a targe and for a vouge for the lord [and] their making as well as two ostrich feathers to place on the chapeau de Montauban, [20 July] Jehan Quinnesoit, transporter (of goods), 27*s.* 6*d.* both for his salary as well as his expenses and hire of one horse for three days coming from Angers to Champigny and returning to carry three jousting helms that the lord wished to have, Jehan de Bonnes, the lord's armourer, 55*s.* for his expenses and his horse going from Champigny to Angers to arrange to bring certain harness in the lord's armoury, [8 August] Jehan de Bonnes, the lord's armourer, 27*s.* 6*d.* which he has given to a man who brought the helms with the other harness from Champigny to Saumur, [14 August] Master Fremin, cutler, 55*s.* for a hunting sword, [31 August] Jehan Nicollas, goldsmith, 6*l.* 17*s.* 6*d.* for a silver

43

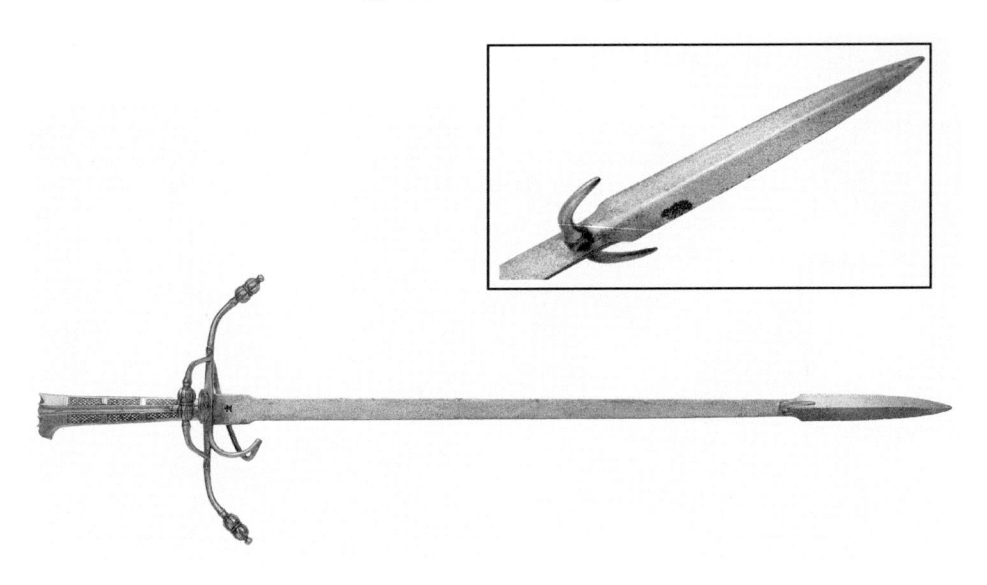

Figure 6. Boar-hunting sword, German, early-sixteenth century
(Glasgow Museums, R. L. Scott bequest, E.1939.65.0j).

fitting weighing 1oz *6gr.* for a sword given to Bernard Monseigneur enamelled with
a violet field with flowers of memory (or pansies) throughout [and] for making this
enamel, [1 September] Thomassin de Baigneux, armourer, 117*s.* 6*d.* for the purchase
of a sword given to Bernard Monseigneur 60*s.*, for having equipped the scabbard
with fringes and with straps 10*s.*, furbished and equipped the scabbard and straps
of another sword which was of the Turkish fashion 20*s.*, for a sword blade for the
lord 27*s.* 6*d.*, [1 October] Jehan de Xaintonge, valet of the wardrobe, 14*s.* 2*d.* for
equipping the crossbow and *mataraz* [a material of some sort?] for it and for
sending to enquire at Launay for another of the lord's crossbows, [8 October]
Philippe de Lenoncourt, squire of the *écuyerie*, 27*l.* 10*s.* both for one horse to carry
the harness given to my lord of Saint-Pol [and] for the purchase of two wicker
panniers as well as for having reimbursed Guillaume Roux, armourer of Angers, [11
October] Balthazar Hirtanhaus, [German and Queen's Secretary], 20 *écus* 27*l.* 10*s.*
in deduction of this which ought to be due for a jousting harness which the lord
had made, [16 October] Master Fremin, cutler, for having painted two swords with
Moorish letters for the lord – one of which is the said Fremin's and the other is the
lord's 40*s.*, making another gilt sword – the pommel and cross – 4*l.* 10*s.*, [26
October] Philippe de Lenoncour 20 *écus* 27*l.* 10*s.* ordered to be granted to him in
deduction and reimbursement of that which must be due for certain jousting
harness which the lord had made beyond the other 20 *écus* granted, [27 October]
Jehan Nicollas, goldsmith, for having refitted the little bosses of the arming corset
and for having riveted the staples and the mordants (tongues) 27*s.* 6*d.*, [20
November] Pierre Bouchard de Villiers, goldsmith [and culverin-maker], 10 *écus* 13*l.*
15*s.* for the purchase of two cast-iron culverins – one with six (loading) chambers

and the other with twelve, [2 January] Gerardin de Vausaillon 4 *écus* 110s. for a steel crossbow taken from him, [7 January] Thomassin de Baigneux, the lord's armourer, 106s. due to him both for wood and making of 33 tourneying bourdons (heavy lances) for the lord and his servants going in his company to Notre Dame de Clery as well as for their ferrules and points – each bourdon costing 3s. 4d., [1 February] Jehan de Baudrecourt, squire, 7 *écus* 6l. 10s. [for various saddlery and] for a war saddle and for certain horse harness, [5 February] Nicollas Grenot, the lord's tapicer, 2 *écus* 55s. for the hire of 50 ells of cloth to make the lists before Casanova and overseeing those who made the wooden (parts), [23 March] Godfrey Barrel, spurrier of Angers, 110s. both for a piece of work of his craft and given to the squire of the *écuyerie* – Bertrand Monseigneur de Baviere – by order of Balthazar de Hirtenhaus for the lord's jousting harness after his going to Notre-Dame de Cléry as well as the work of several other pieces, that is to say: one targe, one padded section, and several other secret things which one does not wish to name – an advantage for the (lance) rest of the said harness as well as for another padded section in which there is likewise several secret (things), [4 April] Thomassin de Baigneux, the lord's armourer, 32s. 6d. for a wooden stand placed in the armoury and also for having dyed an ostrich feather black to place on the helm of Bernard Monseigneur [*sic*] at the jousts held before Casanova, [2 May] Jehan de Bonnes, the lord's armourer, 4l. 5d. t. for having a wooden case made to place a large hoop (head/helmet decoration) garnished with gold 7s. 6d., having had another case made to place swords and one axe 13s. 9d., for purchase of a pipe (i.e., cask) to place the lord's harness that he had brought by water to Provence 6s. 8d., equipping one jousting shield 10s., having remade and reinforced the said pipe 20d., delicate cloth to place with the said harness 2s. 6d., olive oil and pig fat to grease the said harness 2s. 6d., the purchase of another pipe to place harness 10s. 20d., having paid a carter who brought the said necessities from the castle to the river by two journeys 5s., having had a white leather cover lined with blanket (fabric) made for the lord's dress sword 15s., [3 May] to the said Jehan de Bonnes, armourer, 33l. for his wages for the months of January, February, March, and April last at 6 *écus* a month, Philippe de Lenoncour, squire of the *écuyerie*, 5 *écus* given at Tours to purchase a mail gorget for the lord 6l. 17s. 11d., Bertrand de la Haie de Mallelievre, squire of the *écuyerie*, as ordered and granted to him for his journey to Brittany before the Duke for making ten lances, Collas Marchaise, *artilleur* of Angers, 14l. for 4 bows and two quivers of arrows given to Louis Painbleu and Guillaume de Lesnaie, the lord's sergeants-at-arms, [7 May] Thomassin de Baigneux, the lord's armourer, 28l. 10s. due to him both for his wages for the months of June, July, and August 1451 at 110*fr.* a month as well as other things of his craft he has made, Jehan Truon 33l. 5s. for 15 pairs of hunting knives equipped with *poinçons* (i.e., by-knives) and *faucilles* (wide-bladed un-making knives), Jehan Nicollas, the lord's goldsmith, for making and enamelling a gilt chape made for a dagger 10s., for making, material wastage, and enamelling of a gilt fitting for one sword 8*fr.* 5s., making and enamelling a gilt chape for a dagger 10s., making, and material wastage of the gilt fitting for a large hunting knife 68s. 9d., [9 May] Pierre de Lettres, clerk, 41l. 5s. for and purchase and payment for a complete harness bought by him by order of the lord and given to Sir Bertrand de Beauveu, the younger, as well as for the purchase and payment of a mail gorget also bought by him for the King of Sicily, [10 May] Colinet de Fontaines, saddler of Angers, 37s. 6 d. for his pains for having affixed the velvet and satin upon a wooden targe that the lord had carried with him and the grips to carry it 10s., for a leather case fitted with white (leather) to cover it 27s. 6d., [29 May] Master Jehan Fremin, cutler, 6l. 10s. above that due to him for fittings and making of two espieux (espieu: a type of lance/spear), [26 June] Jehan Nicollas, goldsmith, for having newly enamelled the fittings of the bicoquet with visor as well as having riveted it 8 écus, having made the fittings of the sword in the manner of tears as well as for two gold gross that he was due 8 écus, having made the fittings for the bicoquet and also the armet that weigh together 2 marcs 6gr. – 28 écus, having made (and) enamelled one sword 50 écus, for satin and leather to place within the straps of the bicoquet as well as for having had it furbished 50 écus, for the gold which he has placed on the fittings of the gorget as well as for his pains in having made the fittings 2½ écus, for gold and making of 54 arming aglets (metal tips for arming points) weighing 12 écus, for gold and making of another 14 arming-point aglets weighing 3½ écus – 5 écus, [27 September] Sir Bertrand de Beauvau, the younger, 7 ducats 13 florins 2gr. 5p. that the King gave him to have one (horse) bard, Stefano della Mane, merchant of Milan, for one arming journade (a fabric overgarment, but here poss. means arming doublet) for the lord and Sir Bertrand 51fl., Joulques Dagolt, seigneur de Mison, 18fl. 10gr. 5p. for a corset at Milan, [28 September] [Sorleone] Spinola [di Spinoli, Maître d'hôtel], 18fl. 10gr. 5p. for another arming corset, Jehan de Bonnes, the lord's armourer, 22fl. 8gr. for providing the wine to the valets of Missaglia the armourer, Jehan de Baudrecourt, squire, 6fl. 8gr. to assist him to arm and equip himself, Ypolide de Housenen, squire, 184fl. 10gr. 5p. both for his wages as a man-at-arms for the months of July and August last as well as to assist him to arm and equip himself, Louis de Fouleux, échanson (cup-bearer), 36fl. 8gr. to assist him to equip and arm himself in Milan, Chales de La Grant, squire, man-at-arms of the company of the lord of Mallelievre, 100 écus 183fl. 4gr. both to assist him to have a horse in consideration of the one killed by the men of Lord Guillaume before Alexandria as well as to assist him to arm and equip himself, [29 September] Jehan de Plessis, called 'Le Begue', [squire of the lord's écuyerie], 65fl. 7gr. 7p. for two bards for the horses of the lord's person 29fl. 9gr. 2p., for three new saddles for three horses of écuyerie 17fl., two shaffons for two horses of the écuyerie 5fl. 8gr., for the feather-maker who made the two black plumes for the lord 13fl. 2gr. 5p., to the said 'Le Begue' 150 ducats to grant to Missaglia, armourer of Milan, in deduction and reimbursement of the sum of 300 ducats which the lord owes him both for harness for his own person as well as for several gentlemen of his household, Jacques, Bastard of La Trémoïlle, 94fl. 5gr. 2½p. to assist him to arm and equip himself in Milan, [30 September] Sir Bertand de Beauvau, knight, 37fl. 9gr. 2p. to assist him to arm and equip himself in Milan, [2 October] Guillaume de Lesnaie and Louis Painbleu, sergeants-at-arms, 7fl. 8gr. 5p. for the cases for their maces, Jehan de Bonnes 1fl. 2gr. for the purchase of two lanceheads, Jehan de Bonnes 1fl. 10gr.

4p. for the purchase of a sword for the lord in Milan, [17 November] Jehanin Cabut of Rébé and André Bobert (the lord's keeper of the furs and *valet de chambre*), 4 ducats and 16 Milanese *parpaillole* [currency] by reason of 22gr. 4 *petits* for [one?] ducat 8fl. 4gr. 5p. for part of the transport of brigandines which were brought by Daniel Arrigi from Genoa to Lombardy, [20 November] Jehanim [*sic*] de Maslines, poursuivant (a herald), 11fl. 3gr. for covering his expenses going from Gabbione (in Lombardy) to Florence carrying the lord's letters to my lord of Missaglia and Jehan Cossa, lord of Grimaldi, being for the lord's business [both there and return], [1 January] Jehan de Amans, armourer, 5fl. 6gr. for covering his expenses going to Provence, Sorleone Spinola 26fl. 10gr. for [various merchandise including] one steel mail *panziere* [Ital. haubergeon] which was given to 'Le Begue', Claux [de Bellemont] 3½ ells of black (fabric) to line an arming jacket (i.e., arming doublet) and a black velvet *journade* [prob. means fabric overgarment here] 9fl. 4gr.

11

Paris, Archives nationales de France, Y//7: Registres des bannières du Châtelet de Paris, fol. 89r–fol. 90v

Royal Ordinances made concerning the Acts of the Craft of the Armourers, Brigandine-Makers, Makers of Swords and Other Things pertinent to War Equipment of the City of Paris, 20 March 1452 (new style)

Ordonnances Royaulx faictes sur le fait du mestier des armeuriers brigandiniers faiseurs despees et aut[re]s choses toucha[n]s habilleme[n]s de guerre de la ville de paris

Loys par la grace de dieu Roy de france Sauoir faisons a tous presens et aduenir Nous auoir Receue lumble supplicacion des maistres et Jurez de la co[m]munaulte des armeuriers brigandiniers forbissuers de harnoys & haubergiers de n[ost]re bonne ville et cite de paris Contenant Que pour obuier aux abus fraudes & malices qui es temps passez ont este co[m]mises esd' mestiers ou preiudice & lesion de la chose publique & dont sensuiuoie[n]t de grans dangers et Inco[n]uenie[n]s Jure Inreparables Feu N[ost]re trescher seigneur et pere que dieu absoille qui en son temps a desire mectre en ordre et police les estaz de ce Royaulme fist Ja pieca faire & drecer certains articles par forme de statut & ordonna[n]ce qui sont contenuz en vng Roolle de parchemin signe de la main de Poton de saintrailles & seelle du seel des ses armes duquel len dit la teneur estre telle Cest lordonnance que le Roy n[ost]re s' veult estre faicte & gardee es villes de son Royaulme sur les mestiers des armeuriers brigandiniers faiseurs despees haches guisarmes ou voulges dagues et autres choses toucha[n]s habilleme[n]s de guerre Premierement Quiconques vouldra estre armeurier ou brigandinier & leuer ouurouer desd' mestiers ou de lun diceulx faire le pourra pourvueu quil soit a ce souffisant et expert par le Raport des Jurez et gardes dudit mestier et payez dentre soixante solz par' Cestassauoir quarante solz par' au Roy n[ost]re dit s[eigneu]r & vint solz a la co[n]frairie n[ost]re dame Si non que ceulx qui ainsi leueront leur dit mestier feussent filz de maistre Lesquelz en ce cas silz sont souffisans pourront franchement leuer leurd' mestier sans payer lesd' soixante solz par' Item Que aucun dudit mestier ne autre marchans ne pourra achecter pour Reuendre en lune desd' villes ne en la banlieue harnois de dehors soit blanc ou noir pour mectre en autre facon q' celle dont Il sera Ne aussi n[...]le pourra Remectre en facon de lune desd' villes ou Il sera demourant sur peine de perdre led' harnoys et de soixante solz paris[i]s damende a appliquer co[m]me dessus Item Seront lesd' armeuriers brigandiniers et autres des mestiers dessusd' tenuz de faire ouurage bon marcha[n]t loyal et Raisonnable cest assauoir lesd' armeuriers & brigandiniers harnoys blanc & brigandines despreuue darbaleste a tillolles ou demie espreuue a tout les moins darbalestre a croq ou darc et sera louurage despreuue merque de deux merques & celui de demie espreuue dune merque sur peine de forfaire et confisquer lesd' harnoys et brigandines & de la dicte admende de soixante solz par' a appliquer co[m]me dessus Item Ne pourra nul desd' ouuriers seduire ne fortraire les varletz & seruiteurs les vngs dauec les autres dura[n]t le temps de leur s[er]uice et loyer sans le congie de leurs maistres ou maistre sur peine de ladicte admende de soixante solz par' Item Que tous marchans venans demourans et apportans ou faisans apporter harnoys & brigandines pour vendre Ne mectent ou esposent en vente lesd' harnois & brigandines et aut[re]s choses des dessusd' mest[ie]rs Jusques a ce quelles ayent estre veues et visictes par les Jurez et gardes desd' mestiers A fin de veoir et sauoir se elles sont bonnes loyalles et marchandes souffisans et de bonnes estoffes ainsi & de lespreuue dessus declairee sur peine de forfaire les choses dessusd' & de ladmende de soixante solz par' a appliquer co[m]me dessus Item que aucun desd' ouuriers ne vendra en la ville ou Il demourra harnoys ne brigandines pour ouurage fait en ladicte ville ne naffermera Icellui ouurage estre neuf pour viel ne avoir este fait en lad' ville sur peine de le confisquer et de ladmende dessusd' a appliquer co[m]me dessus Item Que pour la visitac[i]on dud' ouurage et aussi pour la cons[er]uacion de lordonna[n]ce dessusd' Seront ch[asc]un an esleuz deux preudes hommes Jurez & gardez dud' mestier en cha[asc]un desd' villes Qui Jureront aux sainctes euuangilles de dieu pardeua[n]t Poton seigneur de saintrailles Premier escuier de corps du Roy n[ost]red' s[eigneu]r et maistre de son escuirie ou de son co[m]mis de par lui de bien loyalment & dilige[m]ment visiter led' ouurage et garder lad' ordonnance et et seront Iceulx esleuz Jurez tenuz faire leur Rapport de ce quilz auront trouue en la Justice du lieu pour estre faicte pugnic[i]on des Infracteurs dicelle ordonnance par admendes & peines Indictes corporellem[en]t ou aut[re]me[n]t ainsi que au cas appartendra Et lesquelz Jurez esleuz signeront et m[er]queront louurage quilz auront trouue bon de quelque pays quil soit admene dun signe soit poincon ou autre merque telle quil sera aduise A ce que aucun ne soit fraude ne deceu dudit ouurage et pour obuier aux dangiers et Inco[n]ueniens qui sen pouroient esuiuir

Royal Ordinances made concerning the acts of the craft of the armourers, brigandine-makers, makers of swords and other things pertinent to war equipment of the town of Paris

Louis, by the grace of God, King of France, lets it be known to all present and to come that We have received the humble supplication of the masters and judges of the commonalty of the armourers, brigandine-makers, harness-furbishers, and haubergers (mail-makers) based in Our fair town and city of Paris, that to avoid the abuses, frauds, and evils which in times past has subjected the said masters to the prejudice and hurt of the public weal and the ensuing great dangers and sworn irreparable inconveniences, Our late very dear Lord and Father (who God absolve) who had in his time desired to put in order and govern the states of this realm had, some time ago, made and directed certain articles in the form of a statute and ordinance which were contained in a roll of parchment signed by the hand of Poton de Xaintrailles and sealed with the seal of his (heraldic) arms, of which it is said the tenor is such that this ordinance that Our Lord the King wanted to have done and supervised in the towns of His Realm over the crafts of the armourers, brigandine-makers, makers of swords, axes, gisarmes, vouges, daggers, and other things pertinent to war equipment. Firstly, whosoever wants to be an armourer or brigandine-maker and rise to the position of craftsman of these crafts (or of one of them) in order to do so he must be proven suitable and expert by the report of the judges and wardens of the craft; and they must pay sixty Parisian *sous* ingress – that is to say: forty Parisian *sous* to the King and twenty *sous* to the Confraternity of Notre Dame, but not if they have been raised to their craft being a son of a master they, in this case, if they be suitable, may freely rise to their craft without paying sixty Parisian *sous*. None of the craft, nor any other merchant, may buy to sell in any town or in the outskirts, harness from outside – be it white or black (i.e., polished or unpolished steel) – to place in another fashion to those (harnesses) which shall be found here on pain of forfeiting the harness and a fine of sixty Parisian *sous* as stated above. Armourers, brigandine-makers, and others of the crafts aforesaid are obliged to make their work good, legal, sellable, and reasonable – that is to say: the armourers and brigandine-makers craft white harness and brigandines of the proof of a device-spanned crossbow or of half proof of a belt-hook-spanned crossbow or bow (i.e., longbow). The fully-proofed work shall be marked with two marks and those of half proof with one mark on pain of the forfeiture and confiscation of the harnesses and brigandines and a fine of sixty Parisian *sous*. Let none of the craftsmen draw away or harm valets and servants (nor one the other) during the time of their apprenticeship and employment; and they not be in debt to their masters on pain of the fine of sixty Parisian *sous*. All merchants coming, remaining, or importing, or having imported harness and brigandines to sell, shall not place or put up for sale the harness, brigandines, and other things of the crafts aforesaid until they have been viewed and appraised by the judges and wardens of the crafts in order to see and know if they be thus good, legal, sellable, suitable, of good stuff, and of the proof declared above on pain of the forfeiture of the goods and a fine of sixty Parisian *sous*. None of the craftsmen may sell in the town where they are resident harness or brigandines as work made in that town or affirm this work to be new if it be old on pain of its confiscation and aforesaid fine. For the appraisal of the work, and also for the enforcement of this ordinance, two worthy men shall be elected every year as judges and wardens of the craft in each town who shall swear on God's Holy Gospels before Poton, Lord of Xaintrailles, premier squire of the King's person and master of his *écuyerie* (or his depute), that they shall loyally and diligently appraise the work and enforce the ordinance. They who have been elected judges shall be obliged to make their report of all that they have found in God's judgement and punish those who infringe this ordinance by the fines and corporal punishments or otherwise as shall be deemed appropriate to each case. Those elected judges shall sign and mark the work which they find good from whichever land they have been brought with a sign – be it a punch or other mark – as they shall be so advised so that this work be not fraudulent or deceitful and to thus avoid the ensuing dangers and inconveniences.

12

Durham Cathedral Archives, Accounts of the Sacrists and Hostillers of Durham Priory

Durham Priory Hostiller's Account, 1452–3

sol' pro Araiac[i]one & le Scowrynge diu[er]sor[um] Armor[um] rem' in Sacri[st]o hostillarij cu' vnctione preseruatina eor[un]d[u]m ad rubigine expel[…]nda' iij s' iiij d'

> paid for scrubbing and the scouring of diverse armour remaining in the hostiller's sacristy with oil for preserving the same and for getting rid of the rust *3s. 4d.*

13

Now-Lost Original Document from the Archives municipales de Douai, printed in E. J. Soil de Moriamé, 'Armes et armuriers tournaisiens. Heaumiers, haubregonneurs, forbisseurs, couteliers. Contribution à l'histoire des métiers d'art et à l'histoire militaire de Tournai de XIIIe au XVIIIe siècle', *Bulletin de l'Académie royale d'archéologie de Belgique*, unnumbered (1913), pp. 36–154 (at p. 105)

Account of Jacques Queval, Douai, 1453

ung haubregon, coutiel à clau, une espée et un huvette xl s. une daghe à ung coupiel d'argent 5 s. une dague à ung coespliel d'argent vi s. ung planchon et une macque esquantelée ii s. ung heaume, une huvette […] deux lances et une langue de buef […] ung pan de haubregon vii s. ii hausecols vii s. iii poitrinières xv s. iiii bracelés […] iiii lamettes […] deux vies arbalestres, une targe, ung housiaulx, esporons et fastras ii s. one haubergeon, knife with (decorative) nail, one sword, and one *huvette* (type of helmet) 40s., one dagger with a silver fork 5s., one dagger with a silver fork 6s., one plançon and one spiked mace 2s., one helm, one *huvette* […], two lances and one langue de boeuf […] one haubergeon-paunce 7s., two hounskulls 7s., three breast-plates 15s., four bracers […] four small lames […], two old crossbows, one targe, one (pair of) boots, spurs, and shoes 2s.

14

Paris, Archives nationales, KK//328

Journal *of Maître Jehan Dauvet, King's* procureur général, *Angers, Bourges, Feurs-en-Forez (near Lyon), Montpellier, and Tours, 6 July 1453–5 July 1457*

> Dauvet's Journal *records the business dealings and sale of the goods of Jacques Coeur (d. 1456). Coeur was an extremely wealthy merchant, moneylender, and royal administrator who was brought down by his enemies and tried for various crimes in 1451.*

[Tours, 6 July 1453]

vng colier dor a xxx gros boutons dor vne garnison de salade esmaillee de gris vne garnison de Jazeran esmaillee de blanc a fleurs de Rouge cler conten' six boucles & les tixus qui sont dor esmaillez de mesmes les boucles les boecets & les Riuez et dix gros chatons et Cinquante quat' aut[re]s petiz chatons auec aut[re] menu frutin dor […] et en faire forgez des escuz [7 July 1453] Et le collier dor a xxx gros boutons est a xviij caratz & poise ij M' vij o' deux gros qui Reuiennent a ij M' vne once x d' xij grains dor fin Et la garnison de la salade est a xx caratz & poise vng marc deux gros et demy qui Reuiennent a vj o' xxij deniers vj grains dor fin en ce non comprins deux bocetes de fer qui pesoient neuf gros ou enuir' Et la garnison de Jazeran a xx caratz & poise vj o' v d' qui Reuiennent cinq onces iiij d' iiij grans dor fin […] dont fault Rabat' pour la tare de lesmaile qui estoit tant oud' colier a xxx boutons q' es g[ar]nisons de la salade & du Jazeran xviij d' dor fin val' vj escuz xx s' t'

[Bourges, 16 November 1453]

Balsarin de trez p[rese]nta son compte de la compaignie de harnoiz co[n]traicte ent[re] guillaume de varye & led' balsarin & feu gasparin son fr[er]e lequel compte led' balsarin afferma par s[er]ement estre veritable tant en Re[cep]te que en despence Et les xvj xvij & viijme Jour dud' mois Octo briconnet & moy auons vacque a veoir visiter et exam' led' compte qui est grant & prolix & a verifier les parties tant des Receptes que des despen' dicelluy [18 November] Pour ce que le compte de balsarin nest en bon ordre ne en bon Langaige par laduis de octo & briconnet Jay ordonne audit Balsarin le faire mectre et ordonner en ordre & bon Langaige et y decle[r]er les debates tant des Receptes et despen' que des ventes & amplect' et le plus brief que faire se pourra Il le me Rapporte [20 November] Octo briconnet et moy visitasmes les asteliers forges hostilz et le moulin a harnoiz de balsarin estant en ceste ville de bourges dont Icelluy balsarin compte plus[ier]s grant despences en ses comptes [21 November] nous auons besongne ou compte de balsarin et pour ce que Il y a plusieurs parties de harnois quil dit auoir este deliurees par lordonnance du Roy a plus[ieur]s personnes dont Il se Rapporte au papier du Roy Jay ordonne & appoincte que Je surcoyre de proceder des plus auant a lexamen & conclusion dud' compte Jusques a ce que octo castellan qui brief yra deu[er]s le Roy pour ceste matiere & aut[re]s ay parle aud' S[eigneu]r desd' parties & sceu si par led' papier dud' s[eigneu]r elles se pourront verifier ou nom [sic]

[Tours, 1 December 1453]

Quant aux trois brigandines dont lune estoit couuerte de veloux co[m]me Il mest aduis Laquelle Je donnay Au conte de douglaz & les deux aut[re]s estoient couuertes de drap que Je donnay a deux des gens dud' conte aussi Je les approuue & peuent valoir au plus hault pris que le Roy les a mises xij escus la brigandine qui est xxxvj e' Et le veloux pour la couuerture dicelle dud' conte xiiij e' Pour ce Cinquante e'
[Sale of goods from Jacques Coeur's properties in Montpellier, 25 May 1454]
vne Jaueline Roillee A Estiene boutie ij s' j d' vng voulge a Jehan de flandres xxiij s' viij d' vng aut[re] voulge Roille a Anthoine maleRipe xlj s' iij d' vng autre voulge Roille A loys de chartres xx s' vng aut[re] voulge Roille a Jehan le flament xxj s' j d' vne hache a anth' Juin xxv s' vj d' vne aut[re] hache aud' anthoine Juin xx s' ij d' vne aut[re] hache audit anth' Juin xxv s' ij d' le fust dune Jaueline a sarrilon xiij d' vng haste de fer audit sarrilon x s' vj d' vng aut[re] haste de fer a mess[i]re Jehan de vedel xiij s' vj d' vne salade a loys de chartres xxj s' iij d' deux gantelles & vne baui[er]e a pierre sezelly xx s' [3 June] A girault fouet vne brigandine couuerte de satin violet figure xij l' v s' James boier vne aut[re] brigandine couuerte de satin noir figure xij l' Aud' boyer [sic] vne aut[re] brigandine couuerte de fustaine noire viij l' v s' A saluadour vne aut[re] brigandine couuerte de fustaine noire viij l' bernard de vaulx vne aut[re] brigandine couuerte de fustaine noire viij l' v s' [12 June] a bernard de vaulx dune dozeine & demie de Jus[ar]mes vne xij de haches doze salades deux arbalestres que lesd' chos' ont este ordonn' a lusaige de la gelee saint Jacques laquelle galee auec son yssarse et habillemens de guerre luy onte este vendues

[métairie (smallholding) at Asnières-les-Bourges, 1 February 1456]

vendu et deliure A Raoulet tostain marchant demour' a tours a luy quatre enseignes des estraines dargent vng petit heaume dargent deux boillons de salade et vint petiz cloz de sainture le tout dargent pes' deux onces xl s' a este vendu a mery bueille vne hache darmes toute vsee et Roillee pour le pris de vij s' vj d' vendu a pierre de valenciennes vne vueillez cuisasses [sic, recte cuirasses] couuertes de vielz veloux tout Rompu auec deux ou trois vielles pieces de garde bras le tout xxxv s' vendu vne aut[re] vielle hache tout Roillee & vsee aud' valenciennes v s' vendu & deliure a Jacotin le lieure vng carnequin [*sic, recte* cranequin] de vielle facon tout demambre x s' vendu a Jehan de la granche trois vielles arbalestres dacier auec les teilloles lx s' vendu & deliure a phelippon belon trois hastes de fer xx s'

[Feurs-en-Forez (40 miles west of Lyon), 5 July 1457]

(*These two folios are now illegible but have been printed in* Journal du Procureur Dauvet, *ed. M. Mollat, vol. 2 (Paris, 1953), p. 653)*

Jay fait fin et conclusion es Comptes de Balsarin de laquelle fin & conclusion tele que Je les liuray arrestee en la fin dud' Compte la teneur sensuit Recept de ce present compte faicte par lesdiz Balsarin et Gasparin De traiz dudit Guillaume de Varye en deniers comptans pour employer ou fait de ladicte compaignie, se monte en somme toute 21.841 escu[z] en or, et en monnoye neuf livres seze solz six deniers tournois. Et la despence faicte par lesdiz freres, tant en achactz ou emplecte de harnoiz blanc et de briguandines que on fait de la boutique levee et decree en la ville de Bourges par lesdiz freres, et autres despences deppendans de ladicte compaignie, plus a plain declereez en ce present compte, monte en somme toute 22.327 escuz 10 s. 2 d. t. Et par ainsi seroit deu ausdiz freres, qu'ilz auroient plus mis que receu la somme de 479 escuz 6 s. 2 d. t. Et la recepte faicte par lesdiz freres de la vente par eulx faicte desdiz harnoiz et brigandines, ainsi qu'il appert en ce present compte, se monte, en somme toute, trente mille trois cens quatre vintz six escuz et demi neuf solz onze deniers. Parquoy appert qu'il y a eu de gaing et prouffit ou fait de ladicte compaignie huit mil cinquante neuf escuz et demi, dont les trois quars appartiennent au Roy, pour et ou nom dudit Jacques Cuer, et le quart esdit Balsarin et Gasparin freres, lequel quart dudit prouffit se monte 2.014 escuz 24 s. 1 d. t. Ainsi seroit deu ausdiz freres, tant pour leur porcion dudit prouffit que pour le plus mis et emploie ou fait de ladicte compaignie, la somme de 2.494 escuz 2 s. 9 d. t. Et en oultre leur est deu par ledit Jacques Cuer, pour les parties de harnoiz et brigandines qu'il a prins a sa charge, ainsi qu'il appert par les parties declereez en ce present compte, vint sept mille six cens treze escuz dix sept solz neuf deniers tournois. Ainsi leur seroit deu, en somme toute, trente mille cent sept escuz vint solz six deniers tournois; et ilz doivent, pour la recepte par eulx faicte de la vente dudit harnois, comme il est dessus declaire, trente mille trois cens quatre vintz six escuz et demi neuf solz dix deniers tournois. Ainsi, tout compte et rabatu, doivent lesdiz freres en deniers comptans, deux cens soixante dix-neuf escuz trois solz deux deniers tournois.

[Tours, 6 July 1453]

one gold collar with 30 large gold buttons, one grey-enamelled sallet garnishing, one jazerant garnishing enamelled with white with bright-red flowers, having six buckles and the straps which are gold enamelled the same, the buckles, little-bosses, and the washers, and ten large (jewel) fittings and 54 other little fittings with another little gold decorative settings [these and other goldsmithery] [...] melted and made into *écus* [7 July 1453] and the gold collar with 30 large buttons is 18 karat and weighs 2 *marcs* 7oz 2 *gross* of which there remains 2 *marcs* 1oz 10*d*. 12 *grains* of fine gold, and the sallet garnishing is 20 karat and weighs one *marc* 2½ *gross* of which there remains 8oz 22 *deniers* 6 *grains* of fine gold and this does not include two small iron bosses which weigh 9 *gross* or thereabout, and the jazerant garnishing is 20 karat and weighs 6oz 5*d*. of which there remains 5oz 4*d*. 4 *grains* of fine gold [...] for the wastage of the enamel for both the collar with 30 buttons as well as the garnishings of the sallet and jazerant 18*d*. of fine gold is valued at 5 *écus* 20 *sous tournois*

[Bourges, 16 November 1453]

Balzarino da Trezzo presented his account of the company of harness contracted between Guillaume de Varye [Jacques Coeur's *facteur* (agent)] and the said Balzarino and the late Gasparin, his brother, the which account the said Balzarino affirmed on oath was true both in receipt as in expenses. On the 16th, 17th, and 18th days of the said month Otto [Otto Castellain or Castillani, a Florentine, royal treasurer at Toulouse], Briçonnet [Jehan Briçonnet, King's *sécretaire*], and I have gone to inspect and examine the said account – which is large and prolixious – and to verify the parties both of the receipts as well as its expenses [18 November] Because the account of Balzarino was not in good order nor in good language, on the advice of Otto and Briçonnet, I have ordered the said Balzarino to cause and order them to be put in good order and language and to declare the discrepancies both of the receipts and expenses of both sales and payments and to report it to me in the briefest possible manner [20 November] Otto, Briçonnet, and I have visited Balzarino's workshops, forges, lodgings, and the harness mill in this town of Bourges of which this Balzarino has accounted for several great expenses in his accounts [21 November] out of necessity we have (looked into) Balzarino's account and because there are many orders of harness that he says have been delivered by order of the King to several persons which he has reported on paper to the King, I have ordered and appointed the security of proceeding to the further examination and conclusion of the said account up to that which Otto Castellain who has briefly reported to the King on this matter and others who have spoken with the King about these deliveries and to know if, by the King's paper, these can be verified or not.

[Tours, 1 December 1453]

Of the three brigandines, one of which was covered in velvet as I was instructed which I gave to the Earl of Douglas, and the two others were covered with cloth which I gave to two of the Earl's men. Also, I approved and was able to value them at a higher price than the King had given them 12 *écus* the brigandine which is 36 *écus*, and the velvet for the covering of that of the Earl 14 *écus* – for this 50 *écus*

[Sale of goods from Jacques Coeur's properties in Montpellier, 25 May 1454]

a rusted javelin to Estinne Boutie 2s. 1d., one vouge to Jehan de Flandres 23s. 8d., one other rusted vouge to Antoine Maleripe 41s. 3d., one other rusted vouge to Louis de Chartres 20s., one other rusted vouge to Jehan le Flament 21s. 1d., one axe to Anthoine Juin 25s. 6d., one other axe to the said Anthoine Juin 20s. 2d., one other axe to the said Anthoine Juin 25s. 2d., one javelin-shaft to Sarrilon 13d., one iron spear to the said Sarrilon 10s. 6d., one other iron spear to Messire Jehan de Vedel 13s. 6d., one sallet to Louis de Chartres 21s. 3d., two (pairs of) gauntlets and one bevor to Pierre Sezelly 20s. [3 June] to Girault Fouet one brigandine covered in figured violet satin 12l. 5s., James Boier one other brigandine covered in figured black satin 12l., the said Boier one other brigandine covered in black fustian 8l. 5s., Salvadour one other brigandine covered in black fustian 8l., Bernard de Vaulx one other brigandine covered in black fustian 8l. 5s. [12 June] to Bernard de Vaulx 1½ dozen guisarmes, one dozen axes, 12 sallets, two crossbows, which things were ordered for use aboard the galley *Saint Jacques* which galley with its rigging and its war armaments were sold to him

[métairie (smallholding) at Asnières-les-Bourges, 1 February 1456]

sold and delivered to Raoulet Tostain, merchant at Tours, four silver luck charms, one little silver helm, two boulions (decorative roundels) of a sallet, and five little girdle-buckles all of silver weighing 2oz 40s., sold to Mery Bueille one arming axe completely worn out and rusted 7s. 6d., to Pierre de Valenciennes one old (pair of) cuirass covered in old velvet completely broken with two or three pieces (i.e., lames) of the pauldrons 35s., one other old axe completely rusted and worn out to the said Valenciennes 5s., to Jacotin le Lièvre one cranequin of the old fashion completely disassembled 10s., Jehan de la Granche three old steel crossbows with the pulleys (i.e., windlasses) 60s., Phelippon Belon three iron spears 20s.

[Feurs-en-Forez (40 miles west of Lyon), 5 July 1457]

I have ended and concluded the accounts of Balzarino of which end and conclusion such as I have delivered (and) seized at the end of the said account, the tenor follows:

Receipt of this present account made by the said Balzarino and Gasparino da Trezzo with the said Guillaume de Varye in moneys accounted to employ or run the said company amounts in full sum to 21,841 *écus* in gold, and in coin 9 *livres* 16 *sous* 6 *deniers tournois*. And the expense made by the said brothers, both in purchases as in provision of white harness and brigandines which are made in the workshop built and overseen in the town of Bourges by the said brothers, as well as other expenses owed by the said company, more fully described in this present account, amounts in full sum to 22,327 *écus* 10*s*. 2*d. t.* And thus, would be due to the said brothers, as they would have had put in more than they would have received, the sum of 470 *écus* 6*s*. 2*d. t.* And the receipt made by the said brothers of the sale made by them of the said harness and brigandines, as it appears thus in this present account, amounts in full sum to 3,286½ *écus* 9*s*. 11*d*. Because it appears that there was a gain and profit made by the said company of 8,052½ *écus*, three quarters of which is due to the King for, and in the name of, the said Jacques Coeur, and quarter to the said brothers Balzarino and Gasparino, the said quarter of the said profit amounts to 2,014 *écus* 24*s*. 1*d. t.*, thus would be due to the said brothers, both for their portion of the said profit, as well as for the extra put into and employed in running the said company, the sum of 2,494 *écus* 2*s*. 9*d. t.* And furthermore, they are due by the said Jacques Coeur for the portions of harness and brigandines which he has taken in his charge, as it appears thus by the portions declared in this present account, 27,613 *écus* 17*s*. 9*d. t.* They would thus be due, in full sum, 37,107 *écus* 20*s*. 6*d. t.*, and they must (account) for the receipt made by them for the sale of the said harness, as it is declared above, 386½ *écus* 9*s*. 6*d. t.* Thus, the whole account and rebate the said brothers must account for in coin 289 *écus* 3*s*. 2*d. t.*

15

Nottingham, Nottinghamshire Archives, CA1

Charge of Assault against Henry Venoun, Nottingham, 17 July 1453

henr' vernou' de Not' in Com' ville Not' in guerrino arreiat' ad modu' riote insultu' feceru[n]t sup[er] Rob[er]t[i]m Cade vnu' vigilanc' d[omi]ni Iurat' cu' vno lang de befe & dagar' cont[r]a pacem d[omi]ni R'

> Henry Vernoun, of Nottingham in the county town of Nottingham, arrayed for war in the manner of a riot made an assault upon Robert Cade, one of the sworn watchmen of the Lord (King's) town, with a langue de boeuf and dagger against the Lord King's peace

16

Brussels, Archives de l'État en Belgique/Rijksarchief in België, Chambre de comptes 46397, fol. 8r–fol. 9v

Household Account of Guillaume, Prince-Bishop of Toul, Free Imperial City of Toul (16 Miles West of Nancy), 22 January–20 March 1454

Paye en pres le xxije Jour dud' mois de Januier A lancelot de la tale armoyer par lordo[n]nance de mond' seign[eu]r de thoul xij lyons dor val' xviij l' A henry de

Rossem brigandinier de mons[eigneu]r de Charol' le derr' Jour dud' mois de Januier par lordonnan' c[omm]e dessus iiij escus dor val' iiij l' xvj s' a luy quant Il apporta et deliura a maistre Adrien vander Ee la brigandine toute p[ar]faite xl s' pour la parpaye dud' brigandinier des viij escuz quil doibt auoir paye po[u]r lui et quil deuoit a hey[n]rie [sic] Roelens lvj s' aux compaignons pour le vin iiij s' au varlet dud' henry de Rossem pour auoir dore m cleux s[er]uans a la d[i]c[t]e brigandine xxiiij s' a Jehan blancquart le ve Jour de mars lan dess[us]d' pour iiij asnes et vng quartier de drap de veloux pour la d[i]c[t]e brigandine a iij couro[n]nes dor lasne font xv l' vj s A luy pour les cordes de soye s[er]uans a la d[i]c[t]e brigandine pesans [no no. recorded] onses xvj s' pour assayer le courset & la brigandine po[u]r le corps de mond' seign[eu]r de thoul p[rese]nt mess' gautier de le noot ch[eua]l[ie]r le xj Jour de mars lan dess[us]d' paye a deux arbalestriers po[u]r v vieretons q[ue] Ilz Romperent paye vng chrick' val' xiiij s' po[u]r assayer les aut[re]s trois coursses le xx Jour de mars lan dess[us]d' p[rese]nt franck de le poele paye ausd' deux arbalestriers et pour xj vieretons q[ue] Ilz Rompirent xxiiij s' po[ur] vne asne et vng quart[ie]r de drap de veloux s[er]uans au coursset de mond' s[eigneu]r achete a louuain a berthelmj le lomb' po[u]r iiij l' iiij s' & pour iiij ounces de soye pendans au bas dud' coursset a ix s' ch[asc]une onse val' xxxvj s' a henry de molenbetre orfeure qui a fait & ouure les p[ar]ties qui sens[ui]t s[er]uans tant a la brigandine de mond' seign[eu]r de thoul co[m]me a son coursset pour la brigandine deux grandes blouques dargent dore & viij petites blouques deux grans morgans et viij petis xxx cleux et xxx saudeures xxiiij bosettes et xl cleux cou[er]es tout s[er]uant a la d[i]c[t]e brigandine et peasant en argent viij onces et demie A vng pietre dor lonce dargent autant pour la doreure font ensamble xvij peters qui val' xv l' vj s' a luy pour auoir dore ijm cleux de laton s[er]uans a la d[i]c[t]e brigandine oultr' & p[ar] dess' les m cleux cy dessus dorez par le varlet du brigandinier a vne couro[n]ne ch[asc]un millier font xlviij s' a luj po[u]r les parties qui sens' s[er]uans au coursset de mond' s[eigneu]r de thoul P[re]mi[er]e pour iiij bendes dargent dore xxvij morga[n]s dargent dore vj cleux de fer couuert les testes dargent & dore xlix cleux en facon de Rozes dargent dore lij bosettes d[ar]gent dore iiijxx cleux cou[er]es dargent dore iiijxx <saudeurs> /Rivetz\ da[r]gent dore s[er]uans ausd' cleux liij Jestelets po[ur] atacher les morgans sur le cuir tout peasant xix zonces [sic] <et vng quart> dont fait a Rabatre j z onse po[u]r le pesant des[uss]d' celux de fer demeure en argent xviij\ onse a vng piet' lonse Et autant po[u]r la doreure font xxxvj piet[re]s dor <et demj et po[u]r la doreure desd' cleux de fer vng peter et de[m]ie> / qui val' xxxij l' viij s'\

Paid close to 22 January to Lancelot de La Tale, armourer, by command of my Lord of Toul 12 gold *lions* (currency) worth 18*l.* [prob. *livres tournois*], to Henry to Rossem, brigandine-maker to my Lord (Charles, Count) of Charolais, the last day of January, 3 gold *écus* worth 4*l.* 16*s.*, to him when he carried and delivered the fully-complete brigandine to Maître Adrien vander Ee 40*s.*, for the said brigandine-maker's prepayment of 8 *écus* he was due and that he owed to Heynrie [sic] Roelens 56*s.*, to the companions for wine 4*s.*, to a valet (servant) of the said Henry de Rossem for having gilded 1,000 nails for the said brigandine 24*s.*, to

Figure 7. Detail of a Burgundian tapestry panel, c. 1450
(Glasgow Museums, Burrell Collection, 46.80).

Jehan Blancquart on 5 March the aforesaid year for 4¼ ells of velvet cloth for the said brigandine at 3 *couronnes* the ell that makes 25*l.* 5*s.*, to him for the silk cords for the said brigandine 16*s.*, for assaying the corset and brigandine for the body of my Lord of Toul in the presence of Sir Gautier de Le Noot, knight, on 11 March the aforesaid year, paid to two crossbowmen for the five *viretons* (bolts) they broke, paid (for) one (prob.) cranequin worth 14*s.*, for assaying the other three corsets on 20 March in the presence of Franck de Le Poele, paid to the said two crossbowmen and for the six *viretons* they broke 24*s.*, for 1¼ ells of velvet cloth for my Lord's corset bought at Louvain from Barthélémy the Lombard for 4*l.* 4*s.* and for 4oz of silk for hanging from the bottom of the said corset at 9*s.* an oz worth 26*s.*, to Henry de Molenbetre, goldsmith, who has made and crafted the following both for my Lord of Toul's brigandine and his corset: for the brigandine – two large silver-gilt buckles and eight small buckles, two large mordants (buckle-tongues) and eight small, 30 nails and 30 saltires (X-shaped fittings), 24 small bosses and 40 fully-covered nails all for the said brigandine and weighing 8½oz in silver at one gold *piètre* (Louvain currency) the oz of silver as well as for the gilding that makes in all 17 *piètres* which is worth 15*l.* 6*s.*, to him for having gilded 2,000 latten nails for the said brigandine above and beyond the 1,000 nails hereinabove gilded by the brigandine-maker's valet at one *couronne* for each 1,000 that makes 48*s.*, to him for the following pieces for my Lord of Toul's corset: firstly for four silver-gilt bends, 27 silver-gilt mordants, six iron nails – the heads covered with silver – and gilded, 19 silver-gilt nails in the shape of roses, 52 silver-gilt small bosses, four score nails covered with silver gilt, four score <saltires> silver-gilt *rivets* (i.e., washers) for the said nails, 53 [...] to attach the mordants to the leather all weighing 19oz <and a quarter> taking back 1oz for the aforesaid weight of the iron nails – 18oz the remainder in silver at one *piètre* the oz, as well as for the gilding that makes 36 gold *piètres* <and a half for the gilding of the said iron nails 1½ *piètres*> which is worth 32*l.* 8*s.*

17

London, London Metropolitan Archives, Plea and Memoranda Roll A80, membr. 4

Bill of Debt against Court Pothof, Armourer, late of Southwark, 4 November 1454

Court pothof nup[er] de Suthewerk armurer' [...] vj paria de Curas vij par' de Gardebras & pollerons xxviij par' de vambras vj salettes absq' visours ij saletes cu' visours j nigr' salet xiij Gorgettes de calibde vj par' leggeherneys iiij par' de Ganteletz j helmet ij par' vet' Curas defic' ij hynde tasse & j fore tasse iiij vambras j vet' helmet xviij pesons de maile xj standardes absq' sengles j par' manuc' de mayle westvale j par' manuc' de gestrant j haberieon de mayle j vet' habergeon j habergeon de meleyn j vet' habergeon al' habergeons ij jakett' ij habergeons j vet' habergeon j al' vet' habergeon j jaket de maile j vet' Basenet j brode hatte iiij par' va[m]bras iiij gardebras defic' ij gardes ij pollerons deficient' j garde viij gorgett' de Calibd' iiij wardrer axes vj pesons de maile ij gladios [sic] viij stripes de maile [...] vijxx lb de calibde j habergeon de Calibde Ronde maile j gesserant de maile j gesserant westvale j jaket de maile ap[er]t' j jaket de Flat maile j jaket gesserant tres al' jakett' gesserant ij par' manuc' de maile ij pesons cu' standardes xj pesons & j vet' manuc' de maile j breche & j paunse de maile ij par' gussett' xliij lb de laton vj salett' cu' visours iij visours vij par' poleyns iiij gardes j par' greves ij hab[er]geons gesserant

[Valuation by] Joh[ann]is Garbesham Thome atte wode & laurencij hunt armurar' [...] vj par' de Curas p[re]c' par' xx s s[um]ma inde vj li vij par' de Gardebras & pollerons p[re]c' par' iij s j d s[um]ma inde xxiij s iiij d xxviij par' vambras p[re]c' par' iij s s[um]ma inde v li xiiij s vj salettes absq' visers p[re]c' pec' ij s viij d s[um]ma inde xvj s ij salett' cu' visers p[re]c' pec' iiij s s[um]ma inde viij s j nigra Salet p[re]c' x d xij Gorgett' de Calibde p[re]c' pec' xvj d s[um]ma inde xvij s iiij d vj par' leggeharneys p[re]c' cuiusl[ibe]t par' vj s viij d s[um]ma inde xl s iij par' Gauntelett' p[re]c' par' xvj d s[um]ma inde iiij s j helmet p[re]c' x s ij par' de Curas vet' deficient' ij hynd tasse & j fore tasse p[re]c' viij s iiij vambras p[re]c' xx d j vet' helmet p[re]c' ij s vj d xviij pesons de maile p[re]c' pec' xviij d s[um]ma inde xxvij s xj standardez absq' sengles p[re]c' pec' viij d s[um]ma inde vij s iiij d j par' manuc' de maile westvale p[re]c' xx d j par' manucar[um] Gesserant p[re]c' iij s j haberion de maile p[re]c' v s j vet' haberion p[re]c' xx d j hab[er]ion de meleyn p[re]c' v s j vet' haberion p[re]c' xx d j hab[er]ion [prec'] ij s vj d j al' hab[er]ion p[re]c' xvj d j jaket p[re]c' xx d j al' jaket p[re]c' xvj d ij hab[er]ions p[re]c' ij s j vet' hab[er]ion p[re]c' xx d j al' vet' hab[er]ion p[re]c' xij d j jaket de maile p[re]c' xx s j vet' Basenet p[re]c' xvj d j brode hatte p[re]c' xij d iiij par' de vambras p[re]c' cuiusl[ibe]t par' ij s vj d s[um]ma inde x s iiij Gardebras deficien' ij gardez & ij pollerons deficient' j gard p[re]c' iij s viij d viij gorgett' de Calibde p[re]c' viij s iiij wardrer axes p[re]c' pec' ij d s[um]ma inde viij d [...] de maile p[re]c' pec' vj d s[um]ma inde iij s ij gladij p[re]c' iiij s viij Stripes de maile p[re]c' xvj d [...] vijxx lb de calibde p[re]c' lb vj d s[um]ma inde iij li x s j hab[er]ion de Calibde [...] maile p[re]c' vj s viij d j gesserant de maile p[re]c' vj s viij d j gesserant westvale p[re]c' iij s j jaket de maile p[re]c' iij s iiij d j jaket de Flat maile p[re]c' ij s j jaket Gesserant p[re]c' ij s j al' jaket Gesserant' p[re]c' xvj d [...] de Gesserant p[re]c' xx d j al' jaket Gesserant p[re]c' v s ij par' manucar[um] de maile p[re]c' v s ij pesons cu' standardes p[re]c' ij s viij d xj pesons & j vet' manuc' de maile p[re]c' vij s j breche & j paunse de maile p[re]c' ij s iiij d ij par' de Gussett' p[re]c' xvj d xliiij lb laton p[re]c' lb vj d s[um]ma inde xxij s ij saletz cu' ij visours p[re]c' viij d [...] p[re]c' iij s vij par' poleyns p[re]c' vij s iiij gardez p[re]c' xij d j par' Greves p[re]c' viij d & ij hab[er]ions Gesse[...] p[re]c' xx s

Court Pothof, late of Southwark, armourer [...] six pairs of cuirass, seven pairs of gardebras and pauldrons, twenty-eight pairs of vambraces, six sallets without visors, two sallets with visors, one black sallet, thirteen steel gorgets, six pairs of legharness, three pairs of gauntlets, one helmet, one pair of old cuirass lacking two hind tassets and one fore tasset, three vambraces, one old helmet, eighteen mail pisans, eleven standards without cingles, one pair of mail sleeves of Westphalia (make), one pair

Figure 8. Two views of a sallet, Burgundian or French, late-fifteenth century (Glasgow Museums, R. L. Scott bequest, E.1939.65.ak.[1]).

of jazerant sleeves, one mail haubergeon, one old haubergeon, one haubergeon of Milan (make), one old haubergeon, other haubergeons, two jackets, two haubergeons, one old haubergeon, another old haubergeon, one jacket of mail, one old basinet, one broad hat, four pairs of vambraces, three gardebras lacking two guards, two pauldrons lacking one guard, eight steel gorgets, four warders axes, six mail pisans, two swords, eight strips of mail […] seven score lb of steel, one haubergeon of round steel mail, one jazerant of mail, one jazerant of Westphalia, one open jacket of mail, one jacket of flat mail, one jazerant jacket, three other jazerant jackets, two pairs of mail sleeves, two pisans with standards, eleven pisans and one old mail sleeve, one 'breche' and one paunce of mail, two pairs of gussets, forty-three pounds of latten, six sallets with visors, three visors, seven pairs of poleyns, three guards, one pair of greaves, two jazerant haubergeons

[Valuation by] John Garbesham, Thomas atte Wode, and Laurence Hunt, armourers: six pairs of cuirass price of the pair 20s. thence the sum of £6, seven pairs of gardebras (i.e., pauldron reinforces) and pauldons price of pair 3s. 1d. thence the sum of 23s. 4d., 28 pairs of vambraces price of pair 3s. thence the sum of £5 14s., six sallets without visors price of the piece 2s. 8d. thence the sum of 16s., two sallets with visors price of the piece 4s. thence the sum of 8s., one black sallet worth 10d., 13 steel gorgets price of the piece 16d. thence the sum of 17s. 4d., six pairs of legharness price of each pair 6s. 8d. thence the sum of 40s., three pairs of gauntlets price of the pair 16d. thence the sum of 4s., one helmet worth 10s., two pairs of old cuirass lacking two hind tassets and one fore tasset worth 8s., four vambraces worth 20d., one old helmet worth 2s. 6d., 18 pisans of mail price of the piece 18d. thence the sum of 27s., eleven standards (mail collars) without cingles price of the piece 8d. thence the sum of 7s. 4d., one pair of mail sleeves of Westphalia worth 20d., one pair of jazerant sleeves worth 3s., one mail haubergeon worth 5s., one old haubergeon worth 20d., one haubergeon of Milan worth 5s., one old haubergeon worth 20d., one haubergeon [worth] 2s. 8d., another haubergeon worth 16d., one jacket worth 20d., another jacket worth 16d., two haubergeons worth 2s. one old haubergeon worth 20d., another old haubergeon worth 12d., one mail jacket worth 20s., one old basinet worth 16d., one broad hat worth 12d., four pairs of vambraces price of each pair 2s. 6d. thence the sum of 10s., four gardebras lacking two guards and two pauldrons lacking one guard worth 3s. 8d., eight steel gorgets worth 8s., four warders axes price of the piece 2d. thence the sum of 8d. [...] of mail price of the piece 6d. thence the sum of 3s., two swords worth 4s., eight strips of mail worth 16d. [...] eight score lb of steel price of the pound 6d. thence the sum of £3 10s., one haubergeon of steel [...] mail worth 6s. 8d., one mail jazerant worth 6s. 8d., one jazerant of Westphalia worth 3s., one jacket of mail worth 3s. 4d., one jacket of flat mail worth 2s., one jazerant jacket worth 2s., another jazerant jacket worth 16d. [...] of jazerant worth 20d., another jazerant jacket worth 5s., two pairs of mail sleeves worth 5s., two pisans with standards worth 2s. 8d., 11 pisans and one old mail sleeve worth 7s., one 'breche' and one paunce of mail worth 2s. 4d., two pairs of gussets worth 16d., 44lb of latten price of the pound 6d. thence the sum of 22s., two sallets with two visors worth 8d. [...] worth 3s., seven pairs of poleyns worth 7s., three guards worth 12d., one pair of greaves worth 8d., and two jazerant haubergeons worth 20s.

18

Milan, Archivio di Stato Milano, Notarile 1413, 1455 genn. 2.

Agreement between the Armourers and Armour-Furbishers of the City and Duchy of Milan, 2 January 1455

This document is very badly damaged.

Symonis de medicis Joh[an]ne di[ct]i zini de cortexijs donati de scharauazijs donati de vianoua leonardi de legniano Antonij de burris fr[atr]is di[ct]i Angelini et d[omi]ni Ambr[os]ij de burris et martini ei' filij si[mi]l[ite]r om' magi[str]or[um] armorator[um] et trau[er]sator[um] armor[um] cuiut[ati]s et ducat' m[edio]l[an]i p[ro] quib[us] et quolib' et alt[er]o eor[um] [...] [agree in this legally-binding instrument] In primis Q[uod] nullus [...]s amoratorib[us] [*sic*][6] et trau[...]orib[us] armor[um] sup[er]' no[m]i[n]atis [...] et[...] alique alia p[er]sona [...] eid[...] sit et existat nec aliquis nec aliqui eor[um] [...]ssit nec velat nec eis liceat nec licean' sit [...] fabricare nec placitare facere de nouo aliqua' [...] p[ro] trauersando nec amolando arma in ciui[ta]te nec [...] librar[um] cent[u]m i[m]p[er]' aplicandar[um] venerabile fabrice eccl' [...] pacto Q[uod] aliquis ex di[cti]s amoratorib[us] et trauersatorib[us]

6   The notary often spells this without the first 'r' but meaning is unaffected.

armor[um] s[...] nec aliquis nec aliqui eor[um] non possit nec valeat nec possint nec nec eis liceat nec licean' sit h[ab]ere nec tenere nisi vna' trauersera' [...] plures p[ro] qual' maxnata s[uper]s[crip]tor[um] sup[er]' no[m]i[n]ator[um] singula sing[u]l[i]s referendo vt s' sub pena librar[um] cent[u]m i[m]p[er]' ap[...] pacto Q[uod] nullus ex di[cti]s amoratorib[us] et trau[er]satorib[us] armor[um] sup[er] no[m]in[...] nec aliqui eor[um] non possit nec valeat nec possint nec valeant laborare facere de di[ct] a arte vt s' alicui armorerio ciuit[at]is et ducat' m[edio]l[an]i nec al[...] qui uel que sit debitor alicu' seu aliquor[um] trau[er]sator[um] et amorator[um] sup[er][...] sub pe[n]na flor' vigintiq[uin]q[ue] q' valor[um] ad [com]p[utu]m sol' xxxij i[m]p[er]' p[ro] flor' aplicandor[um] vt [...] pacto Q[uod] si essent vno uel tres uel plures ex s[uper]s[crip]tis trau[er]satorib[us] [...] om[n]es laborantes alicui armorerio vt s' Et q' vnus uel plures eor[um] [...] non vellet aut non posset laborare di[ct]o armorerio et esset creditor creditores di[ct]e armorerij de aliqua denarior[um] quantitate p[ro] alias seu alij [...] non possit nec valeat nec possunt nec valeant laborare di[ct]o armorerio [...] et vsq[ue] quo di[ct]us trauersator seu di[ct]e trau[er]satores credit' vt s' erit satisfac[...] eru[n]t satisfacti de ei' seu eor[um] credit' sub penna flor' xxv p[re]di[ct]e val[...] pacto Q[uod] nullus ex di[ct]us amoratorib[us] et trau[er]satorib[us] armor[um] sup[er]' no[m]i[n]atis nec aliquis nec aliqui eor[um] non possit nec valeat nec possint nec val[...] p[ro] laborando nec ad laboranda' alicui laboratori seu laboratorib[us] alic[...] trau[er]satoris et amoratoris seu aliquor[um] amorat[orum] et trau[er]sator[um] su[...] durante t[em]p[o]re [con]uentionis et acordi di[ct]i laboratoris cum di[ct]o mag[ist]ro [...] et amoratore Ip[s]o tant' mag[ist]ro satisfaci[on]em di[ct]o laboratori de eo' mo[...] penna flor' xxv p[re]d[ict]e valor' aplicandor[um] vt s' pacto Q[uod] nullus ex di[ct]us armoratorib[us] et trau[er]satorib[us] armor[um] nec aliquis nec aliqui eor[um] non possit nec valeat nec possint [...] laborare nec laborare facere alicui armorerio nec alicui al[...] d[ic]ta arte p[ro] minorib[us] p[re]tijs p[re]tijs Inf[r]as Inf[rascript]ior[um] laborarior[um] nou[...] sub penna florenor[um] xxv p[re]d[ict]e valoris aplicandor[um] vt s' Q[uod] [...] Inf[rascript]ior[um] laborar-ior[um] nouor[um] sunt ista sing[u]la sing[u]lis [con]grue refer[...] In primis p[ro] corazia vna sol' viginti sex i[m]p[er]' p[ro] corseta vn[...] vigint[...] p[ro] payro vno arnexiar[um] saldar[um] sol' viginti p[ro] pay' vno a[...] sol' sedic[e]m p[ro] pay' vno brazaliu' saldar[um] sol' vndec[i]m p[ro] pay' vno [...] p[ro] pay' vno spalaziar[um] saldar[um] sol' duodec[i]m p[ro] pay' vno spalaz[...] p[ro] pay' vno guantor[um] saldor[um] sol' qu[in]q[ue] p[ro] pay' vno gauntor[um] az[...] p[ro] armeto vno sol' viginti p[ro] celata vna c[u]m visera sol' [...] ab equo sol' sept[e]m p[ro] celata vna ab oculis sol' octo p[ro] barb[...] Et que vero p[re]tia Inf[rascript]ior[um] laborerior[im] veter[um] su[n]t ista sing[u]la sin[...] In p[ri]m[i]s p[ro] corazia vno trauersatis sol' duodec[i]m i[m]p[er]' et p[ro] [...] et amorata sol' viginti i[m]p[er]' p[ro] pay' vno arnexiar[um] [...] trau[er]sat' et amorat[orum] sol' sed[...] p[ro] pay' vno br[...] amorator[um] et trau[er]sat' sol[...] trau[er]sata et armato vno sol' [...] sol' dec[i]m et p[ro] armeto vno trau[er][...] p[ro] celata trau[er]sata et amorat[...] pacto Q' aliquis ex di[ct]us [...] aliquis nec aliqui eor[um] non possint nec valeant nec possit nec valeat accipere ab armorerijs p[ro] eor[um] mercede aliud q' p[...] sub pena flor' vigintiq[uin]q[ue] p[re]d[ict]e valoris aplicandor[um] vt s' pacto Q' aliquis ex di[cti] s trau[er]satorib[us] et amoratorib[us] sup[er][...] nec aliqui nec aliquis eor[um] non possint nec valeant nec possit nec [...] facere societate' seu [com]pagnia' aliquam de di[ct]a arte trauersand' et am[...] cum aliqua alia p[er]sona nisi Int' se sit sup[er]' no[m]i[n]atos sub pena flor' [...] p[re]d[ict]e valor' vt s' aplicand[um] [...]

Simone de Medici, Giovanni, called 'Zini de Cortexijs' (i.e., nicknamed 'Lacking Courtesy'), Donato de Scaravazzi, Donato de Vianova, Leonardo de Legnano, Antonio de Burris, brother of the said Angelino, and Master Ambrogio de Burris and Martino his son, likewise all the master armourers and furbishers of armour of the City and Duchy of Milan [...] [agree in this legally-binding instrument]: firstly, that none of the above-named armourers and furbishers of armour, nor any other person such as there is, neither any one nor any of them, can nor will, nor will he or they be licensed to, build or cause to be built anew any [prob. workshop] for furbishing or grinding arms in the City or [...] [prob. Duchy of Milan] [under pain of a fine of] 100 *lire imperiali* to be used for the venerable fabric of the Church of [...]. It is agreed that each of the said armourers and furbishers of armour [...] neither he nor any of them, can or will, nor will he or they be licensed to, have or hold more than one furbishing-workshop for any of the above-written aforenamed magnates referring one by one as above under pain (of a fine) of 100 *lire imperiali* to be used [for the purpose as above]. It is agreed that none of the said armourers and armour-furbishers [neither he etc.] may set to work anyone of the above-said craft in the City and Duchy of Milan nor elsewhere if he be a debtor to any furbisher or armourer under pain (of a fine) of 25 florins to the value of 32 *soldi imperiali* the florin to be used as above. It is agreed that should there be one or three or several of the above-written furbishers all (being) workmen for any armourer as above that one or several of them may not nor cannot work for the said armourer if he be creditor and they be creditors of the said armourer of any amount of money for others or [...] he or they may not nor cannot work for the said armourer [...] until the said furbisher's or said furbishers' above creditors be satisfied of his or their creditor under pain (of a fine) of 25 florins aforesaid [...]. It is agreed that none of the said above-named armourers and furbishers of armour nor any one of any of them cannot [etc.] work or put to work any worker or workers (or) furbisher and armourer nor any armourers or furbishers [...] during the time of the contract and agreement of the said worker with the said master [...] and this armourer must to the master's satis-faction of the said worker of his money (i.e., settle the worker's wages) [...] under pain (of a fine) of 25 florins to the value aforesaid to be used as above. It is agreed that none of the above-named said armourers and furbishers of armour may [etc.] work nor set to work any armourer or anyone else of the said craft for less than the price of the price of the new workmanship written below under pain (of a fine) of 25 florins to the value aforesaid to be used as above. The which is written below, referring to one at a time, for new workmanship is this: firstly, for one cuirass 26 *soldi imperiali*, for one corset [...] 20 [*soldi*] [...], for one pair of assembled (leg) harness 20 *soldi*, for one pair of [...] 16 *soldi*, for one pair of assembled bracers (plate arm defences) 11 *soldi*, for one pair of [...], for one pair of assembled pauldrons 12 *soldi*, for one pair of assembled gauntlets 5 *soldi*, for one pair of gauntlets [...], for one armet 20 *soldi*, for one sallet with visor [...] *soldi* [...], [for one poss. sallet?] for a horse (man) 7 *soldi*, for one sallet with sights 8 *soldi*, for one bevor [...] And that the true price written below, one at a time, for old workmanship is this: firstly, for one furbished cuirass 12 *soldi imperiali*, and for [...] and armed (i.e., fitted with linings, straps and buckles etc.) 20 *soldi imperiali*, for one pair of (leg) harness [...] furbished and armed 16 [*soldi*] [...], for one pair of pauldrons [...] armed and furbished [...] *soldi*, [...] furbished and armed 1 *soldi*, [...] 10 *soldi*, and for one armet furbished [...], for one sallet furbished and armed [...] It is agreed that any of the said [workmen?] [etc.] may not accept from armourers for their wages any but that [...] under pain (of a fine) of 25 florins to the value aforesaid to be used as above. It is agreed that any of the above-named said furbishers and armours may not [etc.] form a society or company with anyone of the said craft of furbishing and armouring [...] [or] with any other person unless (it be) between him and the above-named under pain (of a fine of) [25] florins to the said value to be used as above

19

Kew, National Archives C 66/480, membr. 7

Inventory of the Tower of London, 20 May 1455

This is a parte of the goodis that been deli[er]ed' oute of the Armere by the kingis co[m]maundement sythen' the tyme that Joh[a]n Stanley hath' been' Sergeant of the Armurrye as it apperith' here after more playnly by the parcellys that here folowen' First viij swerdis and a long' blade of a swerde made in wasters so[m]me gretter and so[m]me smaller for to lerne the kyng' to play in his tendre age a litel harneys that the Erle of Warwyk made for the kyng' or that he went ouer the see garnysshed' w[i]t[h] gold which' was deliu[er]ed to duc of Suff' for his sone xiiij li' deliu[ere]d' by Joh[a]n mcrston' clerk of the Jewellys to the said' Sergeant for to pay c[er]teyn' armurers which' is done as it apperith' by endentures And the said' money paid' at two tymes that is to say vij li' at a tyme a scottyssh' swerde hilte and pomell' cou[er]ed w[i]t[h] syluer and a smale Corone a boute the pomell' which' was stolen' oute of the kingis Chambre and the blade brokyn' and caste in to Tempse (i.e., the Thames) j banner of Satyn' of Entertaille of the Armes (quartered with the heraldic arms) of Englond' and Fraunce ij banners beten' (decorated) of the armes of Englond' and Fraunce iij banners of Satyn' of Entertaille of the armes of Fraunce iij banners beten' of the armes of Fraunce vj banners of Entertaille of seint George armes vj banners beten' of the Trinite iiij banners beten' of oure lady iij penno[u]ns of the feders of Entertaille v penno[u]ns beten' of the feders CCC ix pensell' of the feders Of the which' banners ij were deliu[er]ed to Joh[a]n Chatewyn' and ij to Thomas Boulde and ij to Joh[a]n Seynloo that tyme Squiers for the kingis body and ij now late to my lord' of Shrewesbury and all' the remanent were delyu[er]ed for the Entiermentis of the iij Quenes [...] a breaste w[i]t[h] a boxe vpon' for the Egle and a pomell' of a swerd' w[i]t[h] armes therin which' was deliu[er]ed to Parker Armurer for to make the kingis herneys by which' he hath' lost ij lytill' Cote Armurs which been' the Sergeantis fee of the Armurry and so deliu[er]ed by the kyngis co[m]maundment to hym by cause that thei were so lityll' and wole' s[er]ue no man for thei were made for him when' he was but vij yere of age xxxiijti standardis of worsted' of the armes of Englond' and Fraunce xxij standardis of worsted' of the Armes of Fraunce The which standardis been' woren' and spendid' in karyng of the kingis hernoys in and oute in to his Chambre for faulte of theire stuff' v banners for Trumpettis deliu[er]ed to the Trumpettis when' the Duc of Glocuestr' went to the rescowe of Caleis viij habergo[u]ns so[m]me of meleyn' and so[m]me of westwale of the which' v of meleyn' were delyu[er]ed' to the College of Eyto[u]n and other iij broken' to make slewys of woyders and yes (i.e., eyes: reinforced holes on the arming doublet for the points) ij yerdis iiij quarters of Corse iij pourpoull' and xv smale poyntis of silke for the kingis briganders which' were deliu[er]ed in like wise ij yerdis iiij quarters of Corse of rede silke d[imidj] yerd' d[imid]j quarters of rede velewet iiij grosses of point[is] vjC armyng' nayle alle spended and moche more to oon' of the kingis herneis ix olde picers j olde paytrill' brode of ledder xj testures iiij frounters of testures iij olde Justing' sadell' peinted of diu[er]s werkys x olde Justing sadell' parcell' broken' for the pese (i.e., jousts of peace) iij olde Justing sadell' for tournament[is] xiij olde bastard sadill' so[m]me parcell' broken' iiij smale olde sadill' xij olde sheldis peynted' xiij olde paveys peynted' x olde banner shaftis bounde w[i]t[h] yren' v olde spereshaftis for pese j spereshafte j longe spere with a hede j olde Trapper of platis broken' in diu[er]se placis a hamer j bequerne j peyre of pynsons iij pounde of wyre which was sold' by Maister William Fox Armurrer l bowestaff[is] wormeeten' deliu[er]ed by the kingis co[m]maundement to my lord of Gloucestr' when he went ouer to Caleys j peyre of trussyng' Coeffers and j peyre of Gardeviant[is] spended longe tyme a goo in the king[is] cariage a wyre hate garnysshed' the bordoure serkill' and a sterre of syluer gilt lakkyng' a poynt in the sterre a peyre of Curasses deliu[er]ed' to the lord Powys that laste died' which' that the king' co[m]maunded' to yeue hym

20

Kew, National Archives, E 404/70/34, Kew, National Archives, E 404/71/1/57

Two Letters from Henry VI to His Treasurer and Chamberlains regarding His Brigandines, 3 December 1455 and 25 February 1457

[3 December 1455]

we haue vndrestande by a supplicacion p[re]sented' vnto vs by Thomas Poleyn' Brigandermaker howe that by the co[m]maundement of Jenkyn' Stanley Sargeant of our' Armu[r]eye made for vs ayenst our' last goying to our' parlement of leycestre iij pair' Bryganders whereof ij peir' of theim were assaied broken' and lost by yomen of our' Coroune with' shot a boute the assaying of the same soo that the seid' Thomas lost his werkmanship of theim And the thridde pair' were sauf' and vnhurt and were cou[er]ed' in p[u]rpull' velwet for our' p[er]sone of which' Bryganders the same Thomas couenanted with' the seid Sargeant to haue xj mark' of which' xj mark' the same Thomas hath' be longe tyme behinde onpaied' of the seid' xj mark' [orders payment to be made]

[25 February 1457]

where as oure welbeloued seruaunt Thomas Poleyn Brygandermaker made for vs at oure goying towardis oure parlement last holden at laycestre a payre of Birgandiers For the making of the whiche payre of Birgandiers and for stuffe that was broken therabout' they were cessid [i.e., assessed] by oure welbeloued Squier Jenkyn Stanley Sergeant of oure Armorie at xj marc' for payment whereof we assignid hym by oure l[ett]res of priue seel vnto oure right' trusty and welbeloued Cousin the lord Bourgchier thanne oure Tresourer of England' That notew[i]t[h]standing the said Thomas couthe not nor yet can not be payed therof to his greet hurt and hindering as he sayth' And more ouer the said Thomas Poleyn by the co[m]maundement of oure said sergeant of oure Armorye did' lengthe enlarge and sette newe the sleuys of the said Birgandiers for werkmanship' and for stuffe of the same oure said Sergeant cessed at xxx s' [orders payment without delay]

21

Glasgow University Library, MS Hunter 252 (U.4.10), fol. 12r–fol. 15r

Les cent nouvelles nouvelles: *A Collection of Stories composed for the Court of Philip, Duke of Burgundy, between 1456 and 1461 (Extracts from the Fourth and Fifth Stories)*

Le Roy esta[n]t nague[re]s en sa ville de tours vng ge[n]til co[m]paigno' escossois archier de son corps et de sa grande garde se[n]amoura tresfort dune tresbelle et gente damoiselle mariee et merciere [Her husband, on discovering the affair, commands her to invite him the following evening so he can exact his] trescriminale venge[n]ce Le mercier se fait armer dun grand lourd et vieil harnois prend sa salade ses ganteletz et en sa main vne gra[n]d hache Or est Il bien en point dieu le scet Et semble b[ie]n q' aultresfoiz Il ait veu hutin co[m]me vng champion venu sur les Rencs de bonne heure et attendant son ennemy en lieu de pauillon se va mectre derriere vng tapis en la Ruelle de son lit et si tres bien se caicha quil ne pouoit estre apperceu Lamoureux malade sentent lheure tresdesiree se met au che[m]in deuers lostel a la merciere mais Il noblya pas sa grande forte et bonne espee a deux mains Et co[m]me Il fut venu leans la dame monte en sa chambre sans faire effroy Et Il la suyt tout doulcem[en]t Et quand Il sest trouue leans Il demande a sa dame si en la chambre y auoit aultre quelle A quoy elle Respondit assez laschem[en]t et estra[n]geme[n]t et co[mm]e no' trop asseuree que no' Dictes verite dist lescossois v[ost]re mary ny est Il pas Nenny dist elle Or le laissez venir par saint trignan sil y vient Je luy fendray la teste Jusques aux dens voire par dieu sil estoient trois Jen s[er]ay bien maistre hardime[n]t Et apres ces criminelles p[ar]olles vous [*sic, recte* il] tire hors du fourreau sa grande et bonne espee et si la fait brandir trois ou quatre foiz et aupres de luy sur le lit la cousche Et ce fait visteme[n]t baiser et accoler et le surplus quapres ce ensuyt tout a son bel aise et loisir acheua sans ce que le pouure cour [*sic*] de la Ruelle sosast oncques monstrer mais si grand paour auoit q' apoir quil ne mouroit Nostre escossois apres ceste haulte aduenture prend sa dame conge Jusques vne aultre foiz et la mercye co[m]me Il scet de sa grand courtoisie et se met au chemin et descend les degrez de la chambre Quand le vaillant ho[m]me darmes sceut lescossois en seur de luy ai[n]si effraye quil estoit sans a peine sauoir parler sault de son pauillon et co[m]mence a censer sa femme de ce q[ue]lle auoit souffert le plaisir de larchier Et elle luy respondit que cestoit sa coulpe et sa faulte et chargie luy auoit luy bailler Jour Je ne vous co[m]menday pas dist Il de luy laisser faire sa volunte Comme[n]t dit elle le pouois Je refuser voyant sa grand espee dont Il meust tuee en cas de Refus Et a ceste coup veez cy bon escossois qui Retourne et mo[n]te arriere les degrez de la chambre et sault dedans et dit tout hault Quest cecy Et bon homme de se sauuer et dessoubz le lit se boute pour estre plus seurem[en]t beaucop plus esbahy que parauant La dame fut Reprinse et de Rechef par lamoureux enferree tresbien et a loysir en la fasson que dessus tousiours lespee aupres de luy Apres ceste Rencharge et pluseurs aultres deuises ent' lescossois et la dame lheure vint de partir si luy donna bonne nuyt et pieque et sen va Le pouure martir estant soubz le lit a peu sil sosoit tirer de la doubta[n]t le Retourner de son aduersaire Ou pour meulx dire son compaigno' A chef de piece Il print courage et olayde de sa femme la dieu m[er]cy Il fut Remis sur piez Sil auoit bien cansee et villainee sa femme auparaua[n]t encores Reco[m]menca Il plus dure lege[...] Car elle auoit consenty apres sa defense le deshonne[u]r de luy et delle Helas dit elle et ou est la femme tant asseuree qui osast de dire vng homme ainsi eschauffe et courage q' cestuy est quand vous qui estes arme embastonne et si vaillant que ceste Rage agui Il a trop plus mesfait q' a moy ne lauez ose assaillir ne moy defendre

When the King (Charles VII) was last in His town of Tours, a gentle Scot – an archer of his bodyguard and his Great Scots Guard (*Garde Écossaise*) – fell deeply in love with a very beautiful and gentile *demoiselle*, a mercer's wife. [Her husband, on discovering the affair, commands her to invite him to her lodgings the following evening so he can exact his] extremely criminal revenge. The mercer had armed himself in a large, heavy, and old harness, taking his sallet and his gauntlets and a large axe in his hand. He was so well equipped that, God knows, it seemed more like the commotion of a champion come early to the lists and awaiting his enemy. In lieu of a pavilion he placed himself behind a tapestry in his bed-nook and hid himself so well that he could not be glimpsed. The lovesick one waited for the most desired hour to come then made his way to the mercer's wife's lodgings, but he did not forget his large, strong, and fine two-handed sword. When he had come to the lady he went up to her bedroom without fear. And he followed most softly. Now when he found himself there, he demanded to know from his lady if she had anyone else in the bedroom. To which she replied 'No' fairly half-heartedly and unusually and not very assuredly.

'Speak truly!' the Scotsman said, 'Your husband, he's not here?!'

'No' she said.

'Why let him come! By Saint Ninian, I'll cleave his head to the teeth! Even if there were three of them, by God, I'd doughtily beat them all!'

And after these criminal words he drew his large and fine sword from its scabbard and brandished it three or four times then placed it on the bed close beside him. Having done this, he swiftly kissed and embraced (her) and all that followed this he carried out at his good ease and leisure without the faint-hearted one of the bed-nook daring to show himself for such great fear that he did not want to die. Our Scotsman, after this 'high adventure', 'took his leave' of his lady one more time and thanked her as – what he imagined to be – his great courtesy and went on his way descending the bedroom stairs.

When the valiant man-at-arms knew the Scotsman was safely away from him – for he was so afraid to even make a peep – he leapt out of his pavilion and began to berate his wife for having endured the archer's pleasure. But she replied that *he* was to blame and it was *his* fault and charged that *he* had given the day (of the visit).

'I didn't command you,' he said, 'to let him have his way with you!'

'How', she said, 'could I refuse him seeing his huge sword with which he would have killed me had I refused?'

And here at this outburst the good Scotsman, who had returned, climbed the bedroom stairs and leapt inside and shouted loudly: 'Whit's gangin' oan?'

Now the good man, in order to save himself, threw himself under the bed, for he was even more terrified than before. The lady was entreated and, once again, was well 'lanced' by the lovesick one and in the same way at leisure as before – his sword being always near him. After this 'exchange' – and several such others – between the Scotsman and the lady the time came to leave so he bid her a 'good night, sleep tight' and left. The poor martyr, being under the bed, was too afraid to come out, fearing the return of his adversary, or to better describe his companion, his 'bedcover'. He took courage and went to his wife's aid, thank God. He got to his feet. As he had badly berated and vilified his wife before he began again but even more harshly for she had consented after her defence of his honour and hers.

'Alas!' said she, 'Where is the wife who is so safe that she dares to say to a man this hot-headed and enraged as this one is, when you are armed, have weapons, and are so valiant that you daren't attack or defend me?!'

[The story ends with the married couple making up, but the cuckolded mercer never discovers that his wife had indeed encouraged the amorous advances of the Scotsman all along.]

Figure 9. MS miniature from *Les cent nouvelles nouvelles*, French, c. 1460 (University of Glasgow Archives and Special Collections, MS Hunter 252 (U.4.10), fol. 12r).

At the start the storyteller hails Lord Talbot, who fell at the Battle of Castillon in 1453, as an 'English captain with such prowess, so valiant, and in (feats of) arms so relentless – as everyone knows' ('capitaine anglois si preux si vaillant et aux armes si eureux co[m]me ch[ac]un scet').

Pendent le temps que la mauldicte et pestilencieuse guerre de france et dangleterre Regnoit et qui encores naprins fin co[m]me souue[n]t aduient Vng francois ho[m]me darmes fut a vng aultre anglois prisonnier Et puis quil se fut mis a finance soubz le saufconduit de monseigne[u]r talebot deuers son capitaine sen Retournoit pour faire finance de sa Renson et a son maistre lenuoyer ou la porter Et comme Il estoit en chemin fut par vng anglois sur les champs Rencontre le quel le voyant francois tantost luy demande dont Il venoit et ou Il alloit Laultre respo[n]dit la verite Et ou est v[ost]re saufconduit dist langlois Et Il nest pas loing dit le francois Lors tire vne petite boyte penda[n]t a sa couroye ou son saufconduit estoit et a la[n]glois le tendit qui dun bout a laultre le leut Et comme Il est de coustume de mectre en toutes l[ett]res de saufconduit Reserue tout vray habillem[en]t de guerre Langlois note sur ces motz et voit encores les aguilletes a armer penda[n]s au po[u]rpoint du francois si va Juger en soy mesmes quil auoit enfract' son saufconduit et que aguillettes sont vray habillement de guerre Et luy dist Amy Je vous fays prisonnier car vo[u]s auez Rompu v[ost]re saufconduit Par ma foy non ay dist le francois sauue v[ost]re grace Vous voiez en quel estat Je suis Nenny nenny dist langloys par saint Jehan v[ost]re saufco[n]duit est Rompu Rendez vous ou Je vous tueray Le pouure francois qui nauoit que son paige et qui estoit tout nu et de ses armes desgarny voyant lautre arme et de trois ou q[uat]re archiers accompaigne pour le desfaire a luy se Rendit Langloys le mena en vne place assez pres de la et en prison le bouta

[The case eventually comes before Lord Talbot who demands an explanation from the Englishman]

Mons[eigneu]r pource que en son saufconduit a et auoit Reserue tout vray habil-lement de guerre Et Il auoit et a encores ses aguillettes a armer qui sont vng vray habillement de guerre car sans elles on ne se peut armer Voire dist mons[eigneu]r talebot Si aguillettes sont donc vray habillement de guerre Et ne scez tu aultre chose par quoy Il puisse auoir enfraint son saufconduyt vrayeme[n]t mons[eigneu]r nenny respond langloys Voyre villain de par vostre dyable dist monseigneur talebot Auez vo' sur mon saufconduyt vng gentil homme pour ses aguillettes Par saint george Je vous feray mo[n]strer si ce sont habillem[ent]s de guerre Alors tout eschaufe et de courroux tresfort esmeu vint au francois et de son pourpoint print deux aguillettes et a langlois les bailla et au francois vne bonne espee darmes fist en la main liurer Et puis la belle et bonne et sienne du fourreau tira Et a langlois va dire Defendez vous de cest habillement de guerre que vous dictes si vous sauez Et puis dist au francois frappez sur ce villain qui vous a Retenu sans cause et sans Raison on verra comme[n]t Il se defendra de v[ost]re habilleme[n]t de guerre Si vous lespergnez Je frapperay sur v[ost]re teste par saint george Alors le francois voulsist ou non fut contraint de ferir sur langlois de lespee toute nue quil tenoit Et le pouure anglois sen couroit par la chambre le plus quil pouoit et talebot apres qui tousiours fasoit ferir par le francois sur laultre et luy disoit defendez vous villain de v[ost]re habillement de guerre A la verite langlois fut tant batu que presque Jusques a la mort et crya mercy a talebot et au francoys quj par ce moien fut deliure et de sa Renson par monseigneur talebot acquicte Et auecques ce son cheual et son harnoys et tout son bagaige q' au Jour de sa prinse auoit luy fist Rendre et bailler

During the time the accursed and pestilential war raged between France and England – that still hasn't come to an end as often happens – a French man-at-arms was taken prisoner by an English one. He was then put to ransom under my Lord Talbot's safe-conduct so he could go to his captain then return to arrange payment of his ransom and send it, or carry it, to his captor. Now while he was *en route* he was come upon by an Englishman in the fields who, seeing the Frenchman, immediately asked him whence he had come and where he was going – to which he gave a truthful answer.

'Right, where's your safe-conduct?' said the Englishman.

'It's not far off (i.e., he didn't have to travel far to arrange the ransom)' said the Frenchman.

He then drew a little box hanging from his belt where his safe-conduct was kept and gave it to the Englishman who read it from start to finish.

Now, as it is the custom to state in all letters of safe-conduct 'Save all true habiliments of war', the Englishman took note of these words and looked again at the arming points hanging from the Frenchman's pourpoint, and so judged that by having just these he had broken (the terms of) his safe-conduct and that points were 'true habiliments of war', so he said to him:

'Alright mate, I make you my prisoner for you've broken your safe-conduct.'

'By my faith I *have not*!' said the Frenchman, 'Saving your grace, cannot you see *what* state (of defencelessness) I am in!'

'Nah, Nah!' said the Englishman, 'By Saint John, your safe-conduct *is* broken! Give yourself up or I *will* kill you!'

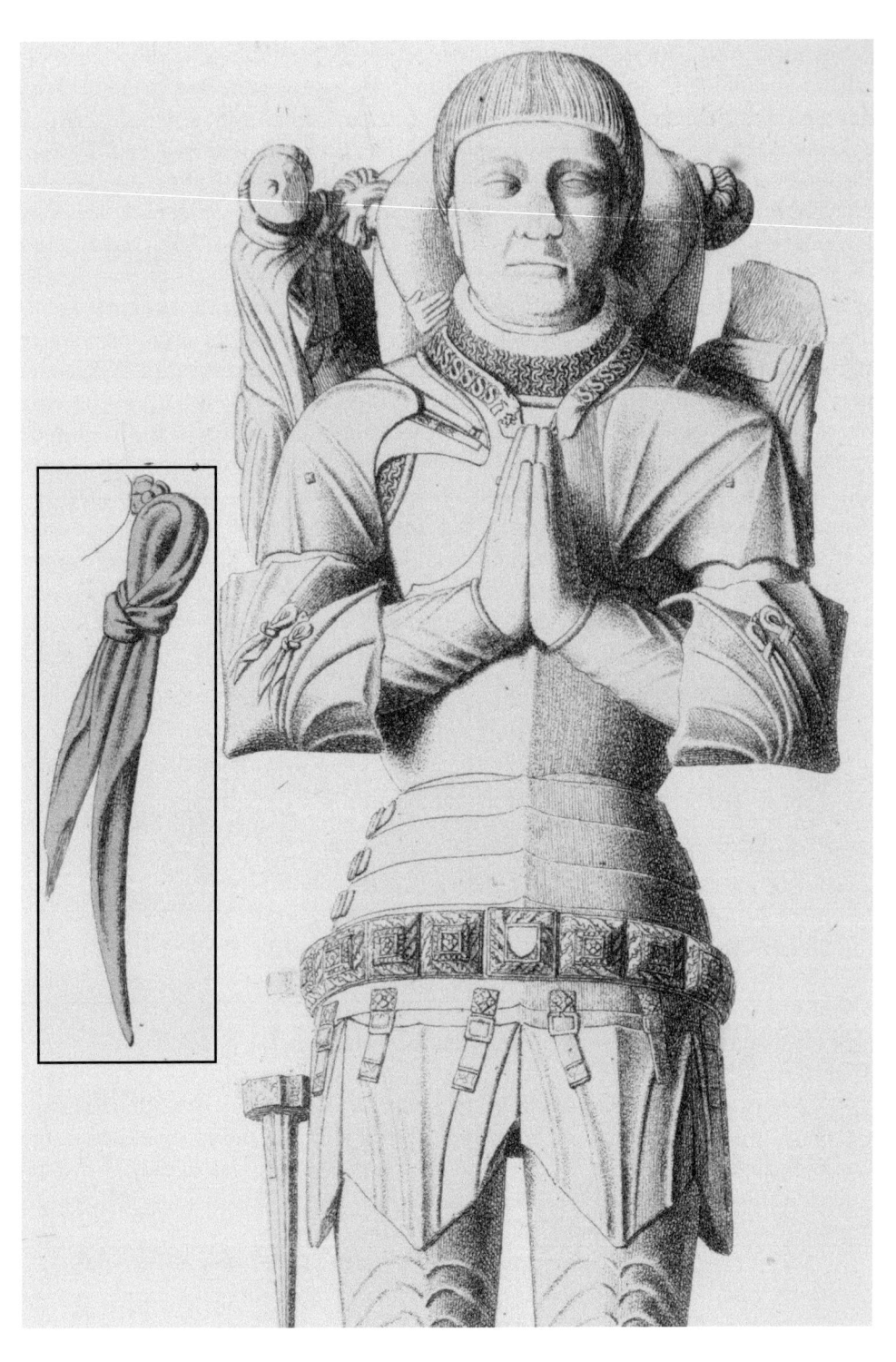

Figure 10. Etching of the tomb effigy of Robert,
Lord Hungerford (d. 1455), Salisbury Cathedral.

The poor Frenchman had naught but his page (for backup) and as he was completely naked (i.e., without armour) nor was he equipped with any of his weapons, seeing the other armed and accompanied by three or four archers, to avoid it (injury or death) gave himself up to him. The Englishman led him to a nearby place and threw him in prison.

[The case eventually comes before Lord Talbot who demands an explanation from the Englishman]

'My Lord, it's because in his safe-conduct it says, 'Save all true habiliments of war.' And he had – and still has – his arming points which is a "true habiliment of war", for without them one *cannot* arm.'

'Ah so,' said my Lord Talbot, 'points are therefore "true habiliments of war", and you can't think of *anything* else by which he's broken his safe-conduct?'

'In truth my Lord, no,' replied the Englishman.

'Why, you villain, what devilry is this of yours!' said my Lord Talbot, 'Have *you*, under *my* safe-conduct, (captured) a man-at-arms because of his *points*? By Saint George! I'll show you if they be "habiliments of war!"'

Then, all hot-headed and indignant, and moving very forcefully, he came up to the Frenchman and yanked off two points and threw them at the Englishman, and shoved a good arming sword into the Frenchman's hand. Then he drew off its beautiful and good scabbard and threw it at the Englishman shouting:

'Defend yourself with *this* if you say it's a "habiliment of war" – if you know how!'

Then he said to the Frenchman:

'Strike this villain who has detained you without good cause and without reason! We will see if *he* can defend himself with *your* "habiliment of war"! But if you go easy on him I'll smash it over *your* head, by Saint George!'

So, the Frenchman, willing or not, was obliged to hit the Englishman with the completely naked sword he held. So, the poor Englishman scarpered around the room as best he could with Lord Talbot after him – who continually made the Frenchman hit him – and he shouted at him: 'Defend yourself villain with *your* "habiliment of war!"'

I tell you no lie that the Englishman was beaten so badly that he was near death! So, he cried for mercy from Lord Talbot and the Frenchman who was by this means excused payment of his ransom by my Lord Talbot. And his horse and his harness and all his baggage he had on the day of his capture he had returned and granted to him.

Figure 11. MS miniature from *Les cent nouvelles nouvelles*, French, c. 1460 (University of Glasgow Archives and Special Collections, MS Hunter 252 (U.4.10), fol. 14r).

22

Glasgow Museums, R. L. Scott Library, MS E.1939.65.1144, fol. 1r–fol. 6r

Paris, Bibliothèque nationale, MS fr. 2692, fol. 18v–fol. 28v and MS fr. 2695, fol. 21v–fol. 43v

Extract from René, Duke of Anjou's Tournament Treatise, written between 1457 and 1472

> *Duke René (1409–80) completed one of his major literary works in 1457. He must, therefore, have finished his treatise sometime after this. He dedicated his 'petit traictie' to his 'treschier tresame et seul frere germain' Charles, Count of Main (1414–72).*[7]

la facon et maniere dont douient estre les harnoys de teste de corps et de bras timbres et lambequins que on appelle en flandres et en brabant et en ses haulx pays on les tournoys se vsent com[m]unem[en]t coctes darmes selles hours et housseures de cheualx masses et espees pour tournoyer Et pour mieulx le vous declairer Icy dessoubz sera figure lune piece apres laut' ainsi q[ue]lles doyuent estre

le timbre doibt estre sur vne piece de cuir boully laquelle doibt estre bien faulcree dung doy despez ou plus par le dedens et doibt co[n]tenir lad' piece de cuir tout le so[m]met du heaulme et s[er]a couuert lad' piece du lambequin armoye des armes de cellui qui le portera Et sur led' lambrequin plus hault de so[m]met s[er]a affis led' timbre et autour dicellui aura vng tortiz des couleurs que vouldra led' tournoyeur du gros du bras ou plus ou moins a son plaisir

---

7   Paris, Bibliothèque nationale, MS fr. 2695, fol. 1r.

le heaulme est en facon dung bacinet ou dune cappeline Res[er]ue que la visiere est
aut[re]ment ainsi que cy dessoubz est paint Et pour mieulx faire entendre la maniere
du timbre du cuir boully et de heaulme Ilz s[er]ont cy dessoubz pourtraiz en troys
facons

Icy apres sensuit la facon et maniere du bacinet du cuir boully et du timbre
le harnoys de corps est co[m]me vne cuirasse ou co[m]me vng harnoys a pie quon
appelle to[n]nellet Et aussi peult on bien tournoyer en brigandines qui vieult Maiz
en quelque facon de harnoys de corps que on vueille tournoyer est de neccessite sur
toute Riens que led' harnoys soit si large et si ample que on puisse vestir et mectre
dessoubz vng porpoint ou courset & fault q' le porpoint soit faulcre de troys doiz
despez sur les espaules & au long des braz Jusques au col et sur le dos aussi pource que
les coups des masses et des espees desc[en]de[n]t plus voulentiers es endroiz dessusd'
que en aut[re]s lieux Et pour veoir la principale et meilleure facon pour tournoyer
s[er]a figure cy dessoubz vne cuirasse pertuisee en la meilleure et plus propre facon et
maniere quelles peut estre pour led' tournoy

[The arm defences ought to be thus:] [C]estassauoir gardebraz auantbraz et gantelez
lesquelx auantbraz et gardebraz fait on voulenti[er]s tenans ensemble et y en a de deux
facons [D]ont les vngs sont de harnoys blanc et les aut[re]s de cuir boully lesquelles
deux facons tant de harnoys blanc que aussi de cuir boully sont paintes cy dessoubz
LA forme et facon des ganteles est telle que on peult veoir cy dessoubz en figure

Icy apres est pourtractie la facon & la maniere des gantelez
lespee Rabatue doibt estre en la forme et manie[re] cy apres painte Et semblabem[en]t
la masse

Icy apres est pourtraicte la facon & la maniere de lespee & de la masse
De la mesure et facon des espees et des masses ny a pas trop a dire fors que de la
largeur et longueur de la lumelle Car elle doibt estre large de quatre doiz a ce quelle
ne puisse passer par la veue du heaulme et doibt auoir les deux tranchans larges dung
doy despez Et affin quelle ne soit pas trop pesante elle doibt estre fort Widee par
le meilleu et mosse dauant et toute dune venue se bien pou non depuis la croisce
Jusques au bout Et doibt estre la croisee si courte quelle puisse seulem[en]t garentir
vng coup qui par cas daue[n]ture descendroit ou viendroit glissant le long de lespee
Jusques sur les doiz et toute doibt estre aussi longue que le braz auec la main de celluy
qui la porte et la masse par semb[lab]le Et doibt auoir lad' masse vne petite Rondelle
bien clouee deuant la main pour Icelle garentir Et peult on qui veult atacher son espee
ou sa masse a vne deliee chaesne tresse ou cordon autour du braz ou a sa sainture a
ce que si elles eschappoient de la main on les peust Retrouuer sans cheoir a terre Au
Regard de la facon des po[m]meaulx des espees Cela est a plaisir Et la grosseur des
masses et la pesanteur des espees doyeuent estre Reuisitees par les Juges la vigille du
Jour du tournoy lesquelles masses [et espees?] doiuent estre signees dung fer chault
par lesd' Juges a ce quelles ne soient point doultrageuse pesanteur ne longueur Aussi

LE harnoys de Jambes est ainsi et de semblable facon co[m]me on le porte en la
guerre sans aut' differance fors que les plus petites gardes sont les meilleurs et les
sollerez y sont tresbons cont' la poincte des esperons LEs plus cours esperons sont

plus co[u]uenables que les longs a ce que on ne les puisse arracier ou destordre hors les piedz en la presse

La cocte darmes doibt estre faicte ne plus ne moins co[m]me celle dung herault Res[er]ue quelle doibt estre sans ploictz par le corps affin que on congnoisse mieulx de quoy sont les armes

[Here Duke René provides a brief excursus on different tourneying equipment]

En brabant flandres et haynault et en ces pays la vers les almaignes ont acoustume deulx armer de la personne aut[re]ment au tournoy Car Ilz prennent vng demy pourpoint de deux toilles sans plus du faulx du corps en bas et lace sur le ventre Et puis sur ce la mectent vnes bracieres grosses de quatre doiz despez et Remplies de couton Sur quoy Ilz arment les auantbras et les gardebraz de cuir boully Sur lequel cuir boully y a de menuz bastons cinq ou six de la grosseur dung doy et collez dessus qui vont tout au long du bras Jusques aux Jointes Et quant pour lespaule et pour le coude sont faiz les gardebraz et auantbraz de cuir boully co[m]me cy deuant est deuise fors quilz sont de plus lorde et grosse facon Et sont dedans bien faulcrez Et de lun en laut' est vne toille double cousue qui les tient ensemble co[m]me vng manche de mailles Puis ont vne bien legiere brigantine dont la poitrine est pertuisee co[m]me cy dessus est deuise Et quant a leurs armeures de teste ont vng grant bacinet a camail sans visiere lequel Ilz atachent par le camail dessus la brigandine tout au tour a la poictine et sur les espaules a fortes agueilletes Et par dessus tout cela mectent vng grant heaulme fait dune venue lequel heaulme est voulentiers de cuir boully et pertuise dessus a la largeur dung tranchouer de bois et la veue en est barree de fer de trois doiz en troys doiz lequel est seulement atachie dauant a vne chaesne qui tient a la poictrine de la brigandine en facon que on le peult gecter sur larczon de la selle pour soy Refrechir et le Reprandre quant on veult Et pendant que on a led' heaulme hors de la teste nul ne ose frapper Jusques ad ce que on lait Remis en la teste Sur lequel heaulme on mect le lambequin des armes la Rorte ou torteis de la deuise et le timbre des armes du tournoyeur atachie a agueilletes co[m]me daua[n]t est deuise Et sur la brigandine mectent la cocte darmes Et quant tout cela est sur lo[m]me Il semble estre plus gros que long pour quoy me passe de plus auant en parler Et au Regard de leurs selles elles sont de la haulteur dont on les souloit porter a la Jouxte en france anciennem[en]t et les pissieres et le chanfrain de cuir [boully] aussi Et mauis deulx a len veu en cest habillement lesquelx quant Ilz esoitent a cheual ne se pouoient aider ne tourner leurs cheuaulx tellement estoient gours [*sic*] ET Au Regard de leurs masses espees et harnoys de Jambes elles sont semblables de celles dont deuant est deuise[8]

Et pour Reuenir a la vraye et plusgente facon la maniere darmer les p[er]sonnes ainsi que dessus est touchie est dassez plus belle et plus seure Et les selles de guerre aussi sont bonnes pour tournoyer quant elles sont bien fort closes derriere et ne veullent pas estre trop haultes darczon dauant

---

[8] I have moved this sentence from its original position in the following paragraph as it makes more sense here.

Oult' plus y est tresneccessaire vne facon de hourt que on atache dauant a larczon de la selle tant hault que bas en plusieurs lieux le mieulx que on peult & le plus seurem[en]t Et descend le long des aulnes de la selle dauant en ambrassant la poictine du cheual lequel hourt est bon po[u]r garentir le cheual ou destrier despauler cont' le hurt quant on vient de choc et pres[er]ue aussi la Jambe du tournoyeur de tout' estorses Le hourt est fait de paille longue ent' toilles fort po[u]rpoinctees de cordes de fouet et dedans led' hort y a vng sac plain de paille en facon dung croissant atachie aud' hourt qui Reppose sur la poictrine du cheual et Relieue led' hourt ad ce quil ne hurte cont' les Jambes du cheual Et en oult' led' pourpoinctem[en]t y a qui vieult bastons cousuz dedans qui le tiennent Roide sans gainchir Et est la facon dud' hourt cy dessoubz pourtraicte tant a lenuers que a lendroit affin que on voye lune & laut' et co[m]me on mect led' sac dedans led' hourt la facon du quel sac est ainsi

Icy apres est pourtraicte la facon & la maniere du sac pour mectre dedans le hourt
Icy est pourtraicte listoire du hort a lenuers
LE hourt a lenuers est tel que cy dauant est semblablement pourtrait
Icy est pourtraicte listoire du hourt a lendroit
on couure led' hort dune couuerture armoyee des armes du seigneur qui le porte et faictes baterie co[m]me cy apres est hystorie
Icy apres est pourtraicte listoire de la couuerte du hourt

How the fashion and manner ought to be of the armour for the head, the body, and the arms; the (heraldic) crests and (fabric) *lambrequins* – as they are called in Flanders and in Brabant and in such high (i.e., Northern) lands where tourneys are commonly held – and coat armours; horses' saddles, *hourts* (padded chest defences), and trappings; clubs[9] and swords for tourneying. And to better describe to you how they ought to be, one piece after another shall be drawn here below.

The crest ought to be (mounted) on a piece of cuir bouilli which ought to be very well reinforced by an inch or more on the inside. And this piece of leather ought to encompass the whole top of the helm. And this piece shall be covered with the *lambrequin* emblazoned with the (heraldic) arms of he who bears it. Now the crest shall be affixed higher up on top of this *lambrequin*; and around this shall be a torse[10] of an arm's thickness – or more or less – of such colours as pleases the tourneyer.

The helm is in the fashion of a basinet or capelline save that the visor is different as is thus painted here below. And to better understand the manner of the crest, the cuir bouilli, and the helm they shall be painted below in three types.

Hereafter follows the fashion and manner of the basinet, the cuir bouilli, and the helm (fig. 12i).

The body armour is akin to a cuirass or a harness for foot (combat) which is called a tonlet. Whoever wants to can also tourney well in brigandines. But in whatever fashion of body armour that one wants to tourney in, it is necessary

---

9   Duke René uses the term *masse*. I have translated it as club to avoid confusion with the sharp-flanged mace wielded in battle.

10 A heraldic term for a wreath made of a twisted roll of fabrics.

– above all – that this harness be so large and so roomy that one can wear and fit a pourpoint or corset beneath. Now the pourpoint must be reinforced to the thickness of three inches over the shoulders and the length of the arms and as far as the neck and over the back also because the club- and sword-stokes often tend to land on these places aforesaid as well as in other areas. And to see the foremost and best fashion for tourneying there shall be drawn here below a pierced cuirass in the best and most suitable fashion and manner as can be for the said tourney (fig. 12ii).

[The arm defences ought to be thus:] that is to say, pauldrons, vambraces, and gauntlets – these vambraces and pauldrons should be attached together. Now there are two types: the first are of white harness and the others are of cuir bouilli. Both of these two types – white harness as well as cuir bouilli – are painted here below (fig. 12iii).

The form and fashion of the gauntlets can be seen in the design below.

The fashion and manner of the gauntlets is hereafter portrayed (fig. 12iv).

The rebated sword ought to be in the form and manner as painted hereafter, and likewise the club.

The fashion and manner of the sword and club is portrayed hereafter (fig. 12v).

There is not much to say about the fashion of the swords and clubs save the width and length of the blade. For it ought to be four inches wide so that it cannot pass through the helm's sight and ought to have one-inch-thick edges. And so that it be not too heavy, it ought to have a strong void through the middle (i.e., a substantial fuller) and front tapered and be all of one piece – so good that it be no less (weak) from the cross (guard) to the end. And the cross ought to be so short that it can only protect against a blow which lands accidentally or comes skyting the length of the sword to over the fingers. And also, the whole thing ought to be as long as the arm and hand of the wielder – and likewise the club. Now the club ought to have a little rondel well nailed before the hand to protect it. And whoever wants to can attach his sword or club with a thin chain, tress, or cord around the arm or to his girdle so that should it escape the hand one can retrieve it without falling to the ground. As regards the sword-pommels these are to the pleasure (of the tourneyer). Now the clubs' thicknesses and swords' weights ought to be inspected by the judges on the vigil of the day of the tournament. These clubs (and swords?) ought to be marked with a hot iron by these judges so that there be no excessive weight nor length too.

The legharness is thus of a similar fashion to that borne in war with no other difference save that the smallest guards (i.e., poleyn wings) are best and the sabatons are very good against the spur-goads (i.e., well fitted to allow the goads to make contact with the horse's flanks). Shorter spurs are more suitable than longer ones so that they cannot be torn off or twisted from the feet in the press.

The coat armour ought to be made no more or less (in size) than that of a herald save that it should not have pleats so that the (heraldic) arms thereon can be better recognised.

[Here Duke René provides a brief excursus on different tourneying equipment]

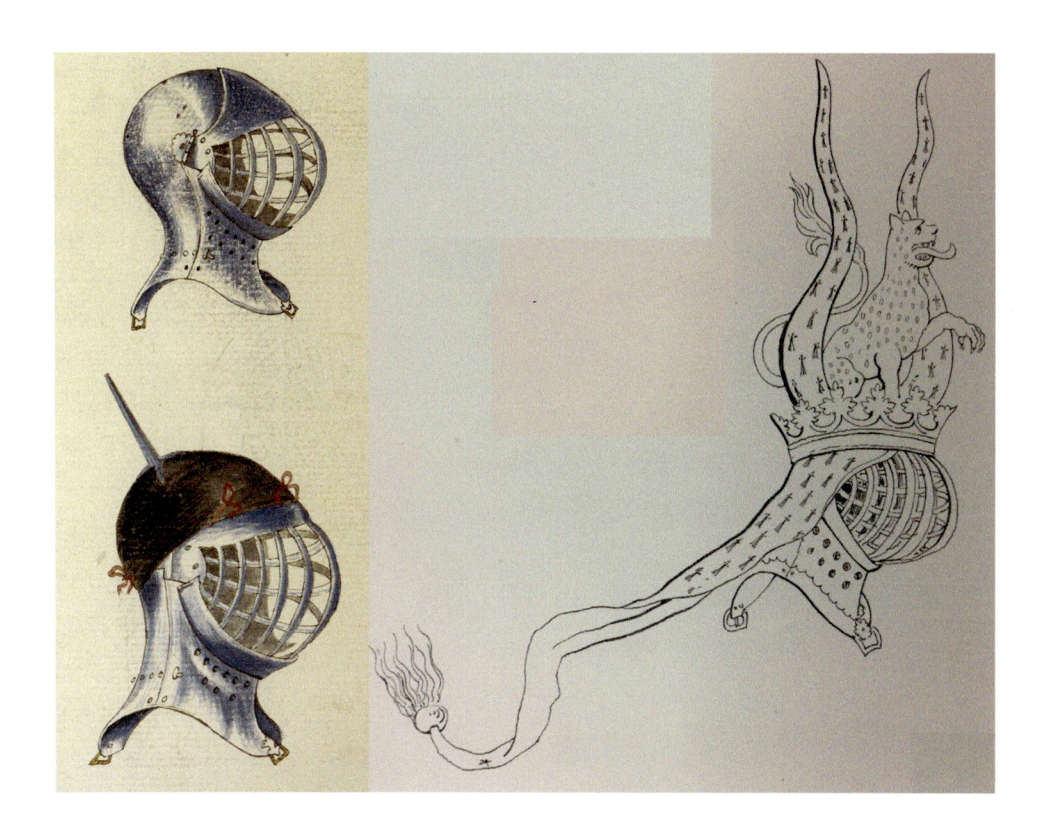

Figures 12i. Illustration from René, Duke of Anjou's Tournament Treatise (Glasgow Museums, R. L. Scott Library, E.1939.65.1144, fol. 11r–fol. 14r).

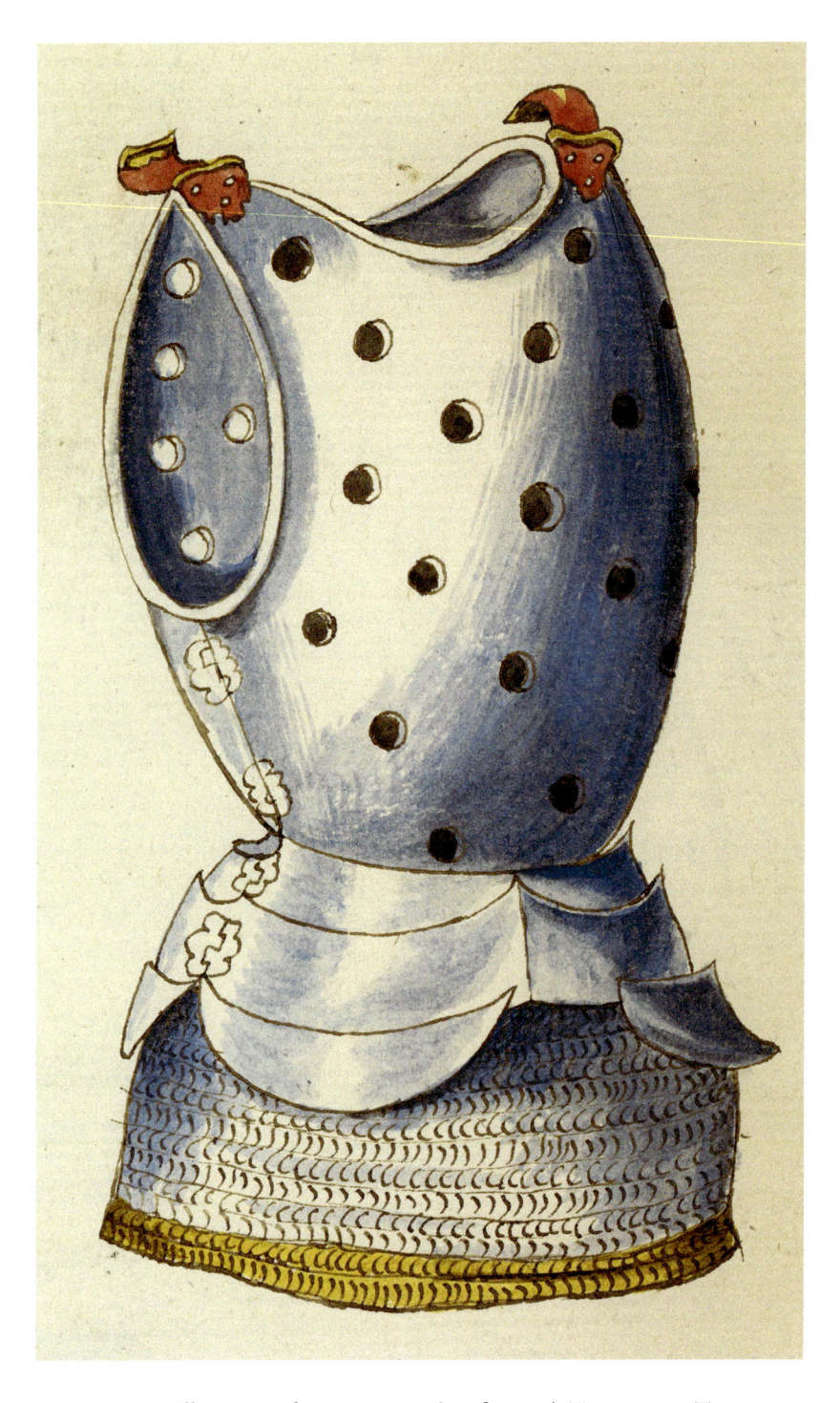

Figure 12ii. Illustration from René, Duke of Anjou's Tournament Treatise.

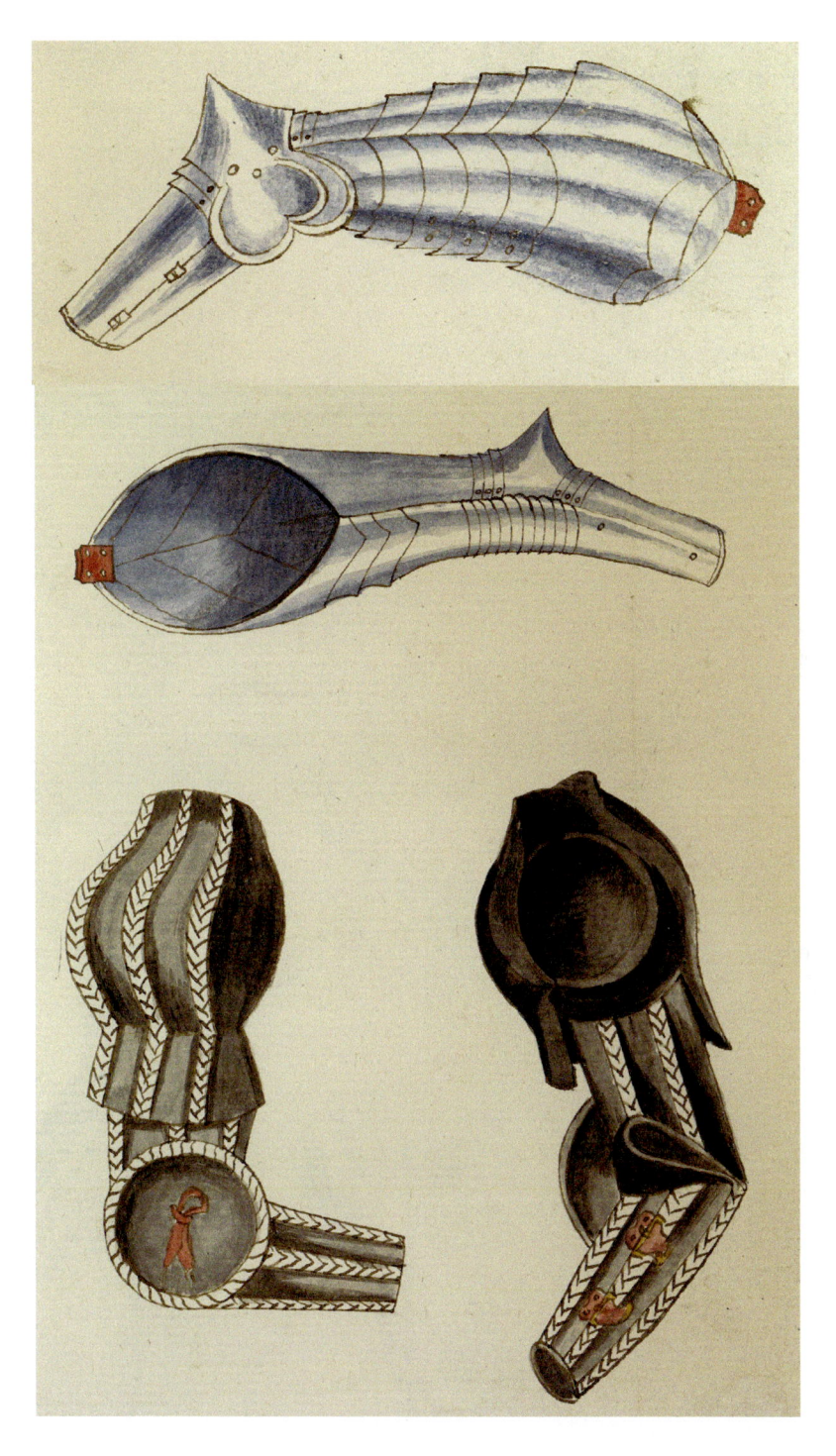

Figure 12iii. Illustration from René, Duke of Anjou's Tournament Treatise.

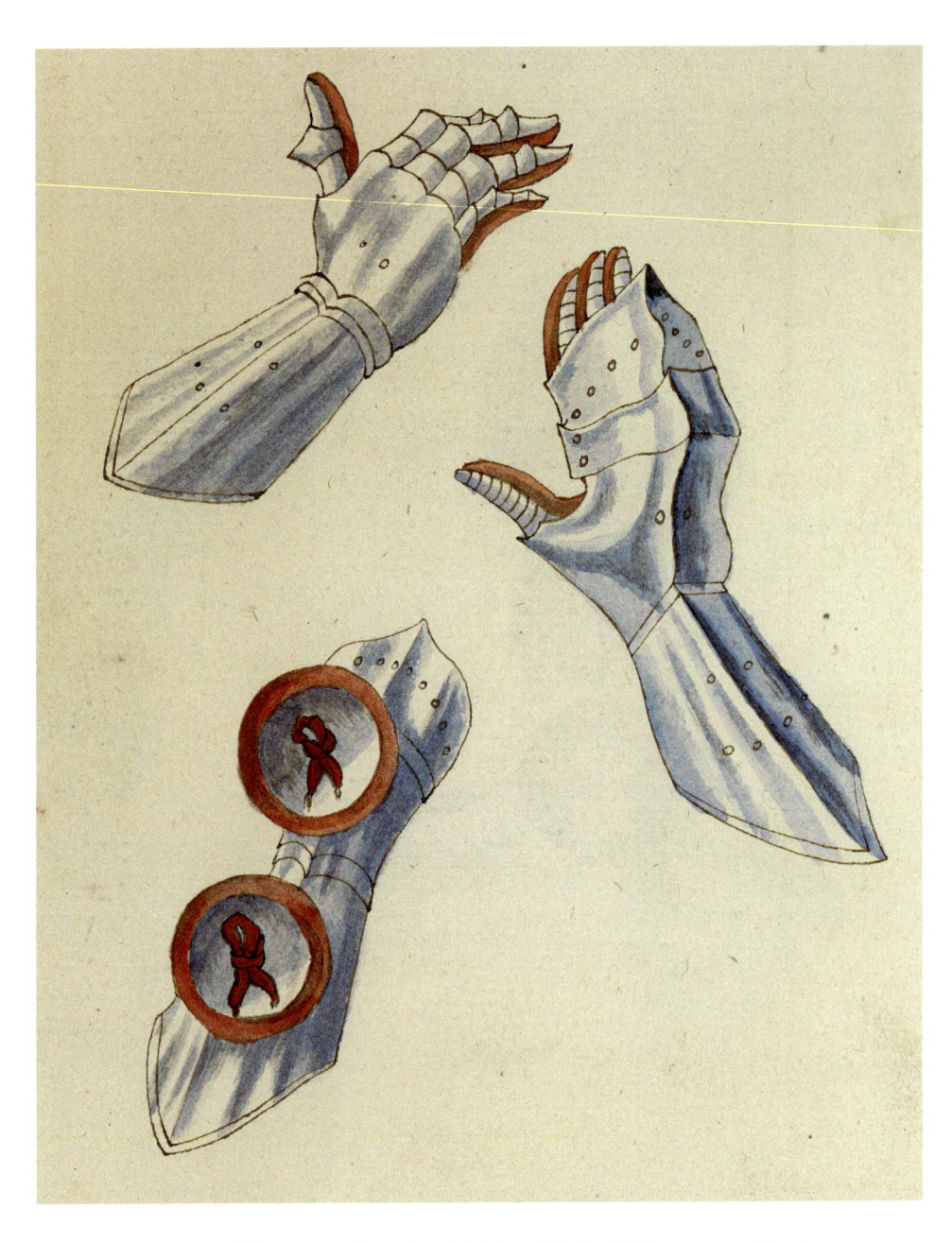

Figure 12iv. Illustration from René, Duke of Anjou's Tournament Treatise.

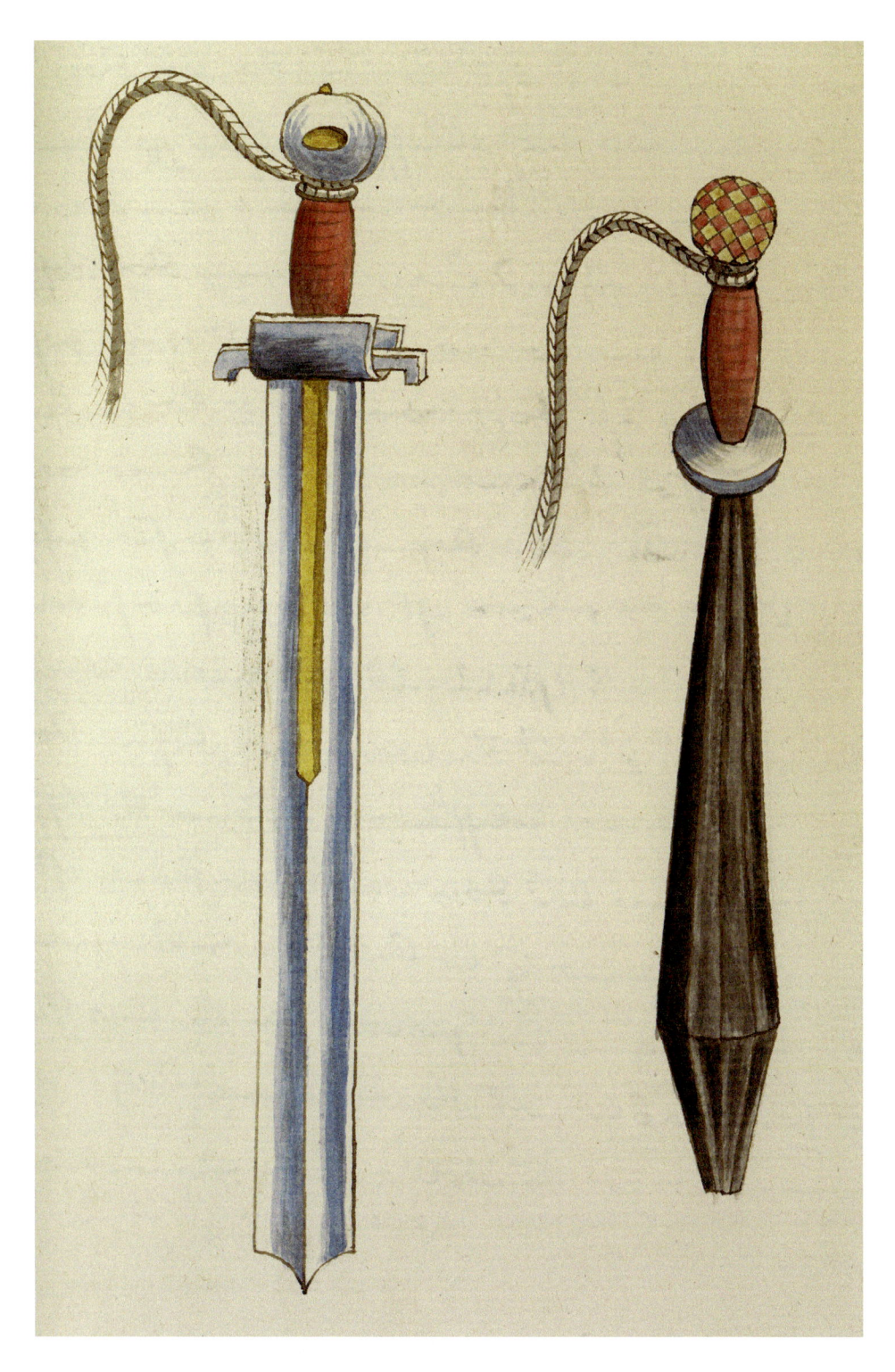

Figure 12v. Illustration from René, Duke of Anjou's Tournament Treatise.

In Barbant, Flanders, and Hainaut, and in the lands towards the German ones (i.e., the Empire) they are accustomed to arm their bodies in the tourney in a different way. For they take a half-pourpoint of two (layers) of cloth no lower than the body's lower torso and laced over the belly. And then over this is fitted a four-inch-thick (pair of) bracers stuffed with cotton. Over which they arm (themselves) with vambraces and pauldrons of cuir bouilli. Over this cuir bouilli there are five or six little inch-thick batons and over the collar which extend the length of the arms up to the (shoulder) joints. Now the cuir bouilli pauldrons and vambraces made for the shoulder and elbow are as described before save that they are of a heavier and thicker type and are well reinforced inside. And from one (component) to the other there is a double-stitched cloth which holds them together like a mail sleeve. They then have a very light brigandine, the breast of which is pierced as is described above. And for head defences they have a large visorless basinet with aventail which they attach by the aventail over the brigandine all around the breast and over the shoulders with strong laces. And on top of all that they place a large helm made in one piece – this helm is wont to be of cuir bouilli and pierced above to the thickness of a wooden trencher (i.e., with holes the circumference of a wooden serving dish) and the sight is barred with iron three inches by three inches (i.e., in a grid of these dimensions). This (helm) is only attached at the front by a chain from the brigandine's breast in such a manner that one can throw it over the saddle-bow to take a breather and then replace it when one wants. Now during the time the helm is off the head none dare strike until it has been put back on the head. On this helm is placed the *lambrequin* (emblazoned) with the (heraldic) arms, the torse of the device and crest of the tourneyer's (heraldic) arms attached with laces as described before. And the coat armour is placed over the brigandine. Now when all of that is on the man it seems to be more thick than long (i.e., elegant), because (of this) I shall say no more. But as regards their saddles they are of the height of those which were wont to be borne in France in the joust of yore and the *pissieres* (chest defences, i.e., peytrals) and shaffrons are also of cuir bouilli. They are a sorry sight to see in this habiliment. When they are on horseback they cannot guide or turn the horse when it goes off course. And as regards their clubs, swords, and legharness they are similar to those described before.[II]

But to return to the true and finer fashion of the previous manner of arming the body thus touched on above, which is more beautiful and more secure. Now war saddles are also good for tourneying when they are strongly closed at the rear and the saddle-bow at the front be not too high.

In addition, it is very necessary to have a type of *hourt* which is attached to the front of the saddle-bow both as high and low in several places as best and as securely as possible. And it extends the length of the saddle's measure at the front and encompasses the horse's breast. This *hourt* acts well to protect the horse or

---

[II] I have moved this sentence from its original position in the following paragraph as it makes more sense here.

destrier from shoulder dislocation against the shock of impact and also prevents the tourneyer's leg from being in any way twisted. The *hourt* is made of long straw between strongly-pourpointed cloth (and) whipcord. And inside this *hourt* is a crescent-shaped, straw-filled sack attached to the said *hourt* which rests on the horse's breast and prevents the *hourt* from clashing against the horse's legs. And in addition to the said pourpointing there are, for those who want it, batons stitched inside which hold it rigid without losing its shape. The fashion of the *hourt* is portrayed here below – both the inside and outside – so one can see both, and how the sack is thus fitted inside the *hourt*.

The fashion and manner of the sack for fitting inside the *hourt* is portrayed hereafter (fig. 12vi).

The design of the inside of the *hourt* is portrayed here (fig. 12vii).

The outside of the *hourt* is similar to that portrayed before.

The design of the outside of the *hourt* is portrayed here (fig. 12viii).

This *hourt* is covered with a trapper emblazoned with the (heraldic) arms of the lord who bears it (on his mount) and is made of beaten (fabric decoration) as in the design hereafter.

The design of the trapper of the *hourt* is portrayed hereafter (fig. 12ix).

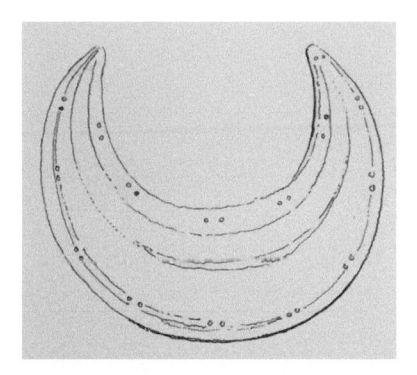

Figure 12vi. Illustration from René, Duke of Anjou's Tournament Treatise.

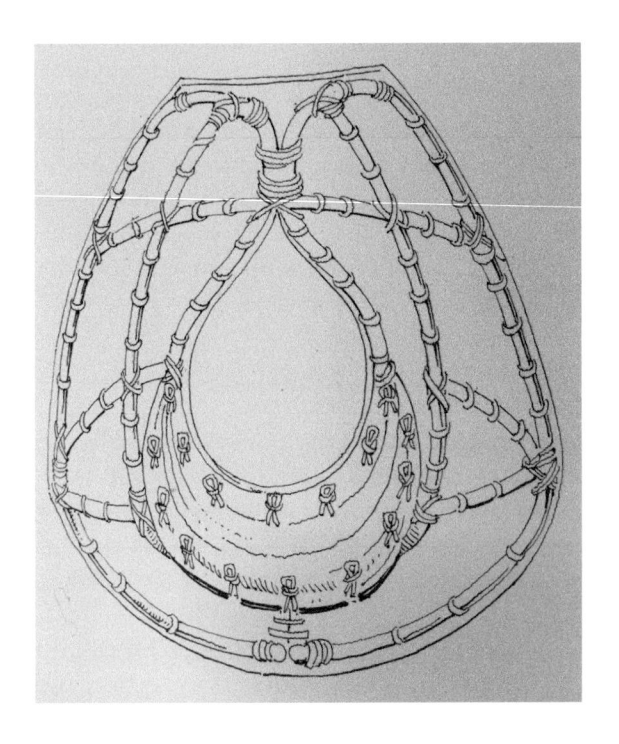

Figure 12vii. Illustration from René, Duke of Anjou's Tournament Treatise.

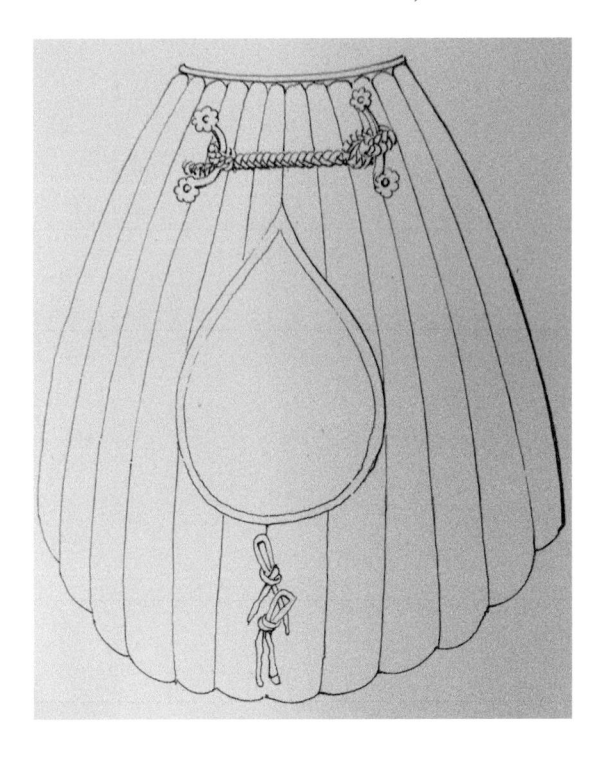

Figure 12viii. Illustration from René, Duke of Anjou's Tournament Treatise.

Figure 12ix. Illustration from René, Duke of Anjou's Tournament Treatise.

23

Now-Lost Original Document from the Archives municipales de Douai, printed in E. J. Soil de Moriamé, 'Armes et armuriers tournaisiens. Heaumiers, haubregonneurs, forbisseurs, couteliers. Contribution à l'histoire des métiers d'art et à l'histoire militaire de Tournai de XIIIe au XVIIIe siècle', *Bulletin de l'Académie royale d'archéologie de Belgique*, unnumbered (1913), pp. 36–154 (at p. 105)

Account of Jacquemart Lyon, Douai, 1457

une sallade, une cappeline, deux bracheles, deux harnas de gambes, deux garde bras, deux tonneles et deux wanteles xxv s. un bachinet de lombardie v s.

one sallet, one capelline, two bracers, two (pairs of) legharness, two (pairs of) pauldrons, two tonlets (i.e., paunces of plate), and two (pairs of) gauntlets 25s., one basinet of Lombardy (make) 5s.

Figure 13. Two views of a sallet, German, c. 1480
(Glasgow Museums, R. L. Scott bequest, E.1939.65.ai).

24

Dorchester, Dorset History Centre, DC-BTB/FG/3f

Muster Roll of Bridport, Dorset, in the presence of William Oliver and Richard Ball, Bailiffs, and Robert Scarlet and Thomas Stockfysshe, Constables, 6 September 1457

This roll, which is very fragmentary, lists 78 names (including a 'Margaret' Atkyn") with no equipment recorded, therefore these have not been included.

Rob[er]tus Capper glad' [Lat. *gladius*: sword] & ordinab[i]t [Lat. 'he is to provide'] arc' & d[imid]j shefe sagitt' [bow and a half-sheaf of arrows] Wil[he]lm[u]s Stowbrygge a custell' [*sic*, Lat. *cultellus*: knife] arc' & ordinab[i]t xviij sagitt' salet dagger' Wil[he]lm[u]s Nele [com]p[ar] [Lat. citizen] Jack salet j gladiu' & j daggar' & ordinabit j arcu' & sagitt' xviij Joh[ann]es Gye [com]p[ar] j Jack salet gladiu' j daggar' j glefe ij arc' & ij shefe sagitt' Thomas Tracy j Jack salet j gladiu' & bokeler' j arc' & j shefe <de arows> sagitt' Wil[he]lmus Bremyll' Jack salet arc' & shefe sagitt' glad' & dagger' Alex' yonge Jack salet arc' shefe sagitt' glad' bokeler' dagger' Joh[ann]es Bollyng[er] arc' & shefe sagitt' Walt[er]us Smyth' glad' bokeler' salet dagger' & ordinab[i]t Jack arc' shefe sagitt' sub pen' xx s' citat' p[ro]x' [Lat. 'under pain (of a fine) of 20s. at the next summons'] Thomas Smith' Rob[er]tus[12] Joh[ann]es S[...] [surname illegible] [...]d' a prarige [*sic*] & ordinab[i]t pavys henr' mill'[...] a [...]ff cu' cruce [prob. a staff with a cross. See the entry for Johannes Bryght' below] & dagger' & ordinab[i]t pavys Wil[he]lm[u]s hill' smith' arc' shefe sagitt' glad' hap[er]chyn' [i.e., haubergeon] salet Wil[he]lm[u]s Wykys Jack salet arc' & shefe

---

12 These last three names are with braces on left.

sagitt' glad' dagger' Wil[he]lm[u]s Churchstile j Jacke salet j arc' & j shefe sagitt' j gladiu' Jacob[us] Bertram j Jacke j gladiu' j bokeler' & j bylle ij arc' & ordinab[i]t shefe sagitt' citat' p[ro]x' sub pen' xiij s' iiij d' & ordinab[i]t salet henr' laurens [brace with Jacobus above] henr' marnys Jack salet j arc' j shefe sagitt' glad' dagger' legge harnys Joh[ann]es horys j peyr' brycandyrys [i.e., brigandine] j arc' j shefe sagitt' j pollex [& j] Jacke Joh[ann]es Benet barbo[u]r arc' & shefe saggit' custell' Rogg[er]us hore a peyr' of brygandyrys Thomas Bayly j Jack salet j glefe j arc' & j shefe sagitt' Joh[ann]es Sterr' j Jacke salet glad' j ax & ij arc' & ij shefe sagitt' & j haberchyn' Joh[ann]es Newton' j Jacke j arc' & j shefe sagitt' j gladiu' & daggar' & ordinab[i]t citat' Fin' Exaltac[i]o[n]is S[an]c[t]i cruc' [the end of the Feast of the Exaltation of the Holy Cross (14 September)] sub pen' xl d' Joh[ann]es Crokehorn' Jack salet Ric[ard]us Burgh' ij Jack' ij salett' iiij arc' & iij shefe sagitt' ij pollax ij glefis ij daggar' Walt[er]us helyer' j Jack salet j arc' & j shefe sagitt' daggar' glefe j gladiu' Joh[ann]es Trycaldy ij Jackes ij salet' ij arc' & ij shefe saggit' a peyr' of gawndelett' [i.e., gauntlets] Wil[he]l[mu]s Godeyer' [braces to left of last two] R[...] [name illegible] [...] j hole whyte harnys j ax ij Jackys ij salett' & ij arc' & ij shefe sagitt' ij daggar' Ro[...] [...]t [name illegible] no' [com]p[ar] & ordinab[i]t arc' & d[imid]j shefe sagitt' glad' v[e]l [Lat. or] ax Joh[...] [surname illegible] [...]dav' Rog[er] [last three names linked by braces on left] Rob[er]t[...] Burgh' Jacke salet j arc' & j shefe sagitt' j daggar' glad' & bokeler' Joh[ann]es Marincell' arc' shefe sagitt' a salet a peyr' of gawntelett' & daggar' & ordinab[i]t Jack citat' Fin' Exalt S[an]c[t]e cruc' sub pen' xx s' Joh[ann]es Godewyn' glad' glefe a kytell' hatte [i.e., kettlehat] Walt[er]us Padmore pavys sper' & ordinab[i]t dagger' Joh[ann]es Boleyn' sen' [senior] a hap[er]chyn' [haubergeon] glad' pollax & [...]rdinab[i]t arc' & d[imid]j shefe sagitt' v[e]l payvs Alic' hare [i.e. Alice] iiij peyr' curas no' [com]plet' [i.e., incomplete cuirass] Thomas hanne a staffe cu' ferr' i' fine [staff with iron/spearhead at the end] pollax & ordinab[i]t pavys v[e]l arc' & d[imid]j shefe sagitt' Thomas mill[e]war[...] j shefe sagitt' dagger' [...] [name illegible] sagitt' daggar' [name illegible] j glefe [...] j bokeler' & daggar' & ordinab[i]t citat' Fin' Exaltac' S[an]c[t]e cruc' sub pen' xl d' [name illegible] [...] sper' & ordinab[i]t [...]rc' & shefe sagitt' [name illegible] [...] a glefe glad' & ordinab[i]t pavys [name illegible] [...]e style [sic] j sper' & j custell' [name illegible] [...] j daggar' j glefe j custell' & ordinab[i]t citat' Fin' p[re]d[ictu]m Jacke salet sub pen' xx s' Joh[ann]es Wryght' j arc' & xviij sagitt' daggar' & ordinab[i]t Jack' & salet citat' Fin' Exaltac' S[an]c[t]e cruc' sub pen' xx s' Wil[he]lm[u]s Beche Jack salet j arc' & xij sagitt' pollax custell' & daggar' Joh[ann]es Salman' ordinab[i]t citat' Fin' Exalt' S[an]c[t]i cruc' j pavys sub pen' xx s' v[e]l j mall' de plu[m]bo [lead mallet] Joh[ann]es Elys arc' & glad' salet & ordinab[i]t d[imid]j shefe sagitt' Thomas Stockfyssh' ij Jackys ij salett' ij arc' ij shefe sagitt' ij daggar' ij glad' Nich[ol]us Fletcher' arc' & shefe sagitt' dagger' Elia [i.e., female name] Payer' glad' glefe & ordinab[i]t pavys citat' p[ro]x' Joh[ann]es Kete arc' & d[imid]j shefe sagitt' glad' dagger' & ordinab[i]t vn' pavys citat' p[ro]x' Joh[ann]es pryckprowte Jacke glad' bokeler' ij arc' & shefe sagitt' dagger' & ordinab[i]t salet citat' p[ro]x' sub pen' xl d' Joh[ann]es Smith' weber arc' & d[imid]j shefe saggit' pollax & dagger' & ordinab[i]t j pavys citat' p[ro]x' Wil[he]lm[u]s T[...]yssh' arc' xij sagitt' j hanger' & ordinab[i]t j pavys citat' p[ro]x' Joh[...]s Prior[...] arc' [...]

efe sagitt' glad' dagger' S[...]ph[an]us [i.e., Stephen] Davy[...] & ij salett' ij arc' & ij sagitt' & j pollax J[...] [name illegible] [...] iij Jackys iij salett' & iij <bow> arc' & iij shefe sagittas W[...] [name illegible] [...]agitt' glad' & dagger' T[...] [first name illegible] Trevys j arc' xxti sagitt' glad' bokeler' pollax dagger' & ordinab[i]t Jack' & salet citat' Fin' Exaltac[i]o[n]is S[an]c[t]i cruc' sub pen' Joh[ann]es hille Jack salet ij arc' ij shefe sagitt' ij glad' j ax & ordinab[i]t Jack salet ij daggar' j arc' & j shefe sagitt' erga citat' p[ro]x' Wil[he]lm[u]s powr' ax glad' & ordinab[i]t arc' shefe sagitt' salet dagger' Joh[ann]es atte wer' j arc' xijor sagitt' glad' & ordinab[i]t Jack salet citat' p[re]dic[ti]s sub pen' Thomas Gramond' j arc' & d[imid]j shefe sagitt' salet ij peyr' gawndelett' & ordinab[i]t citat' & c' Jacke glad' & dagger' Rob[er]tus [no surname] [linked by braces with Thomas above] Joh[ann]es hulle Jack' salet arc' xviij sagitt' glad' & ordinab[i]t daggar' citat' p[ro]x' Joh[ann]es davy taylor' glefe & dagger' & ordinab[i]t j pavys

[left margin] Alic' [main text] Joh[ann]es kynge j Jacke salet j arc' & shefe sagitt' <math[ew]e [...]> hewys Jacke salet [last two names linked by braces to Alic' in margin] <Alic' pav[...]> Wil[he]lm[u]s Jrying[er] [sic] j arc' & xij sagitt' glad' & bokeler' j Gun & ordinab[i]t xij sagitt' citat' p[ro]x' Rob[er]tus Shephurd' a sper' dagger' & ordinab[i]t <pavys> arc' & d[imid]j shefe sagitt' citat' p[ro]x' sub pen' vj s' viij d' [...]h[ann]es Bryght' a staffe cu' cruce' [staff with a cross] dagger' & ordinab[i]t arc' & d[imid]j shefe sagitt' J[...]h[...] [prob. Johannes] [...]kyr' [surname illegible] [com]p[ar] [...] ordinab[i]t arc' & shefe sagitt' glad' ax bill' & salet Wil[he]lm[u]s hows Jack salet arc' & shefe sagitt' glad' & bokeler' & ordinab[i]t salet [i.e., sallet] Nich[ol]us hoore Jack salet arc' & shefe sagitt' glad' & bokeler' dagger' Rog[er]us Frankeleyn' Jack salet arc' shefe sagitt' glad' bokeler' dagger' Rogg[er]us Batt' glad' bokeler' & sper' & ordinab[i]t Jack salet arc' & shefe sagitt' citat' p[ro]x' Andr' weber' & [sic] ordinab[i]t j arc' & d[imid]j sagitt' citat' p[ro]x' Joh[anne]s hamell' Jack glad' bokeler' & ix sagitt' arc' & ordinab[i]t salet & d[imid]j shefe sagitt' S[...]eph[an]us [i.e., Stephen] Gregory Jack & salet arc' & shefe sagitt' glad' & bokeler' Rob[er]tus Batt Jacke & salet glad' & bokeler' ax dagger' & ordinab[i]t arc' & shefe sagitt' Joh[ann]es sewell' arc' & iij takell' [sic] dagger' & ordinab[i]t xvj sagitt' [&] pavys Joh[ann]es denys masyn' ordinab[i]t pavys a mall' de plu[m]bo Joh[ann]es Keche an ax glad' & ordinab[i]t pavys Wil[he]l[mu]s Edmu[n]de arc' & shefe sagitt' glad' dagger' & ordinab[i]t Jacke salet citat' p[ro]x' Joh[ann]es Rendall' Jacke salet j arc' & j shefe sagitt' j glad' & j daggar' Joh[ann]es strayte j arc' & d[imid]j shefe sagitt' glad' daggar' pollax Joh[ann]es mayowe arc' & d[imid]j shefe sagitt' dagger' & ordinab[i]t pavys citat' p[ro]x' Joh[ann]es A Blw [sic, i.e., surname] Jacke salet sper' glad' daggar' & ordinab[i]t arc' & shefe sagitt' Joh[ann]es Blu[n]payn' ordinab[i]t arc' & shefe sagitt' staffe & salet Thomas wey Jack salet arc' & shefe sag[...] Joh[ann]es williams Jack bille glad' & bokeler' Joh[ann]es dun Jacke salet glad' & bokeler' arc' & shefe sagitt' Thomas parker' & [sic] ordinab[i]t arc' & d[imid]j shefe sagitt' Thomas warn[er] arc' & d[imid]j shefe sagitt' glad' & ordinab[i]t Jacke salet dagger' & d[imid]j shefe sagitt' Joh[ann]es Crips Jacke salet arc' & shefe sagitt' glad' dagger' & ord' Jacke salet arc' & shefe sagitt' glad' & dagger' Jo[hann]es Palmer' Jacke arc' & d[imid]j shefe sagitt' glad' & ordinab[i]t j salet Joh[ann]es Tugge[er] arc' & d[imid]j shefe sagitt' & ordinab[i]t

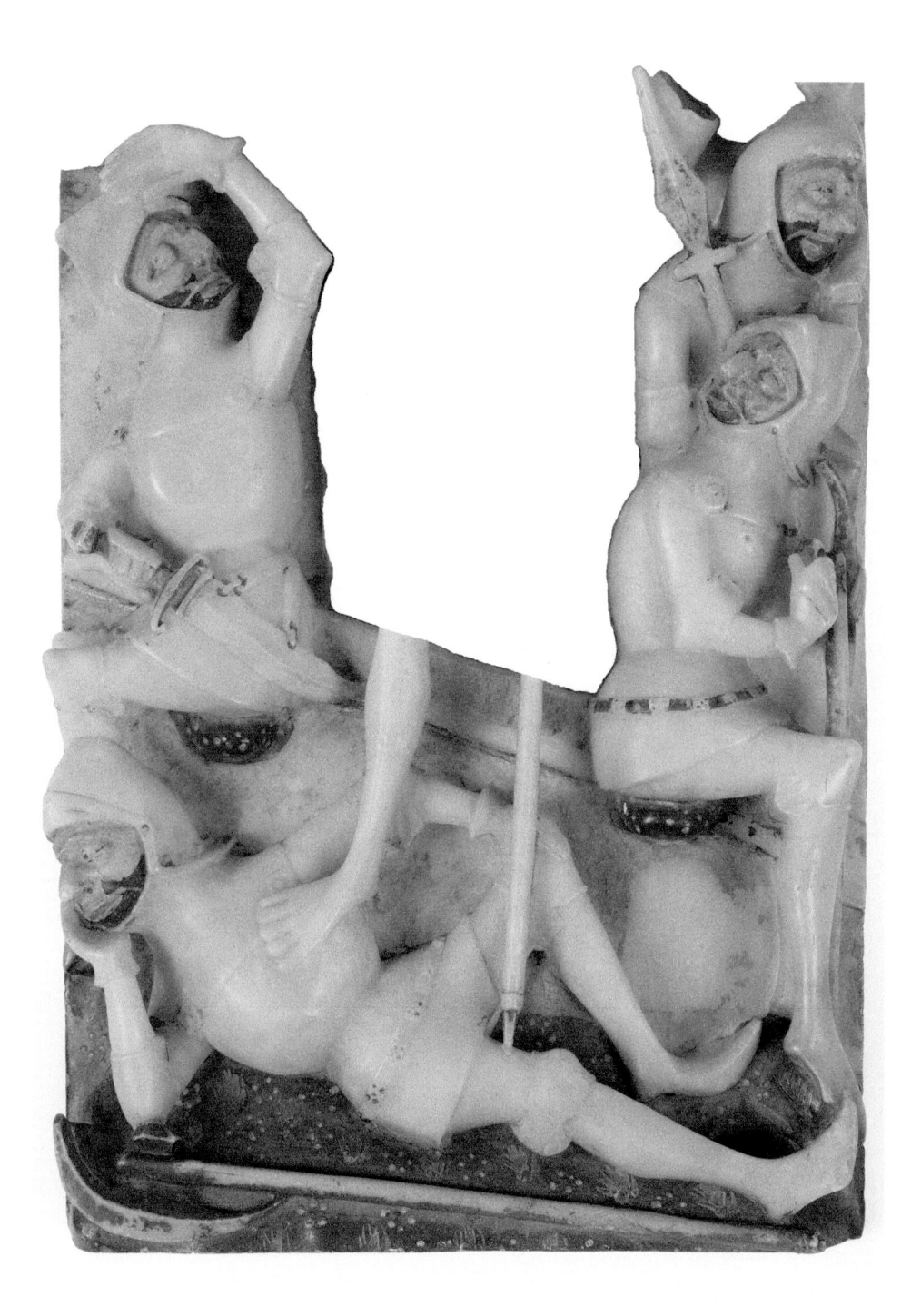

Figure 14. Detail of an alabaster panel depicting the Resurrection, English, late-fifteenth century (Glasgow Museums, Burrell Collection, 1.17).

j pavys Joh[ann]es Algar' salet ij arc' & shefe sagitt' glad' glefe & ordinab[i]t ij Jackes ij shefe sagitt' salet ij daggar' sub pen' citat' p[ro]x' Wil[he]lm[u]s sheter' Jacke salet arc' & shefe sagitt' glad' & bokeler' dagger' Rad[ulph]us Towker' arc' & shefe sagitt' & ordinab[i]t Jack [&] salet Joh[ann]es Bremyll' arc' & shefe sagitt' glad' dagger' & ord' Jacke [&] salet Edwardus Tracy Jacke salet arc' & shefe sagitt' glad' hap[er]chyn' [haubergeon] palet [i.e., pallet] Joh[ann]es harrjs Jacke salet glad' bokeler' ij arc' & ij shefe sagitt' a peyr' of gawndelett' [gauntlets] Ric[ard]us marchall' Jacke salet arc' & shefe sagitt' glad' & bokeler' sper' pavys Joh[ann]es doget Jack salet j arc' shefe sagitt' glad' bokeler' dagger' glafe Joh[ann]es Tengmarch' Jacke salet arc' & shefe sagitt' glad' bokeler' dagger' Joh[ann]es Forsey Jacke salet arc' & shefe sagitt' glad' & ordinab[i]t p[ro] al' ho[m]i[n]e [Lat. 'he is to provide for another man'] citat' p[ro]x' Joh[ann]es Batisgate Jack' salet glad' bokeler' dagger' glefe & ordinab[i]t arc' & shefe sagitt' sub pen' xiiij s' iiij d' citat' p[ro]x' Joh[ann]es Benet Bowerer' Jack salet glad' & daggar' & ordinab[i]t citat' p[ro]x' arc' & shefe sagitt' sub pen' sex solid' & oct' denar' Wil[he]lm[u]s Brown' Jack salet glad' bokeler' glefe arc' & shefe sagitt' [first name illegible] wase Coweser' [sic] arc' & sagitt' glad' bokeler' Thomas Fulbreke Jacke salet arc' & shefe sagitt' glad' & bokeler' Rob[er]tus Byrche a whyte harnys w[i]t[h] a basenet Henr' wychybroke arc' & xvj sagitt' ordinab[i]t a mall' de plu[m]bo Rob[er]tus Tyley arc' & d[imid]j shefe sagitt' dagger' & ordinab[i]t ax [&] pavys Ric[ard]us Glover arc' & d[imid]j shefe sagitt' glad' dagger' Joh[ann]es Skyrven[er] a sper' & dagger' & ordinab[i]t pavys Joh[ann]es Pycher arc' & shefe sagitt' dagger'

25

Now-Lost Document, printed from a Copy made before 1752 in *The Paston Letters, A.D. 1422–1509*, ed. J. Gairdner, vol. 3 (London, 1904), pp. 176–86

Inventory of the Goods of Sir John Fastolf, Caister Castle, Norfolk, 31 October 1459

Garderoba Domini

j. pece of skarlot for trappars for horsys with rede crossis and rosys, ij. cote armours of silke aftir his own [heraldic] armys, j. cote armour of whyte silke of Seynt George, j. bollok haftyd dager harneysd wyth sylver and j. chape thertoo, j. lytyll schort armyng dager withe j. gilt schape [i.e., chape]

Clothis of Arras and of Tapstre warke

j. newe banker [bench cover] of arras with a bere holdyng j. spere in the middys of the clothe, j. clothe of ix. Conquerouris [the Nine Worthies], j. clothe for the nether hall of arras with a geyaunt in the myddell beryng a legge of a bere in his honde, j. clothe of arras with iij. archowrys on scheting a doke in the water with a cross bowe,

Figure 15. Detail from 'The Stag Hunt' by Lucas Cranach, 1529
(Glasgow Museums, Burrell Collection, 35.73).

j. banker of arras with a man schetyng at j. blode hownde, ij. clothis of arras for the chamboure over the nether halle of huntyng and of haukyng, a coveryng of a bedde of aras withe hontyng of the bore a man in blewe with a jagged hoode white and rede

Garderoba in domo Superiori

xxj. bowys, viij. schefe arrowys of swanne

Magna Camera ultra Aulam Estevalem

j. coveryng with j. geyaunt smytyng a wilde bore with a spere

[No location recorded]

j. jakke of blakke lynen clothe stuffyd with mayle, vj. jakkes stuffyd with horne, j. jakke of blake clothe lyned with canvas mayled, xxiiij. cappes stuffed withe horne and sum withe mayle, vj. payre glovys of mayle of schepys skynne and of doos, iij. grete crosbowes of stele with one grete dowble wyndas [windlass] ther too, j. coffyre full of quarrellys of a smale sorte, xij. quarrellis of grete sorte feddered with brasse, vj. payre curassis, j. payre of breggandires, iij. harburyones of l'Milayne, v. ventaylettes [i.e., aventails] for bassenettes, vj. peces of mayle, j. garbrasse, j. polleson. [*sic, recte* 'polleron': pauldron], vj. payre grevys, iiij. payre thyes [thighs, i.e., cuisses], xj.

93

Figure 16. Burgundian tapestry panel, c. 1435–50
(Glasgow Museums, Burrell Collection, 46.57).

bassenetts, j. payre coschewes [cuisses], j. payre bregandines helyd with rede felwet, j. spere, ij. bassenetts, ij. saletts withe ij. visers, viij. saletts white withe oute vesoure, v. payre vambras, iij. spere heddys, j. swerde with a gyld chape, j. prikkyng hat covered withe blake felwet, ij. tarcellys of hym be hynde,[13] iij. gonnes called serpentins, ij. white payre of brigaundiris, ij. payre hosyn of blak kersey, [j.] payre bounde wyth lether, ij. payre of skarlat, j payre of blake vampayed withe lether, ij. chaynes for the draught brigge [drawbridge]

Magna Aula

xj. crosbowes whereof iij. of stele and v. wyndas, j. borespere, vj. wifles [a type of knife], j. rede pavys, j. target, xxj. speris, j. launce gay

26

Kew, National Archives, E 403/823, membr. 3

Royal Payments for Equipment, 2 July 1461

henrico Grand de london' Fletcher' m[i]l Garb' Sagitt' p[re]c' Garbe xviij d' & p[ro] xij Groc' de Bowstrynge' p[re]c' Groc' vj s' viij d' ad opus d[omi]ni Regis lxxix li' Nich[ol]o Wodener' de london' Arcuar' DC Arcub[us] ab ip[s]o empt' ad opus d[omi]ni Regis p[re]c' vni[us] Arcus xviij d' xiiij li' xiij s' iiij d' Petro lynelanger' Godfrido Artonys & alijs Gu[n]ners tam p[ro] custub[us] & expens' suis q[u]am p[ro] cariago de Gunpoudre & aliar[um] rer[um] p[ro] d[omi]no Rege v[er]sus p[ar]tes boriales xliiij li' xviij s' viij d' Joh[ann]i Nicholl' de london' Grocer' p[ro] diu[er]s' Barell' de Gunpouder' ab ip[s]o empt' p[ro] staur' Regis lx li' Joh[ann]i Armorer' de london' p[ro] diu[er]s' Armaturis ab ip[s]o empt' & miss' d[omi]no Regi v[er]us p[ar]tes Wallie xxv li'

> Henry Grand, fletcher of London, 1,000 sheaves of arrows at 18d. a sheaf and 12 gross of bowstrings at 6s. 8d. the gross £79, Nicolas Wodener', bowyer of London, 600 bows for the use of the lord King at 18d. a bow £14 13s. 4d., Peter Lynelanger', Godfrey Artonys, and other gunners, both for their keep and expenses as well as for carriage of gunpowder and other things for the Lord King to Northern parts £44, 18s., John Nicoll, grocer of London, for divers barrels of gunpowder bought from him for the King's store £60, John, armourer of London, for divers armours bought from him and sent to the Lord King in Welsh parts £25

---

[13]   This is very unlikely to be Middle Eng. tercel (falcon). It is poss. a mistranscription of tascettys, i.e., hind tassets.

27

Paris, Archives nationales, Chartrier de Thouars 1AP/1669

Inventory of the Goods of Olivier de Coëtivy, Seigneur de Taillebourg, Hôtel de Fay, County of Saintonge, 26 December 1461

quatre arbalestes de passe g[ar]nies ch[asc]une de son tour po[u]r les bender vsix escuz dor deux aut[re]s petites arbalestes portatiues g[ar]nies ch[asc]une dun baudrie Six escuz dor Six douzaines de gros trait lx s' iiij douzaines de menu trait xxij s' vj d' deux couleurines de mestal xx esc[u]z dor vng ca[n]non de fer C sol' vng Ribaudeq[ui]n de fer C sols deux arcs et deux trossez iiij esc[u]z dor deux espioulx de chasse ij escuz dor vng espioul darmes vng escu deux voulges iiij esc[u]z troys brigandines xviij escuz dor troys sallades dont lune esoit g[ar]nie darg' xxij escuz deux espees ij esc[u]z deux Jauelines et vne languedebeuf vng escu deux dagues val' deux esc[u]z

> four heavy crossbows each equipped with its torsion device for spanning 6 gold *écus*, two other small portable crossbows each equipped with a baldric 6 gold *écus*, six score of large shot (i.e., crossbow bolts) 60 *sous*, three dozen small shot 22 *sous* 6 *deniers*, two metal (i.e., cast iron) culverins 20 gold *écus*, one iron cannon 100 *sous*, one iron ribauldequin (field gun) 100 *sous*, two bows and two quivers 4 gold *écus*, two *espieux* for hunting 2 gold *écus*, one *espieu* for fighting 1 *écu*, two vouges 4 *écus*, three brigandines 18 gold *écus*, three sallets one of which is garnished with silver 22 *écus*, two swords 2 *écus*, two javelins and one langue de boeuf 1 *écu*, two daggers 2 *écus*

28

Tours, Archives départementales d'Indre et Loire, 3E1/1, fol. 18r

Legal Agreement regarding an Armourer's Harness Mill recorded by the Royal Notaire at Tours, 18 May 1462

Jehan de galles laisne armeurier et varlet de chambre du Roy n[ost]re S[eigneu]r confesse auoir vendu et transporte et par ces p[rese]ntes vend' et transporte des maint' a tousioursmais p[er]petuelement a h[er]itaige A Jehan de galles le Jeune son filz a ce p[rese]nt et acceptant agre tant pour lui que pour ses h[eriti]ers &c' vng molin a harnoys assis sur la Riuiere de la choisille au fief de labasse de beaumont Item plus lui vend' et transporte le lieu fief terre & seigneurie de franche ville la petite auecques ses app[er]ten' & dependen' situez & assis lez a clomiers en brie A auoir &c' laquelle vendon' a este & est faicte par led' Jehan de galles laisne aud' Jehan de galles son filz pour demouier quicte enuers sond' filz de la somme de Cent cinquante escus dor sur la somme de iijC iiijxx xvj escus dor en quoy sond' pere lui est tenu & oblige soubz le seel de ceste mesme court de laquelle s[omm]e de cent cinq[uan]te escus dor led' Jehan de galles le Jeune sest tenu et tient pour content & bien paie quicte &c' Promet' garantir &c' en paiant les charges & denoirs deuz a cause desd' chos' a lui ausd' vendues comme dit est Oblig' &c' &c' Rend' &c' &c' p[rese]n[te]s vincent Julien & Roulin godart tesmoing[e]s

Jehan de Galles, the elder, our Lord King's armourer and *valet de chambre*, has confessed to have sold and transported and by these present (letters) sold and conveyed hereafter and always in perpetuity as inheritance to Jehan de Galles, the younger, his son, as this present and account agrees both for him and for his heirs etc. a harness mill set up on the River Choiselle in the fief of the Abbey of Beaumont. Furthermore, he has sold and conveyed the place, fief, land, and lordship of Francheville-La-Petite with its appurtenances and dependants and those set up at Coulommiers-en-Brie and has etc. the said sale has been and is made by the said Jehan de Galles, the elder, to the said Jehan de Galles, his son, to remain quitclaimed towards his said son of the sum of 150 gold *écus* over the sum of 396 gold *écus* which his said father is owed and due to him under the seal of this same court of which sum of 150 gold *écus* the said Jehan de Galles, the younger, is obliged and held to be content and well paid, quitclaimed etc., promised, guaranteed etc., in paying the charges and dues due for the arrangements of these matters to him has thus been sold as is said. Obliged etc. etc., rendered etc. etc. in the presence of Vincent Julien and Roulin Godart witnesses

29

Kew, National Archives, E 122/128/1, fol. 2v, fol. 6v–fol. 7v

Record of the Subsidy (Import Duty) paid by Alien Merchants, Port of Sandwich, 2 November 1462–18 October 1463 (Extracts)

[2 November] na' vn' Joh[ann]es Walsh' e[st] m[agister] Joh[ann]e loye Al' p[ro] j maunde cu' j pak' & j cist' cu' lxxxj hatt' xij dos' Gladijs xxj dos' & d[imid]j dagg[er] es viij dos' x gorgett' de mail' xviij Salett' de Stele x pair' bumbard' [*sic*] p[re]c' xx li' S[u]bs' xx s' [17 January] Galea vn' matheus loridan[us] e[st] pat[r]on[us] George de polyngryn' Al' p[ro] j barr' olei ij polaxis vj bac[u]lis cu' dagg[er]s x vln' tel' lin' ij fraill' Fygg' p[re]c' xxv s' S[u]bs' xv d' Alegreto de lago Al' p[ro] l vln' tel' lin' ij d[imid]j bar' sagate vj Salett' xvj paxbred' xv dos' zon' fil' ij dos' pawtens' xl dos' cult' iiij gros hatband' p[re]c' xl s' S[u]bs' ij s' Georgio de Spalato Al' p[ro] C vln' tel' lin' ix Awt[er] cloth' ij dos' zon' fil' vj dos' glass' ij glad' j salet ij peir' card' p[re]c' xliij s' iiij d' S[u]bs' ij s' ij d' Nich[ol]o Georgio Al' p[ro] iiijxx vln' tel' lin' iij pan' pict' v g[r]os lac' xviij lb' fil' diu[er]s' color[um] xl m[i]l cl' p[ro] brygandynes p[re]c' xxxiij s' iiij d' S[u]bs' xx d' Patrono [*sic*, only one name given] Al' p[ro] m[i]l Bowestaff' p[re]c' xiij li' vj s' viij d' S[u]bs' xiij s' iiij d' Galea vn' Thomas Casyn' e[st] patron[us] S[an]c[t]o de Splato [*sic*] Al' p[ro] viij gladijs viij dagg[er]es viij dos' shers ij pap[er] poynt' xl vln' tel' lin' p[re]c' xx s' S[u]bs' xij d' [18 October] na' vn' Joh[ann]es Fers e[st] m[agiste]r Andree dontynar' Al' p[ro] vj ketyll' vj Salett' j p[ar]u' bar' triacl' p[re]c' xiij s' iiij d' [Subs'] viij d' Allere de ludryn' Al' p[ro] j pece tel' lin' iij g[r]os lac' corij ij bowes de Stele p[re]c' xiij s' iiij d' S[u]bs' viij d'

[2 November] Ship of John Walsh: John Loye, alien, for one basket with one pack and one chest with 81 hats, 12 dozen swords, 1½ dozen daggers, eight dozen and 10 mail gorgets, 18 steel sallets, 10 pairs of bumbards[14] worth £10 – subsidy 20s. [17 January] Galley of Mathew Laridanus: George Polyngryn', alien, one barrel of oil, two pollaxes, six staffs with daggers, 10 ells of linen cloth, two baskets of figs worth 25s. – subsidy 15d., Allegretto de Lago, alien, for 50 ells of linen cloth, a half-barrel of grease, six sallets, 16 pax-boards, 15 dozen thread belts, two dozen pattons, 40 dozen knives, four large hat-bands worth 40s. – subsidy 2s., Giorgio de Spalato, alien, for 100 ells of linen cloth, nine altar cloths, two dozen thread belts, six dozen glasses, two swords, one sallet, one pair of cards [for wool] worth 43s. 4d. – subsidy 2s. 2d., Niccolò Giorgio, alien, for four-score ells of linen cloth, three painted panels, five gross of lace, 18lb of thread of divers colours, 40,000 brigandine nails worth 33s. 4d. – subsidy 20d., Patrono [only one name given], alien, for 1,000 bow-staves worth £13 6s. 8d. – subsidy 13s. 4d. Galley of Thomas Casyn': Santo de Spalato for eight swords, eight daggers, eight dozen (pairs of) shears, two paper styluses, 40 ells of linen cloth worth 20s. – subsidy 12d. [18 October] Ship of Johannes Fers: Andrea Dontinari, alien, for six kettles, six sallets, one small barrel of treacle worth 13s. 4d. – subsidy 8d., Allere de Lundryn', alien, for one piece of linen cloth, three gross of leather laces, two steel bows worth 13s. 4d. – subsidy 8d.

30

Now-Lost Original Document from the Archives municipales de Douai, printed in E. J. Soil de Moriamé, 'Armes et armuriers tournaisiens. Heaumiers, haubregonneurs, forbisseurs, couteliers. Contribution à l'histoire des métiers d'art et à l'histoire militaire de Tournai de XIIIe au XVIIIe siècle', *Bulletin de l'Académie royale d'archéologie de Belgique*, unnumbered (1913), pp. 36–154 (at p. 106)

Account of Nicolas Dimenche, called 'The Lombard', Douai, 1463

une targe, ii arbalestres iii s. vi planchons, ii macques escancheliés, ung arebalestre et uns chimielles iii s. ii hauseco[l]s, une hache, ung gorgerin, deux haub[r]egons et une espée iiii lb. une targe et un bouquelier ii s. x d. deux macques à ronde viroelle

---

14 A component of a plate shoulder-defence. See the illustrated glossary.

iiii s. unq mailliet de queuvre et i arch xxvi d. ung harnas et un heaume xv s. deux espouloires ix d. ung plain harnas de guerre, une capeline, unq bonnet d'achier xxix s. ung pourpoint de cuyr de ziem xvii s.

one targe, two crossbows 3s., six plançons, two spiked maces, one crossbow and one *jumelle* (twin or double crossbow) 3s., two hounskulls, one axe, one gorget, two haubergeons, and one sword 4l, one targe and one buckler 2s. 4d., two maces with round ferrules, one copper mallet, and one bow 26d., one harness and one helm 15s., two (pairs of) spaudlers 9d., one simple war harness, one capelline, one steel bonnet 29s., one pourpoint of leather of 'Ziem' 17s.

31

Kew, National Archives, E 122/128/4, fol. 8v–fol. 9r

Valuation of Goods landed by Alien Merchants at the Port of Sandwich, 6 December 1463

Carraca vn' Thomas Justynuan' e[st] patron[us] Joh[ann]e de Barde Al' p[ro] lxix bal' harneys cu' Curas complet' Cix peir' iiij Curas broken' w[i]t[h]out Any g[ar]nysshyng' j peir' bolsters for the kyng' ij peir' polrons xxviij salett' iij hatt' de Stele vij peir' legharneys An helmet p[ro] Rege xxxvij harneys for horsehed' xj gorgett' w[i]t[h] mayle xxix peir' gauntelett' viij burlett' for Sperys to Just with xliij spere heed' ij masus of Stele v botell' of glasse closid in ledir w[i]t[h] lok & key ij horse harneys of boyled ledir j p[ro] Rege & j p[ro] d[omi]no warr' xxx gorgett' of Mayle vj Rest' viij peir' vambrac' p[re]c' CCC li' Thoma Justynyan' Al' p[ro] xv cass' Suger xxxvj oll' cu' Suger xvij Jarris olei C bowstauys iij p[ar]u' sacc' pip[er]is pond' C lb' p[re]c' iiijxx li'

Carrack of Tommaso Giustinian: Giovanni de' Bardi, alien, for 59 bales of 109 complete harnesses with cuirasses (and) four broken cuirasses without any fittings (i.e., the cuirass components need to be assembled rather than them being damaged), one pair of bolsters for the King, two pairs of pauldrons, 28 sallets, three steel hats, seven pairs of legharness, a helmet for the King, 27 defences for horses' heads (i.e., shaffrons, and possibly crinets), 11 gorgets with mail, 29 pairs of gauntlets, eight burrs (grips) for jousting lances, 43 spearheads, two steel maces, five glass bottles enclosed in leather with lock and key, two horse harnesses of boiled leather – one for the King and one for the lord (Earl) of Warwick, 30 mail gorgets, six (lance) rests, eight pairs of vambrace worth £100, Tommaso Giustinian, alien, for 15 cases of sugar, 36 pots with sugar, 17 jars of oil, 100 bow-staves, three small sacks of pepper (corns) weighing 100lb worth £80

32

Kew, National Archives, E 404/73/45A and 45B

Royal Payments for Jousts, Tower of London, 24 May 1465

o[u]r trusty & welbeloued s[er]uant Johan Wodd Squyer mast' of oure ordynaunce to provide & ordeine for such stuffe as shall' s[er]ue & suffice for þe Justes to be holden before vs on moneday next co[m]myng CC speres xv li' Cl Graters [grappers] viij li' xv s' C l Cornalles viij li' xv s' the wages of xxiiij Joynours for ij daies xxxij s' wages of xij men Awaiters (attendants) for the graters & Cornalles of eu[er]y broken spere in þe felde the Day of þe Just' vj s' for bryngyng togidre & cariage of all' the speres and other stuff ij s'

33

Extract from Jehan de Bueil's *Le Jouvencel* (c. 1466)

Paris, Bibliothèque nationale de France, MS fr. 192, fol. 179r

> *Jehan de Bueil (b. c. 1405–6, d. c. 1478), was a veteran of the Hundred Years War, serving from as early as 1424. He was appointed amiral of France in 1450 and oversaw the defeat of the English at Castillon in 1453. His* Le Jouvencel *is a piece of fiction but is clearly informed by his vast experience.*

Je vous aduertys que moy estant ieune ie vey deux hommes darmes faire rencontre de lance et lun osta a lautre sept fois la visiere de son armet de la pointe de sa lance & se neust estre vng ancien homme darmes qui la estoit des le s[e]cond coup que cellui qui couroit contre son amy estoit en dangier de sa lance Je croy sceurement quil eust estre tue et le conseil quil lui donna lui fist oster les veruelles qui tenoient la visiere de son armet et la fist atacher a vne agueillete & o [*sic*] de la cire et lui suffissoit seullement quelle tenist pour le gallop du cheval Et toutes les fois que son aduersaire le rencontroit il lui donnoit tousiours a la visiere de larmet sans faillir et pource quelle ne tenoit gueres lautre lemportoit et sa lance ne prenoit point

Let me tell you that when I was young I watched two young men at arms run (mounted courses) with the lance. And one struck up the visor of the other's armet seven times with his lance. And had it not been for the intervention of an aged man-at-arms who happened to be there, I firmly believe that he would have been killed. For he (the older man) realised after the second (lance) strike that the man who ran against his friend was very skilled and that his friend was in great danger of (being injured by) his lance. This was the advice he gave: he should remove the staples which held his armet's visor and instead affix it with wax and a lace as this would suffice to hold (the visor in place) as the horse galloped. And at every

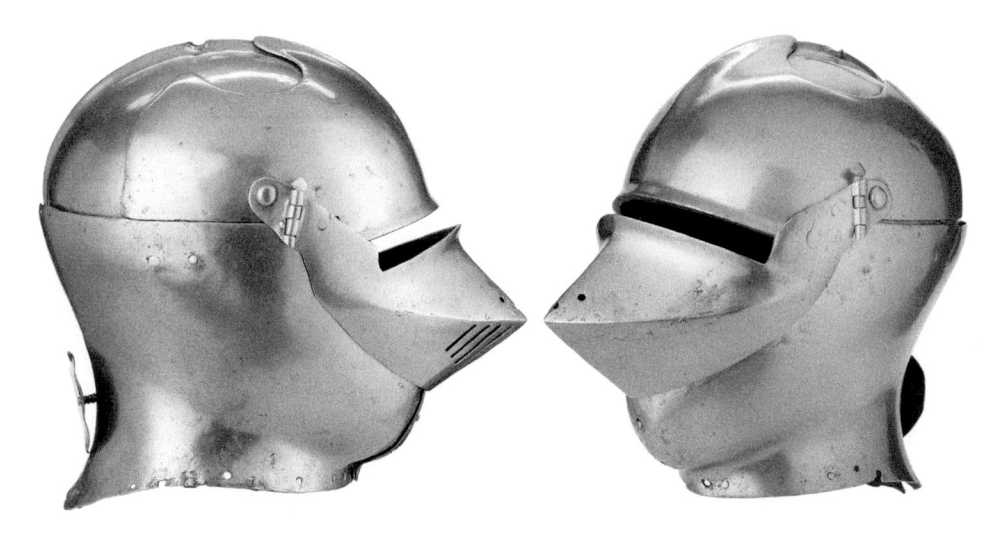

Figure 17. Armet, Italian, c. 1500 (Glasgow Museums, A.1965.39).

encounter his adversary always tried without fail to strike his armet's visor. But because it (the visor) was not completely attached, no matter how much the other (man) struck it, his lance did not catch (on it)

34

Unlocated Document from the Registers of the Dukes of Milan, printed in W. Boeheim, 'Werke Mailänder Waffenschmiede in den kaiserlichen Sammlungen', *Jahrbuch der Kunsthistorischen Sammlungen des Allerhöchsten Kaiserhauses* 9 (1889), pp. 375–418 (at p. 390)

Letter to the Duke from Giovanni Pietro Panicharolla, His Ambassador to the French Court, 27 April 1466

Zonse inquete parti del mese di marzo proximo passato Francesco dil [*sic*] Missaglia come la Signoria Vostra he informata per armar questo signore Re; quanto piacere la maseta soa ne havesse credo quella per mie lettere lo habia inteso; piu volste lo ha facto andare in camera soa di giorno et di nocte, et quando andava a dormire, adcio vedessa la persona soa et cognossesse el volere suo et l'aptitudine bisognava de l'armatura che non li facesse male in modo alchuno; percha ha una persona molto delicata; et continue lo ha tenuto per questa casone. Hora dicto Francesco informato de la persona volere et desiderio di essa maseta si parte questo di, al quale ha commisso, che con ogni diligentia et cura expedisca le soe arme, secondo che li ha ordinato et subito luy le porti, perche se non fossero in tuto piacere et gusto di essa soa maesta haverli molto aplicato l'animo; poi a parte quella a me ha replicato dicte parole, instando che con diligentia et studio esse arme sieno facte et reporate. Et me ha dicto sprerare che serano alconzo de la persona soa; perche li pare che esso Missaglia intenda quanto he el desyderio di quella; et per quanto dicte la prelibtata soa maesta fino qui ne resta molto satisfatta. Si che me he parso avisarne la vostra excellenza per il debito mio, adcioche meglio possi provedere et satisfare ad quanto questo signore Re desidera che he di esser armato al destro et agio de la persona soa.

Last March, Francesco da Missaglia arrived in these parts [i.e., France], as Your Lordship knows, to arm [i.e., make armour for] this Lord King. How pleased His Majesty has been, Your Lordship has understood from my letters, I believe. He made him (Francesco) go to His room many times by day and by night, and when He went to sleep, in order to observe His person (i.e., frame) and understand His will and the necessary fit of the armour so that it does not hurt him in any way; because He has a very delicate frame; and He continues to retain him for this reason. Now the said Francesco, being informed of the frame, will, and desire of His Majesty, leaves today and he has committed to send His [the King's] arms with all diligence and care, as they have been ordered and he will immediately bring the armour, because [otherwise] it would not be completely pleasing and to the taste of His Majesty who has greatly applied his mind [*anima*] to the matter. Then in private, He [the King] repeated these words to me, insisting that, with all diligence and study, the said armour will be made and brought back. And the King has told me that He hopes that it will fit his frame, because it seems to Him that this Missaglia understands how much He desires to have it; and having said this, His Majesty is very satisfied with the matter so far. So, I thought it appropriate to inform Your Excellency, as is my duty, so that You can best provide and satisfy what this Lord King desires, namely that he be armed to suit the nimbleness and ease of His frame.

35

Entry from the Now-Illegible Registers of the Notaries of the County of Dunois (Chartres, Archives départementales d'Eure et Loire), printed in L. Merlet, *Registres et minutes des notaires du comté de Dunois (1369 à 1676)* (Chartres, 1886), p. 25

Inventory of the Arms of Roger de Lobié, Man-at-Arms of the Company of the Sénéchal of Saintonge, at Châteaudun, between 1467 and 1468

une cuirass complette, les gardebraz, les harnois de jambes, les avantbraz, une bauière à salade et un armet avec la bauière d l'armet, deux chanfrains de cheval, une petite espée d'armes, ung esperon et ung autre rompu, ung fer de lance, deux plumes de chanfrains noire double, deux plumes de chanfrains, une plume blanche garnie de paillettes d'or, trois harnois de chevaulx de drap violet deschicqueté

> one complete cuirass, the pauldrons, the legharness, the vambraces, one sallet-bevor and one armet with the armet-bevor (i.e., wrapper), two horse shaffrons, a small arming sword, one spur and one other broken, one lancehead, two black double shaffron-plumes, two shaffron-plumes, one white plume decorated with gold pales (vertical stripes), three horse harnesses of violet cloth with dagged fringes

36

Kew, National Archives, E 159/243, membr. 8r

Letter from Edward IV to the Treasurer and Barons of the Exchequer excusing Foreign Merchants from Import Duties, End of Hilary Term (January–March), 1467

For asmoch' as Fraunces Massallia (Francesco Missaglia) and Joh[a]n de Barde (Giovanni de' Bardi) m[er]chaunt' alient' [*sic*, Lat. (sing.) *alienigenus*: alien/foreigner] of late tyme brought' in to the porte of Sandewych' in a Carrak wherof Thomas Justinan' (Tommaso Giustinian) was patron' lxix bales harneys wyth' Curas complete Cix payre [and] iiij Curas broken' wyth' oute eny garneshyng (i.e., the cuirass components need to be assembled rather than them being damaged) wyth other c[er]tayne hayrneys [*sic*] and abilement' of werre for the felde the which' been entred' in the p[ar]ticuler bookes of the accompte' of William Rose and Joh[a]n Shukburgh' late Collectours of oure Custumes and Subsidies in oure said' Porte the Sexte day of decembr' the iijde yere of oure Reigne [6 December 1463] vnder the name of the said' Joh[a]n de Barde vnde[r] the forme that folowyth' Joh[an]e de Barde Alienigen' p[ro] lxix bales harneys cum Curas Complete Cix payre iiij Curas broken wyth' oute eny garnysshyng j paire bolsters for the kyng ij paire polrons xxviijti Salett' iij hattes de Stele vij paire of legge harneys an helmet p[ro] Rege xxxvijti harneys for horsehedys xj Gorgett' wyth' mayle xxixti parye gauntelett' viij burlett' for Speres to iuste [i.e., joust] wyth' xliij Spere hedys ij mases of Stele v botellys of Glasse closed' in ledyr wyth' lok and key ij horseharneys of boyled' ledyr j p[ro] Rege & j p[ro] d[omi]no Warwic' xxx Gorgett' de Mayle vj restis [i.e., lance-rests] viij payre vambraces p[re]c' CCC li' Wherof the Custume and Subsidie to vs due amounteth' to the so[m]me of xviij li' xv s' the which' so[m]me the said' Frannceys and Joh[a]n de Barde nor either of them hath' not yete payed' nor satisfied vn to the said' William Rose and Joh[a]n Shukburgh' nor to either of them We consideryng howe that p[ar]cell' of the said' harneys was p[u]rueid' and brought' in to this oure Reaume vn to the vse and for the seuertee and defence of oure p[er]sone and the remenant therof for the defence of this oure said' Reaume to oure greet pleasyr We thefore of oure grace esp[ec]iall' by other oure l[ett]res yeuan' vnder oure Priue Seal the xxvjti day of Aprill' the iiijth yere of oure Reigne [26 April 1464] to the said' William Rose and Joh[a]n Shukburgh' direct haue

p[ar]doned' and releassed' vn to the said' Fraunceys and Joh[a]n de Barde and to either
of them the so[m]me of xvij li' x s' to vs due of the Custume and Subsidie of the said'
harneys entred' and writen' in oure said' l[ett]res of Priue Seal to the said' William Rose
and Joh[a]n Shukburgh' directe by the name and entree of lxix bales wyth' Cxiij harneys
of Meleyn' complete for the feld' [complete harness of Milan (make) for the field] wyth'
other diu[er]se smale [i.e., small] harneys and iij Sadeles and ij bordes Curyboyli [*sic*,
i.e., horse bards of cuir bouilli] and where we by the same oure l[ett]res yeuen' vnder
oure Priue Seal to the seid' William Rose and Joh[a]n Shukburgh' directe haue wolled
and straitely charged' theim that they nor neither of theim shuld' aske or demaunde of
the said' Fraunceys and Joh[a]n de Barde nor either of theim the said' so[m]me of xvij
li' x s' for the Custume and subsidie of the said' harneys and m[er]chandisez nor of eny
p[ar]cell' tharof but that they shuld' suffre the said' Fraunceys and Joh[a]n de Barde and
either of them or the deputee or deputees of theim or either of theim in that behalf to
take and carie a waye fro the said' Porte the said' harneys and m[er]chandises to eny place
of this oure Reame at thaire will' wyth' oute eny Custume or subsidie tharof or eny other
duetee to oure vse to be payed

37

Paris, Archives nationales de France, JJ//195, fol. 25v

Extract from a Royal Letter of Remission to Jehan de La Perrelle, franc-archer, given at Paris, June 1468

> *The* franc-archers *were a royal army mobilised from the population by exempting its fighters from taxation. The incident took place in the town of Vire, Normandy.*

The supplicant Jehan asks fellow members of his unit for 'several pieces he has lost from his harness and war equipment' ('plus[ieur]s pieces quil luy failloit de son harnoys et habillem[en]t de guerre'). He is met with this response:
giret touroulde qui estoit ho[m]me fort Rigoureux cauteleux et Rebelle de couraige
mal meu dist audit supp[li]ant que depuis quil auoit este fait franc archier Il auoit
fait do[m]maige en ses habillem[en]s et aut[re]ment de plus de cent solz tourn' ou
aut' so[m]me et que sil le veoit mener au gibet pendre quil en s[er]oit bien Joyeux
et nen donneroit Riens auec plus[ieur]s aut[re]s p[ar]olles Rigoureuses et Iniurieuses
[…] lequel Jeh' qui estoit lors en la tauerne courrouce de ce que led' feu gilet [*sic*]
touroulde le blasmoit et villenoit ato[…] et sans cause de chaulde colle luy donna
vng cop sur la teste dun baston appelle Jaueline ou pourtisaine duquel cop Il luy fit
sang ez playe et lors se dep[ar]tirent lun de laut' et sen ala led' feu giret touroulde
plaindre a aucuns de noz offic[ier]s […] po[u]r Rais' dud' cop emp[ri]sonna led'
supp[li]ant en noz p[ri]son[…] Il fut deliure p[ar] aucuns de nosd' offic[ier]s po[u]r
ce que on veoit led' tournoulde aler p[er]my la ville co[m]me tout sans et aussi quil
disoit quil ne vouloit empescher la deliuran' dud' supp[li]ant et neanmoins vng moys
apres led' cop ou enuir' combien que les barbiers ou cirurgens qui auoient pense led'

tournoulde deissent que dud' cop Il estoit tout sain toutesuoys p[er] s[...] mauuaix
gouu[er]nem[en]t ou autr[e]m[en]t Il ala de vie a t[re]spas

> Giret Touroulde – who was a strong, harsh, crafty man and of indomitable dispo-
> sition – was ill provoked (and) said to the supplicant that ever since he had been
> a *franc-archer* he had knackered his equipment and otherwise to more than 100
> *sous tournois* (or some such sum) and that if he saw him led to be hanged from the
> gibbet he would be most happy and he would give him nothing, with several other
> harsh and injurious words [...] this Jehan who was then in the tavern was angered
> by that which the said late Giret Touroulde blamed and slandered him without
> cause. With hot-blooded choler he gave him a blow to the head with a weapon
> called 'javelin' or 'partisan', this blow drew blood. And then they left each other
> and the said late Giret Touroulde complained to one of Our officers [...] because of
> this blow he imprisoned the supplicant in Our prison [...] he was released by one
> of Our officers because the said Tournoulde was seen to go about the town as if in
> good health and because he did not want to impede the release of the supplicant.
> But nevertheless, a month afterwards (or thereabouts) when the barbers or surgeons
> who had assessed the said Tournoulde said that he was completely healed from this
> blow, suddenly – by poor care or something else – he passed from this life

38

Milan, Archivio di Stato Milano, Notarile 869, 1467 gui. 4

Agreement between Master Pier Innocenzo da Faerno and Pietro de Ghisfola, Milan, 4 June 1467

> *This document has many deletions and insertions. I have only included those most relevant.*

d[ict]us petrus Innocens de ferno filius quon' do[m]ini Joh[ann]is p[arochia]lj s'
marie belt' m[edio]l[an]i p[ar]te vna Et petrus de ghixulfis f' q' do[mi]ni Conrad'
p[aro]c[hial]j s' laurentij maioris foris m[edio]l[an]i p[ar]te altera [...] pacta et
Conuent' p[er] et Int' eas p[ar]tes [...] Imp[ri]mis Q' di[ct]us petrus de ghixulfis
teneat' & obligatus sit p[er] Annum vnum p[ro]x' fut' Inceptur[am] in callendis
me[n]sis Jullij p[ro]x' fut' stare /et morare\ cum di[ct]o d[omi]no petro Innocente
ad laboram et eidem d[omi]no petro Innocenti de arte armor[um] /laborare bene &
fidelit'\ et in eius petri Innocen' stationa et domo in faciendo /armaturas Infrar[um]
manerier[um]\ Corazias ab Armigero Italianas Corazias franzoxias corazias spagniolas
corazias teotonicas ad Computum et ratione' librar[um] quatuor i[m]p[erio]r[um]
bone mon' m[edio]l[an]i pro qualib' petia s[uper]s[crip]tar[um] manerier[um]
armor[um] corsitos franzoxios et teutonicos cum scarselis et afoldatis de retro et
ascarlionatis de antea ad [com]putum et r[ati]onem librar[um] quatuor cum dimeda
i[m]p[erio]r[um] pro quolib' Corazinas secretas ad comput[u]m et r[ati]onem
librar[um] trium i[m]p[erio]r[um] pro qualib' corazina pectoras teotonicas de qualib'

factione ad computum et r[ati]onem soldor[um] decem octo i[m]p[erio]r[um] pro qualib' pezia spalas teotonicas de qualib' facione ad [com]putum et ratione' soldor[um] vigintiquatuor i[m]p[erio]r[um] p[ro] qualib' petia Pro quib[us] quide' armis fiendis p[er] eum petrum ut s' ip[s]e d[ict]us petrus Innocens no' teneat' eidem petro dare aliqua' aydam ad fuxina' nec alibi q' ip[s]e petrus teneat' face' scontraris pectosa et spallas v[i]z vnum cu' alt[er]o q' si di[ct]us petrus fecerit aliquam Coraziam franzoxiam teotonica' Italiana' spagniolam et eas Corazias approbauerit ad p[er]sonas homin' q' di[ct]us d[omin]us petrus Innocens teneat' et obligatus sit dare & solucie eidem petro soldis decem i[m]p[erio]r[um] plus p[ro] qualib' p[e]tio s[uper]s[crip]to pacto ut s' q' durante di[ct]o t[em]p[o]re di[ct]i anni ut s' ip[s]e petrus no' possit nec debeat discedere ab eo d[omi]no petro Innocente nec p[er] se nec cum alio laborare sine sp[eci]ali licentia et volunt' ip[s]ius d[omi]ni petri Innocenti Et q' teneat' ip[s]e petrus laborare eidem d[omi]no petro Innocente in yeme et in estate dieb[us] et horis debitis et [con]suetis s[e]c[un]d[u]m [con]suetudino dicte artis armor[um] Et v[er]sa uice di[ct]us d[omin]us petrus Innocens teneat' et obligatus sit cum petrum retinere p[er] totum ip[s]us dicti anni Et eidem petro manutencie ad laborand' p[er] tot[u]m p[re]di[ct]um tempus Et eidem petro soluc' & satisfac' de m[er]cede sua om[n]i me[n]se et in fine cui[us]lib' me[n]sis Et vlt[er]ius dare ip[s]i petro tant' drapum lane ad donum petri de lacine aut in alia draparia qui ascindat ad s[um]am librar[um] sex i[m]p[erio]r[um] et que libris sex i[m]p[erio]r[um] cedant seu vadant sup[er] ayda extende[n]te deor[um] Armour[um] teneat' ip[s]e d[omin]us petrus Innocens mutuare di[ct]o petro l[i]bras quinquaginta i[m]p[erio]r[um] ad callen' mensis aug[ust]i p[ro]x' fut' sine aliqua exceptione Et quas quid' libras quinquaginta i[m]p[erio]rum teneat' ip[s]e petrus schuxare in laborerio suo seu in m[er]cede sua cum di[ct]o d[omi]no petro Innocente a festo s[anc]ti Mich' p[ro]x' fut' in antea ad ratam p[ro] rata p[ro]ut tanget sing[u]lla' ibide moda usq[ue] in fine di[ct]i anni q' di[ct]us d[omin]us petrus I[n]noce[n]s teneat' dare ip[s]i petro lectum v[nu]m p[ro] se et duo laboratore p[ro] dormendo surs[u]m in fondegheto d[ict]i d[omi]ni petri I[nno]cen' sito de redente stallas

The said Master Pier Innocenzo da Faerno, son of the late Master Giovanni in the parish of Santa Maria Beltrade of Milan, on one part, and Pietro de Ghisfola, son the late Master Conrado in the parish of San Lorenzo at the Great Gate (*porta*) of Milan, on the other part […] [it is] agreed and contracted by and between them […] Firstly, that the said Pietro de Ghisfola is held and obliged for one year next to come from the beginning of the kalends of the month of July next to come to stay /and remain\ with the said Master Pier Innocenzo to work for this same Master Pier Innocenzo in the craft of armour (making) /to work well and faithfully\ based in Master Pier Innocenzo's workshop making /armours of the manner below\ Italian (style) cuirasses for men-at-arms, French cuirasses, Spanish cuirasses, German cuirasses costed at the rate of 4 *lire imperiali* of good Milanese currency for any piece of the above-written manner of armour, French and German corsets with tassets and fitted with faulds at the rear and fitted with tassets at the front[15] costed at the rate of 4½ *lire imperiali* for any, secret little cuirasses (or brigandines) (i.e., to be borne beneath civilian clothing) costed at the rate of 3 *lire imperiali* for any little cuirass, German breastplates of any making costed at the rate of 18 *lire imperiali* for any piece, German pauldrons of any making costed at the rate of 24 *lire imperiali* for any piece, for any of the arms made by this Pietro as above this said Pier Innocenzo is not held to give this Pietro any aid at the forge nor elsewhere, that this Pietro is held to assemble breastplates and pauldrons viz: one with the other, if the said Pietro should make any French, German, Italian, (or) Spanish cuirass and these cuirasses are proofed by men's bodies (i.e., prob. proofed by crossbow-shot) then the said Master Pier Innocenzo is held and obliged to give and pay this Pietro 10 *soldi imperiali* more for any piece above-written, it is agreed as above that during the said time of one year as above this Pierto cannot nor ought not to leave the said Pier Innocenzo – neither he himself nor with any worker – without this Master Pier Innocenzo's special licence and permission, and this Pietro is held to work for the same Master Pier Innocenzo in contract and in the set days and hours given and agreed according to the custom of the said craft of armour (making), and *vice versa* the said Master Pier Innocenzo is held and obliged to so retain Pietro for the whole of this said year and maintain this Pietro to work for the total of the aforesaid time and pay and settle this Pietro's wages every month and at the end of every month, and (or) otherwise give this Pietro such linen drapery from the gift of Pietro de Lacine or other drapery that amounts to the sum of 6 *lire imperiali* and that six *lire imperiali* is passed or goes toward the aid extending to his armours, this said Master Pier Innocenzo is held to loan the said Pietro 50 *lire imperiali* from the kalends of the month of August next to come without any restriction, and that this 50 *lire imperiali* this Pietro is held to be excused in his work or in his wages with the said Master Pier Innocenzo from when feast of Saint Michael next to come is past at the individual rate for the rates exactly as mentioned in the same way until the end of the said year, that the said Master Pier Innocenzo is held to give this Pietro one bed for him and two workers to sleep on in the said Master Pier Innocenzo's foundry-forge situated in the scouring (or polishing) stalls

---

[15] The word 'scarselis' can be interpreted as a Latinised form of the Fr. noun *escarcelle*: a girdle-hanging purse, the Fr. is ultimately derived from Lat. *excarpsus* (lit. to pluck out). *Dictionnaire du moyen français*, ed. R. Martin and others (Nancy, 1998–), online edn. For the strong influence of Fr. martial vocabulary, see T. E. Hope, *Lexical Borrowing in Romance Languages: A Critical Study of Italianisms in French and Gallicisms in Italian from 1100 to 1900*, vol. I (Oxford, 1971), pp. 128–9. If expanded to 'ascarselionatis', this might well be the same word in past-participle form – thus the pseudo-Lat. suffix *-atis*.

39

Now-Lost Original Document from the Archives municipales de Douai, printed in E. J. Soil de Moriamé, 'Armes et armuriers tournaisiens. Heaumiers, haubregonneurs, forbisseurs, couteliers. Contribution à l'histoire des métiers d'art et à l'histoire militaire de Tournai de XIIIe au XVIIIe siècle', *Bulletin de l'Académie royale d'archéologie de Belgique*, unnumbered (1913), pp. 36–154 (at p. 106)

Will of Jean Danetières, Douai, 1470

à Jacques Danetières, mon frère, ung harnas de guerre tout complet, Jennin de la Foye unes brigandines, Jehan de Clermés un haubregon, la confrerie S. Georges mon arbalestre appelée la clocquette, la compagnie nommée Bon Espoir, à S. Jehan, une jumelle à tout le dos nud [*sic, recte* nux d'os]

> to my brother Jacques Danetières one complete war harness, Jennin de la Foye one (pair of) brigandines, Jehan de Clermés one haubergeon, the Confraternity of Saint-Georges my crossbow called 'La Clocquette' ('The Little Bell'), to the Company called 'Bon Espoir' ('Good Hope') of Saint-Jean one *jumelle* (twin or double crossbow) complete with the bone nut (i.e., trigger nut)

40

Kew, National Archives, C 81/832/3110

Royal Permission for Olivier de La Marche to import Armour, issued at the Palace of Westminster, 20 June 1470

Rex &c Sciat' q[uo]d cum dilectus et fidelis m[agiste]r Oliuerus de la marche miles Consiliarius et magister domus predilectissimi fratris n[ost]ri ducis Burgu[n]die in Regnu' n[ost]rum Anglie quingentos integros harneyses completos cum quingent' Brigandines garniziat' et complet' de Salettis cum bavyers gardes gardebraces et legharneis ac mille Salett' pro sagittarijs ibidem vendend' mittere intendat' prout nobis monstrau[er]it Nos nedum premissa verum eciam fidelem diligenciam et labores quos prefatus Oliuerus nobis multotiens veniendo a prefato fratre n[ost]ro in Ambassiata impendit considerantes de gracia n[ost]ra speciali concessimus et licenciam dedimus et per p[rese]ntes concedimus et licenciam damus prefato Oliuero q[uo]d ip[s]e aut eius factores siue attornati vel eorum aliquis dictos quingentos intergros herneyses complet' cum dictis quingentis brigandines garniziat' et complet' de Salettes cum baviers gardes gardebraces et legharneys ac dicti mille Sallett' p[ro] sagittarijs a partibus ex[...] in Regnu' n[ost]r[u]m Anglie et in portum Cuntatis n[ost]re

London' aut portum ville Sandwici siue ville South[amp]t' in quacumq[ue] Naui seu quibuscumq[ue] nauibus vna vice vel diuersis vicibus ad libitum suum adducere valeat et valeant absq[ue] aliquibus Custumis seu subsidijs

> The King, etc., lets it be known that Our beloved and loyal Maître Olivier de La Marche, knight, counsellor and maître d'hôtel of Our most beloved brother the Duke of Burgundy, may send to Our Realm of England 500 complete harnesses with 500 brigandines completely equipped with sallets with bevors, pauldrons, pauldron-reinforces, and legharness, and 1,000 sallets for archers which he intends to sell there. As he has shown to Us not only true diligence and labours which the aforesaid Olivier has often expended for us coming in embassy from our forsaid brother (of Burgundy), in consideration of Our special grace, We have granted and given licence and by these present (letters) We grant and give licence to the aforesaid Oliver – to he himself or his factors or attorneys or to any of them – to bring the said 500 complete harnesses with the said 500 brigandines equipped and complete with sallets with bevors, pauldrons, pauldron-reinforces, and legharness and the said 1,000 sallets for archers from other parts into Our Realm of England and (land them) in the harbour of Our Port of London or the Port of the Town of Sandwich or Town of Southampton in whatever ship or ships by a single way or divers ways he or they wish without any customs or (alien) subsidies

41

Tours, Archives municipales, CC 39, fol. 18v and CC 40, fol. 101v

Payments to goldsmiths for making punches for marking harness and brigandines, Tours, 1470 and 1471

A pierre lambert orfeure la so[m]me de cinquante cinq solz tourn' qui deue lui estoit pour auoir fait et graue six poinsons de fer acerez pour marquer les harnois et brigandines qui seroient faiz et deliurez en lad' ville de la facon que le Roy lauoit ordonne et pour auoir Retaille et Ressue deux desd' poinsons qui estoie[n]t fonduz en marquant les harnois […] [paid 31 October 1470]

> To Pierre Lambert, goldsmith, the sum of 55 *sous tournois* due to him for having made and engraved six steeled-iron punches to mark the harness and brigandines which are made and delivered in the said town of the making that the King has ordained and for having refitted and restored two of the said punches which were cast for marking the harnesses [paid 31 October 1470]

[1471]

A Jehan haranc orfeure pour auoir graue les armes de la ville en deux poinsons de fer pour marquer les harnois et brigandines vendus en lad' ville xxx s'

To Jehan Haranc, goldsmith, for having engraved the (heraldic) arms of the town on two iron punches for marking the harness and brigandines sold in the said town 30 *sous*

42

London, Society of Antiquaries of London Library, MS SAL/MS/211, fol. 94r

Liber Niger Domus Regis Angliae … Edw. IV: Ordinances governing the Household of Edward IV, c. 1471–2 (Extract)

> *A 'henxman' or 'hengest-man', the editors of the* Middle English Dictionary *inform us, is 'an attendant upon a king, nobleman, lord mayor, etc., a high-ranking servant (usually of gentle birth)'.*[16]

Henxmen vj enfauntez or mo as hit shall please the king

Mastyr of Henxmen to show the scoolez of vrbanitie and nourture of Inglond to lern them to ride clenly and surely to drawe them also to justes to lerne [t]hem were theyre harneys to haue all curtesy in wordez dedes and degrees dilygently to kepe them in rules of goynges and sittinges after they be of honour Moreouer to teche them sondry langages and othyr lernynges vertuous to herping to pype sing daunce and with other honest and temperate behauing

43

London, British Library, Additional MS 27445, fol. 72r

Letter from Martin Rondelle, Armourer of the Bastard of Burgundy at Bruges, to Sir John Paston, 28 August 1473

Monsegnieur Jehan Paston chevalier dEngletere per Martyn Rowndell armorer de Bruggys A[nn]o E' iiijᵗⁱ xiijᵒ

Mon tres chier et honnore segnieur je me recomande a vous outant que je puis ne scay Et vous plaise sauoir que je ay oy nouelles de vous par vung de vo marchans de Calais touchant unne armura de [*recte* et] unna sella [*sic*] que vous doy et de vna barbuta la quelle est en diferansce entre vous et moy de la quelle je vous ay aultre foix dist que je estoie contant de fere toute rexon et enquore le vous dige prexentement que je suis prest de fer tout chou quil apartient en tout rexon set asauoir de la barbute et de larmura de sella

---

[16] *Middle English Dictionary*, ed. R. E. Lewis and others (Ann Arbor, MI, 1952–2001), in *Middle English Compendium*, ed. F. McSparran and others (Ann Arbor, MI, 2000–18), online edn, under 'hengest-man'.

Daultre chiox ne vous suis en riens tenut for[s]que en toute les chiox que me seroint posible de faire pour larmour de vous a vostre honneur et a vostre profit je suis toute jour prest a vostre comendement

Item en houltre je ay entendut que vous voulles auoir unng harnax complet Com je pris vostra mexure dernierement quant vous fustes en ceste ville de Bruges saichies que je ay enquor vostre mexure de toutes lez piesces pour quoy se il vous plaist que je la vous fasa je la vous faray de bon ceur et tout cella que il vous plaira auoir fait et au regard du pris je faray tellement que vous seres content de moy Pour tant quant il vous plaira lesiem sauoir queles piesses que vous voles auoir et la faisson et le jour que vous la voles auoir par quelcun a qui je puis inchauder en nom de vous et qui me ballia argent de sus je feray si bein que se Dieu plaist vous vous loeres de moy

Aultre chiox ne vous s[c]ay que mander pour le prexent se non que je prie a Dieu que il vous doint ce que vostre ceur desir Escript a Bruges le xxviij jour de ahoust lan lxxiij

Le tout vostre seruiteur Martin Rondelle
Armurier de Monsire le Bastart de Bourgogne

My most dear and honoured lord,

I do not know how I might commend myself more to you. May it please you to know that I have had news of you from one of your merchants of Calais touching an armour, and a sallet you are owed, and a barbute which is in difference between you and I for which I have said, on another occasion, that I am happy to reasonably make. And again, I say to you, for the time being, that I am ready to make all suitable things in all reason. That is to say, for the barbute, and for the armour, and sallet. I have no choice except to be obliged to do that which I can possibly do for the love I bear you, for your honour, and to your profit, I am always ready at your command.

Item, furthermore, I understand that you wish to have a complete harness. As I took your measurements when you were last in this town of Bruges, know you that I still have your measurements for all the pieces (i.e., plates) because – should it please you – that which I shall make for you, I shall make it with good heart and (with) all that which shall please you to have made. And in regard to the price, I shall make it such that you shall know that I am happy. For – when it should please you – do you thus know which pieces you wish to have, and the fashion, and the day [on] which you wish to have it, by which and to whom I can entrust (the harness) in your name, and who shall pay me? For that (harness) which I shall make shall be so good that (God willing) you shall praise me.

Know you of (any) other things that are ordered at present? If not, I pray God grant your heart's desire.

Written at Bruges on the twenty-eighth day of August in the year [14]73

Your servant in all things,

Martin Rondelle
Armourer to my lord the Bastard of Burgundy

Figure 18. Barbute, Milanese, mid-fifteenth century
(Glasgow Museums, R. L. Scott bequest, E.1939.65.am).

44

Kew, National Archives, E 405/59, membr. 4

Royal Payments for Equipment, Calais, Michaelmastide (29 September–25 December) 1474

Joh[ann]i Wodde mag[ist]ro ordinance[i]oni R' sup[er] officio suo in p[re]cio Cxxxvj milleyn' herneys complet p[re]c' le harnes iiij li' xiij s' iiij d' Sic p[er] Regem empt' de Thoma Graston' marcat' Staple' Calis videl[ice]t in p[ar]tem soluc' dict' Cxxxvj harnes &c den' p[ar] man' d[i]c[t]i Thome Graston' – CCCC li' Rogero Kelshall' valett' de Corona p[ro] tot' den' p[er] ip[si]m solut' p[ro] cariag' diu[er]s' arcuu' Sagitt' & Bowestring' de villa Suth[amp]t' vsq[ue] london' p[er] mandat' R' &c' den' de Wil[he]lmo Kerver' & Rob[er]to Cousyn' Coll' Cust' & Subs' Regis in portu' Suth[amp]t' – lx s'

To John Wood, Master of the King's Ordnance, upon his office for the cost of 136 complete Milan harnesses – price of the harness £4 13s. 4d. – so bought by the King from Thomas Graston, Merchant of the Calais Staple, viz.: in part payment for the said 136 harnesses etc. by the hand of the said Thomas Graston – £400, to Roger Kelshall, Valet of the Crown, for all monies paid by him for carriage of divers bows, arrows, and bowstrings from the town of Southampton to London by order of the King etc., paid from William Carver and Robert Cousins, Collectors of the King's Customs and Subsidies in the Port of Southampton – 60s.

45

Kew, National Archives, E 101/198/13

Account of William Rosse, Victualler of Calais, 5 December 1473–29 September 1475

Pro iij m[i]l lb' pulu[er]is gunnor[um] voc' Towche poudre [fact'] p[er] gunnat' R' Apud Cales' scil[ice]t ex m[i]l m[i]l C lb' pulu[er]is sal[is]petr' pur' xlix li' xiij s' iiij d' st' CClx xiij lb' Sulphur' viu' xv s' ij d' qua' CCClvij lb' pulu[er]is carbon' salic' xv s' x d' st' Et pro m[i]l m[i]l m[i]l m[i]l lb' pulu[er]is gunnor[um] voc' hakbuss' poudr' fact' p[er] gunnat' R' p[re]dict' ex ij m[i]l DC lb' pulu[er]is sal[is]petr' lxj li' x s' viij d' st[er]l' Ex DClx lb' pulu[er]is Sulphur' viu' xxxvj s' viij d' st[er]l' Et ex DCCxl lb' pulu[er]is carbon' de lynde xxxij s' ix d' qu' st' Et pro xv m[i]l CCCCxliiij lb' pulu[er]is gunnor[um] voc' Serpentyn' powdre fact' p[er] gunnat' R' villo s' Cales' p[re]dict' videl[ice]t ex ix m[i]l CClxv lb' pulu[er]is sal[is]petr' pur' CCxix li' ix s' ix d' st[er]l' Ex iij m[i]l CCC iiijxx j lb' pulu[er]is Sulphur' viij li' xvj s' j d' qua' st[er]l' Ft ex m[i]l m[i]l DCC iiijxx xviij lb' pulu[er]is carbon' de lynd' vj li' iiij s' iiij d' st[er]l' Et pro m[i]l m[i]l lb' pulu[er]is gunnor[um] voc' Bomberd powdre fact' p[er] dict' gunnat' R' ville s' Cales' Scil[ice]t ex m[i]l lb' pulu[er]is sal[is]petr' pur' xxiij li' xij s' iiij d' st[er]l' Ex CCCClxiij lb' pulu[er]is Sulphur' viu' xxvj s' vj d' ob' st[er]l' Et ex CCCClxviij lb' pulu[er]is carbon' de lynde xx s' x d' ob' st' pellett' de ferro CClx pond' int[er] se m[i]l ixC lb' ferr' p[re]c' iiij li' iiij s' v d' ob' st' Hailshot de ferro Clxxij lb' lvij s' iiij d' st' Clau' de ferr' voc' Spike' gross' CCCC iiijxx xviij pond' int' se CCxxxvij lb' p[re]c' xix s' vij d' st' Scaling ladders xij p[re]c' xx s' st' Handgunnys de ferro vj pond' int' se CC iiijxx xij lb' xl s' x d' st' Marespik' cu' capit' de ferro DC xviij li' xvij s' v d' st' Serpent' de ferro ij cu' duab[us] camer' pond' int' se cu' bolt' pouchis & forelock' DCClxx lb' ix li' xij s' vj d' qua' j p[ar]u' s[er]pent' de ferro pond' lx lb' p[re]c' xv s' qua' ij s[er]pent' p[ar]u' de ferro vnde j cum iijb[us] camer' & j sine cam[er]a pond' int' se cu' gaffull' powches & forelock' m[i]l m[i]l DCClxvj lb' xxvij li' xiij s' ij d' qua' j s[er]p[en]t' de ferr' pond' cu' bolt' pouchis & forelock' ixC x lb' xj li' vij s' vj d' qua' ij p[a]ru' s[er]pent' de ferro vtroq[ue] cu' ij cam[er]is pond'

cu’ ligat’ bolt’ pouchis & forelock’ CClxiij lb’ xxxv li’ ij s’ vij d’ qu’ st’ Hakegonnys
de ferro lxxvj ponderant’ int’ se iij m[i]l C iiijx v lb’ xxvij li’ vij s’ vj d’ st’ Botill’ ex
marermio fact’ viij iiij li’ st’ Saltpet’ gross’ m[i]l DCCC xlvij lb’ xxxvj li’ xviij s’ vij
d’ ob’ qu’ st’ Salispetr’ pur’ DCCCClxiiij lb’ xxiij li’ x s’ vj d’ ob’ st’ Balist’ de calibe
xxj viij li’ viij s’ st’ wyndelac’ duplic’ pro Balist’ tendend’ l ix li’ xj s’ j d’ st’ wyndelac’
singul’ pro balist’ tendend’ xij xxj s’ iiij d’ st[er]l’ Hagebergh[i]s [sic] xviij lx s’ st[er]l’
whyte bill’ iiij x s’ viij d’ st’ Hakegonnys de Ere v pond’ int’ se C iiijxx xij lib’ lxiiij
s’ st[er]l’ Capit’ quarell’ DCCCClxj xix s’ v d’ st’ Trenchfyle pro cord’ Balist’ lviij lb’
d[imid]i xxvj s’ st’ Syngul’ pro Balist’ tendend’ iiij duoden’ d[imid]i xlij s’ viij d’ st’
Glut’ CCxx lb’ xxiiij s’ v d’ st’ double wynch’ cord’ xxiiij iiij s’ viij d’ st’ Et Colardo
Blaunch’ p[ro] xj m[i]l CC iiijxx ij lb’ sal[is]petr’ inpur’ CCCxxxviiij lb’ [sic, recte li’]
ix s’ vj d’ qua’ Et Joh[ann]i Loste p[ro] m[i]l xx lb’ Sal[is]petr’ pur’ ab eo empt’ apud
Cales’ CClxxiij li’ iiij d’ ob’ st[er]l’ Et pro xj m[i]l lxxv lb’ sal[is]petr’ pur’ empt’ de
dict’ Colardo Blaunche apud Cales’ CClxij li’ vj s’ j d’ st’ Et joh[ann]i de lost pro
m[i]l xx bl’ sal[is]petr’ inpur’ ab eo empt’ xx li’ viij s’ st[er]l’ […] Et pro factur’ iij
m[i]l lb’ pulu[er]is gunn’ voc’ ‘Towch’ powdre iiij m[i]l lb’ voc’ hakebuss’ powdre xv
m[i]l CCCCxliiij lb’ voc’ Serpetnyn’ powdre & m[i]l m[i]l lb’ voc’ bomb[ar]d powdr’
xvj li’ vj s’ st[er]l’ Et pro factur’ vij m[i]l DCCCC lb’ pulu[er]is gunn’ fact’ ex stuffur’
nup[er] R’ E’ iiijti p[er] Joh[ann]em Sturgeon p[re]dict’ Wil[he]lmo Rosse lib[er]at’
p[er] Indent’ tempor’ Regressus d[i]c[t]i nup[er] R’ A viagio s’ Franc’ infra tempus
hui[us] compo’ xxj li’ xj s’ iiij d’ st[er]l’

for 3,000lb of gunpowder called touch powder [made] by the King’s gunners at
Calais namely from 2,100lb pure saltpetre powder £49 13s. 4d., 273lb quick sulphur
15s. 2¼d., 357lb willow-charcoal powder 15s. 10d., and for 4,000lb of gunpowder
called hakebusshe powder made by the said King’s gunners from 2,600lb pure
saltpetre powder 6l. 10s. 8d., from 660lb quick sulphur powder 36s. 8d., and from
740lb linden-charcoal powder 32s. 9¼d., and for 15,444lb of gunpowder called
serpentine powder made by the said King’s gunners in his Town of Calais viz.:
from 9,265lb pure saltpetre powder £219 9s. 9d., from 4,380lb sulphur powder £8
16s. 1¼d., and from 2,798lb linden-charcoal powder £6 4s. 4d., and for 2,000lb of
gunpowder called bombard powder made by the said King’s gunners in his Town
of Calais namely from 1,000lb pure saltpetre powder £23 13s. 4d., from 468lb quick
sulphur powder 26s. 6½d., and from 468lb linden-charcoal powder 20s. 10½d.,
iron pellets: 260 weighing 2,900lb of iron between them £4 4s. 5½d., iron hail shot:
172lb 57s. 4d., iron nails called large spikes: 498 weighing 247lb between them 19s.
8d., scaling ladders: 12 20s., iron handguns: six weighing 292lb between them 40s.
10d., morris pikes with iron heads: 600 £18 17s. 5d., iron serpentines: two with
two chambers weighing 770lb between them with bolts, pouches, and forelocks
£9 12s. 6¼d., one small iron serpentine weighing 60lb 15s. ¼d. , two small iron
serpentines – one with three chambers and one without a chamber – weighing
2,766lb between them with gaffles, pouches, and forelocks £28 13s. 2d., one iron
serpentine weighing 910lb with bolts, pouches, and forelocks £11 8s. 6d., two small
iron serpentines each with two chambers weighing 263lb with (iron) bindings,

bolts, pouches, and forelocks £35 2s. 8¼d., iron hookguns: 76 weighing 2,285lb between them £27 7s. 6d., bottles made of wood: eight £4, large saltpetre: 1,847lb £36 18s. 7¾d., pure saltpetre: 964lb £23 10s. 6½d., steel crossbows: 21 £8 8s., double windlasses for spanning crossbows: 50 £9 11s. 1d., single windlasses for spanning crossbows: 12 21s. 4d., 'Hagebergh[i]s' (prob. halberds): 18 60s., white bills: four 10s. 8d., brass hookguns: five weighing 192lb between them 64s., quarrel heads: 961 19s. 5d., trenchfile for crossbow strings: 58½lb 26s., belts for spanning crossbows: 84½ dozen 42s. 8d., glue: 220lb 24s. 5d., double winchcords: 24 4s. 8d., and [paid to] Colard Blaunche for 11,282lb impure saltpetre £138 9s. 6¼d., and John Loste for 1,020lb pure saltpetre bought from him at Calais £273 4½d., and for 11,075lb pure saltpetre bought from the said Colard Blaunche at Calais £262 6s. 1d., and John Loste for 1,020lb impure saltpetre bought from him £20 8s. [...] And for making 3,000lb of gunpowder called touch powder, 3,000lb called hakebusshe powder, 15,444lb called serpentine powder, and 2,000lb called bombard powder £16 6s., and for making 8,900lb of gunpowder made from the victuals of the late King Edward IV by John Sturgeon given by indenture of the said William Rosse during the time of this account for the King's voyage to France £21 11s. 4d.

46

Kew, National Archives, E 122/128/15, fol. 7v, fol. 8r–fol. 8v, fol. 15r, fol. 23r

Record of the Subsidy (Import Duty) paid by Alien Merchants, Port of Sandwich, 7 May–14 November 1475 (Extracts)

[7 May] Carraca vnde Benedictus de Marin[ius] est Patronus Wil[he]lmo herriott' Ind' pro xxviij ball' wodd iiij kartell' cu' lxxvj p[ar]e bregandynes Et vn' p[ar]u' cass' cu' iij pec' velweʋ' nigr' [con]t' xxiiij u[ir]g' valor' in toto lxiij li' xij s' iiij d' Subs' iij li' xiij s' viij d' [27 May] Nau' vnde Joh[ann]es hamond' est mag[iste]r Nich[ol]o Alwin Ind' pro vn' barell' cu' xxiiij bundell' bokeram[u]s xxvij Roll' bokeram[us] ij marc' gold' thred' Cl clowt' bregandyne naill' p[re]c' x li' S[u]b' x s' [10 April] Nau' vnde Joh[ann]es Courtnay est mag[iste]r Andrea Danckerd' al' pro vn' fard' cu' vj chamfront' [i.e., shaffron] xxx plum' de Ostriche' vj p[ar]ue harneis Argent' & de Aurat' x Angn[us] dei de Argento vn' p[ar]e precar[um] de corral' p[re]c' v li' cust' xv d' Subs' v s' Naui vnde Wil[he]lmus Foche est mag[iste]r Wil[he]lmo Brett' Ind' pro ij Fatt' cu' x herneis complet' iij dos' Salett' ij dos' gorgette' ij dos' gusset' de maill' p[re]c' xxij li' xv s' Subs' xxij s' ix d' [14 November] Carraca vnde Julian[us] Stella est mag[iste]r henrico Bourchier Comit' Essex' Thes' Anglie & Joh[ann]e Say milite p[ar] Wil[he]lm' herriott' Ind' Fact' ip[s]or[um] pro lviij barell' Alome' xxxiiij Sackett' Alome' xlj ball' wodd xij herneis complet' lij p[ar]e bregandynes et Cxxvij pec' co[u]rs Fustian' p[re]c' C li' Subs' [illegible]

[7 May] Carrack of Benedict de Marinus:

William Herriott, denizen, for 28 bales of wood, four kirtles (outer garments) with 76 pairs of brigandines, and one small case with three pieces of black velvet 23 yards (in length) in total worth £63 13s. 4d. – subsidy £3 13s. 8d. [27 May] Ship of John Hamond: Nicholas Alwin, denizen, for one barrel with 24 bundles of buckram, 27 rolls of buckram, two marks of gold thread, 150 flat-headed brigandine nails worth £10 – subsidy 10s. Ship of Johannes Courtnay': Andrea Danckerd', alien, for one pack with six shaffrons, 30 ostrich feathers, six small silver and gilt harnesses [prob. horse harness], 10 Agnus Deis, one pair of coral prayers [religious items] worth £5 – custom 15d., subsidy 5s. Ship of William Foche: William Brett, denizen, for two vats with 10 complete harnesses, three dozen sallets, two dozen gorgets, two dozen mail gussets worth £22 15s. – subsidy 22s. 9d. [14 November] Carrack of Julianus Stella: Henry Bourchier, Earl of Essex, Treasurer of England, and John Say, knight, done on their behalf by William Herriott, denizen, for 58 barrels of alum, 34 sacks of alum, 41 bales of wood, 12 complete harnesses, 52 pairs of brigandines, and 127 pieces of course fustian worth £100 – subsidy [illegible]

47

Kew, National Archives, E 101/198/13

Inventory of the Castle of Guînes, Calais Pale, 28 March 1476 and reviewed 3 January 1477

The reviewers' notes are inserted using slashes (i.e., ∧)

Fyrst in the Arthery (i.e., Archery/Artillery) Cxlj long bowes gode and bad /Reviewed Cxxxvj vn' lxj of the best & lxxvj bad\ iiijxx xiij sheff' of Arowes xxiiij sperys w[i]t[h] owte hedys /whereof lak ij\ iiij grosse of bow streng' /and ix def'\ j barell' full' of Trenchefyle (thread for crossbow-strings) lx mall' of lede [lead mallet] brokyn' and hole /w[i]t[h] owte helvys whereof xl sine [Lat. without] dagger' & xvij w[i]t[h] owte dagger' [*sic*]\ a staff w[i]t[h] a cheyne & a halt' of yron' vij pavices a Chyst [chest] w[i]t[h] <CCC iiijxx> /iiijC\ quarell' hedyd Federyd w[i]t[h] wode a Chest w[i]t[h] vjC /x\ quarell' hedyd vnfederyd an' olde Culu[er]yne w[i]t[h] a cheyne & a powche & no chambre On the wall' betwene the yatehowse and hynto[ne]s to[we]r j Fowler w[i]t[h] iij Chamber' j Fowler w[i]t[h] iij chamber' lyin in the same warde betywxt hyntones towre and the Fane towre j Fowler w[i]t[h] iij Chamber' lying next [to] the Fane towre j Fowler lying in the greate lope w[i]t[h] iij Chamber' a yenst the towne of Guysnes j Fowler w[i]t[h] iij Chamber' lying besyde the postern towre j Fowler w[i]t[h] iij Chamber' lying betwene the prive & the mille towre j serpentyne w[i]t[h] ij Chamber' lying betwene the mille towre and the Chambre warde In the olde Bulwerk ij trestell' gonnes w[i]t[h] vj Chamber' j Fowler w[i]t[h] iij Chamber' lying in the short warde by hyntons towre j Fowler w[i]t[h] ij Chamber' lying by the wache howse sowth[e]ward j greate Fowler w[i]t[h] ij Chamber' lying betwene the kepe and the Castell' j Fowler w[i]t[h] iij Chamber' lying in the Arche of the sowth' syde of the seid Bulwerk j greate Fowler w[i]t[h] ij Chamber' lying on the sowth' syde of the seid Bulwerk toward the towne j greate Fowler w[i]t[h] ij Chamber' lying on' the north' syde of the new bulwerk j Fowler w[i]t[h] ij Chamber' lying in the yate j <pot gon'> Culvryne of brasse lying in the Carpentry j Chambre of yron' in the seid Carpentry j serpentyne w[i]t[h] ij chamber' lying vndre the walle by the postern' yate j bumbard [i.e., bombard] Reman' at Cales /j potgon' Reman' at Cales\ In the Gonpowder towre vj barell' of Gonpowder vj Barell' of Saltpetre [both these barrels] deliu[er]ed by J Sturgon' iij hogg' hed' of Sulphur' ix Barell' of olde gonpowder ij barell' of lynde Cole (linden-wood charcoal) /Gunn' xiij Camer' xxv\

48

Kew, National Archives, E 122/19/12, membr. 7v

Goods exported from Bristol to Ireland, 17 March 1476

Bat' vocat' le Trinit' hay vn' Joh[ann]es haye est m[agister] Nich[ol]us Lewys ind' vj hab[er]gens val' iiij li' vj basnett' val' xxx s' vj Gorgett' val' x s'

> Boat called 'The Trinity' of which John Haye is master: Nicholas Lewys, denizen, six haubergeons worth £4, six basinets worth 30s., six gorgets worth 10s.

49

Kew National Archives, E 101/198/13

Inventory of the Castle of Hames, Calais Pale, 20 June 1476

Fyrst ij smale potgonnes j grate pot gun' j Gon' of Brasse w[i]t[h] iij Chamber' j Smale Serpentyne of brasse w[i]t[h] iiij chamber' xv Fowler' whereof xiiij of yron' and j of brasse and xxviij Chamber' whereof xxiiij of yron' & iiij of Brasse a Serpentyne w[i]t[h] iij Chamber' there ys at Cales j greate gon' of yron' w[i]t[h] iij Chamber' there lakkyth' a greate gon' of yren' w[i]t[h] ij chambers' CC pelett' of lede m[i]l CCCCl gunstonys of diu[er]s' sort' m[i]l CCC Tamponnes In the Arthery [i.e., Archery/Artillery] iiijxx viij long Bowes new and olde C iiijxx sheff' of Arowes xviij mall' of lede [lead mallets] xiiij bill' xxij peyre of brigandinez to be new set j Crow of yron' j Barell' of Crossebow threde vij chest' m[i]l C quarell' hedyd Federyd w[i]t[h] wode & iiij m[i]l ixC quarell' w[i]t[h] owte hed' Federyd w[i]t[h] wode m[i]l D Caltrappys vij Sperys w[i]t[h] owte hedys In the Storehowse An Andevyle & a peyre of Belowes in the Smythy iiij bell' and a wyndymill' [in a different hand at the bottom of the fol.] S[u]ma pag' [sum of the page] viz de potgunn' iij vn' [Lat. *unde* of which] j g[r]oss' Gunn' de ere j cu' iij cam[era]s Serpent' de Ere j cu' iiijb[us] camer' Foulers de Ere j cu' iiijor camer' Foulers

de ferr' xiiij cu' xxiiij camer' pellott' de plu[m]bo Cl lapid' gunn' m[i]l iiijC l Tampon'
pro gu[n]n' m[i]l iijC Arc manual' iiijxx viij mall' de plu[m]bo xviij Crowes de ferro
j Trechefile [*sic, recte* trenchfile] Garb' sagitt' C iiijxx Quarell' m[i]l C cu' capit' et iiij
m[i]l ixC sine capit' Cist' p[ro] quarell' vij Caltrappes m[i]l D Brigandin' xxij par' lanc'
sine capit' vij Aundevil' j Belowes j par' Byll' xiiij Campan' pro vigil' iiij Serp[e]nt' de
ferro j cu' iijb[us] cam[er]' Gonn' de ferr' g[r]oss' j cu' iijb[us] camer' [back to original
hand] In the Arthery ij Crossebowes of wode ij wyndlasse ij Stele bowes j wyndlas vC
quarell' hed' j Fyrdekyn' of gon' powder & a barell' the which' barell' weyeth' CCCCij
lb' j Fyrkyn' of Tarre ij grosse of bow streng' [in the second hand] S[um]ma pag' viz de
Balist' de ligno ij Balist' de Calibe ij windelac' iij capit' quarell' vj [*sic, recte* vC] pulu'
gunnor[um] j barell' & ferthekyn' the barell' pond' CCCvij lb' Barell' de bitume' j
ferthekyn' Cord' pro Arc' man' ij gross'

50

Now-Lost Original Document printed in *Archives législatives de la Ville de Reims*, ed. P. Varin (Paris, 1844), p. 768

War Equipment found and inventoried in the Town of Reims, June 1477

Habillemens de guerre trouves et inventoriés en la ville de Reims, au mois de juin [1477]

Harnois et corsets, quatrevingt deux. – Brigandines, six vingt et onze. – Haut-bergeons [*sic*] et crevisses [*sic, prob. recte* cuirasses], quatre cent quarante-huit. – Salades, bicoquets et bassinets, six cent vingt et un; avec grand nombre de couleuvrines [*sic*], arbalestres, haches d'armes, maillets de plomb, vouges, espieds [*sic, prob. recte espieus*] et aultres bastons de defense, sans les habillemens des cinquante-six francs-archers de la ville

harness and corsets 82, brigandines 131, haubergeons and (prob.) cuirasses 448, sallets, *bicoquets*, and basinets 621; with a great number of culverins, crossbows, arming axes, lead mallets, vouges, *espieux* (type of lance), and other defensive weapons, without (listing all) the equipment of the town's 56 *francs-archers* (archers provided for royal military service)

51

Leeds, Royal Armouries Library, RAR.0241; I.241

A Letter from René, Duke of Anjou (1409–80), concerning the Gift of a Crossbow, written at his Household ('Esc[ri]pt au mesnaige'), 27 August, year not recorded but before 1479 as he died on 10 July the following year

The recipient is a 'Monseigneur du Plesseys'. There were several men with this title. Possible candidates include Estienne Chevalier, Lord of Plessis-le-Comte (c. 1410–74) or Jehan Bourré, Lord of Plessis-Bourré (1424–1506).

Mons' du Plesseys en Reuange des deux belles arbalestes dacier q' mauez donnes & pour ce aussi q' depuis me suis enquis q' vous estes t[re]s bon arbalestier & q' prenez grant plaisir a tirer de larbaleste Je vous aduise q' de ma part tout ma vie y ay prins grant plaisir & affin q' voiez av[ene]ment suis artille Je vo[us] enuoie vne de mes arbalestes laquelle vous c[er]tiffie quelle est' faicte de la main dun sarrazin a barcillonne ne Jamais ne vieult aprende aux crestiens de les faire telles Et Pour ce quelle est destrange facon & quelle tire plus loing selon la petitesse de quoy elle est q' nulle aut' arbaleste de son grauit q' Je veisse oncques Je la vous enoie en vo[us] priant q' la tenez bien chiere & ne la vueillez donner a p[er]sonne q' vint car vous nen trouuerriez point de telle ne Jamais Jour de ma vie nen vis de si belle facon ne de si bonne aussi Il me semble q' le traict q' Je vous enuoie s[er]a trop pesant po[ur] elle mais Je me le vo[us] enuoie q' pour veoir la facon

My Lord du Plessis,

In return for the two beautiful steel crossbows you have given me and also that as I have been informed that you are a very good crossbowman and that you take great pleasure in crossbow shooting – let me tell you that for my part I have taken great pleasure in it all my life – and so that you see what is coming to be useful, I send you one of my crossbows which I guarantee it is made by the hand of a Saracen in Barcelona who never wants to teach Christians how to make them. And as it is of foreign making and it shoots much further than its smallness (suggests), I have never seen another crossbow of its weight (manage this). I send it to you praying that it gives you good cheer and that you should not give it to anyone who comes along for you shall never find one such as this. Never in my life have I seen one of such beautiful making nor so fine. Also, it seems to me that the shot (i.e., bolt) I have sent shall be too heavy for it but I have sent it to you to see the type.

Figure 19. Detail of a Burgundian tapestry panel, c. 1475
(Glasgow Museums, Burrell Collection, 46.61).

52

Now-Lost Original Document from the Archives municipales de Douai, printed in E. J. Soil de Moriamé, 'Armes et armuriers tournaisiens. Heaumiers, haubregonneurs, forbisseurs, couteliers. Contribution à l'histoire des métiers d'art et à l'histoire militaire de Tournai de XIIIe au XVIIIe siècle', *Bulletin de l'Académie royale d'archéologie de Belgique*, unnumbered (1913), pp. 36–154 (at pp. 106–7)

Account of Simon Savary, Douai, 1480

trois vouges, une pertuisane, une hace d'armes, ung espieu, ung pomet, deux maillés de queuvre, une hachette et une javeline l s. une[s] brigandines, deux gardebras et deux gantelets l s. quatre sallades de guerre, une demi sallade et plusieurs pièces de harnas viii lb. une culevrine x s. une javeline, ung gavrelot [*sic*], ung bonnet d'achier et ung tabliel x s. ung cranequin de nerfs, ung arbalestre et ung taquet, une espée garnye d'argent et ung coutel a clau lxx s. ung gorgerin estoffé d'argent iiii lb. Pour haubregerie, ung haubregon de Napples [*sic*] x lb. ung aultre a platte maille d'achier a fachon de paletot vii lb. trois aultres a fachon de palletot platte maille xxi lb. ung hauscol, une brayere, deux collés tout d'achier xxx s. ung haubregon de fer v s.

> three vouges, one partisan, one fighting axe, one *espieu*, one pommel, two copper mallets, one hatchet, and one javelin 50*s*., one (pair of) brigandines, two (pairs of) pauldrons, and two (pairs of) gauntlets 50*s*., four war sallets, one demi-sallet, and several pieces of harness 8*l*., one culverin 10*s*., one javelin, one *gavelot* (*javelot*: casting spear), one steel bonnet, and one little plaque 10*s*., one sinew cranequin [*sic*], one crossbow and one (spanning) hook, one silver-garnished sword, and one knife with (decorative) nail 70*s*., one gorget equipped with silver 4*l*. For mail-makers craft (i.e., mail): one haubergeon of Naples (poss. make) 10*l*. another of flat steel mail (i.e., flat-sectioned wire) fashioned like a *paletot* (overgarment) 7*l*., three others fashioned like *paletots* of flat mail 21*l*., one hounskull, one brayer, two collars all of steel 30*s*., one iron haubergeon 5*s*.

53

Kew, National Archives, E 101/198/13

Indenture recording the Delivery of Arms and Armour to William Comersale, Calais, c. 1480

First a Chariet w[i]t[h] a gret gonne of yron' j Chariet w[i]t[h] the chamb[er] of the said gonne and j chamb' of the long Fowler callid þe Edward j Chariet w[i]t[h] the gret brasyn' gonne j chariet w[i]t[h] a chamb' of the same gonne and j potte gonne of yron' j Chariet w[i]t[h] a gret bombard of yron' j Chariet w[i]t[h] a gret bastard gonne w[i]t[h] her' Chamb' callid the Messanger' j litle chariet w[i]t[h] a bombardell' callid the litle Edward j Chariet w[i]t[h] a Fowler' and her' chamb' callid the Fowler of Chestre ij Chariett' w[i]t[h] ij gret Pott' gonnez of brasse j Chariet w[i]t[h] a Fowler' & her' chamb' callid the megg' j Chariet and a Fowler' w[i]t[h] her ij chamb' callid the Fowler of the Towre j Chariet w[i]t[h] a Fowler' and her' chamb' callid the lesse Fowler of the To[we]r j Curtowe of yron' & j Cart w[i]t[h] iiij whelys CCxv gret shot of stone for the grettest Bombard lxxiiij shot of stone for the ij brasyn' Pot gonnez CCCC iiijxx x shot of stone for bastard gonnez Fowlers & potte gonnez Tamponnez m[i]l iiij Pelowyys of lede w[i]t[h] Ryng' j Crane w[i]t[h] vj pulleis of brasse & the taile w[i]t[h] iij pulleis of brasse to ship' and vnship' the said gret gonnez j Gynne w[i]t[h] a vyce callid a worme w[i]t[h] a Trestill' therto j Gynne callid a stradelyng gynne to cart and vncart the said gret gonnez ij Trokyll' eche w[i]t[h] iiij whelys shod w[i]t[h] yron' Bowes of Ewe m[i]l Cxxxiiij Bowes of wich' [wych elm] CCxxv Bowstring' C iiijxx ij gross' Shevys of Arowes of ix ynches CCCl Arowes of viij ynches m[i]l DCCCl Arowys of vij ynchez vij m[i]l DCCCClx Arowys vnhedid CC xxvij shef' S[um]ma x m[i]l CCC iiijxx vij shef' wherof was wete in the Temps comyng to Cales in a shyp' which' was leyke m[i]l m[i]l CCC xxxij shef' which' come to noo profit Rest Chist' [i.e., chest] for bowys Arowys and bowstring' CCl Shovyll' and Spad' m[i]l iiijxx xij mattokk' and Pyke axes CC iiijxx xvj Felling axes lxvj hand bill' lxxij mall' of lede [lead mallets] CCCvj gonne powd' x barell' pond' [weighing] ij m[i]l Cl lb' Sulphur powd' xij barell' pois' [sic] iij m[i]l lb' brymstone gret vnbrokyn' j hogg' hede [and] ij barell' Salt petre fyne tryed xxxviij barell' pond' xj m[i]l CCCC xvj lb' Cole powd' ij tonnes j hogg' hed' & xxviij barell' gret Crowes of yron' xlvij small' Crowes of yron' xix gret Cuttyng ham[er]s viij gret Cutting pynsonz iij pair' Small' pynsonz j pair' gret hok' of yron' w[i]t[h] cheynez xij j Cheyne w[i]t[h] a hok' forto stay þe potte gon' j Crosbowe of brake [i.e., spanned with a device] j Fowre foted trestill' for the same bowe Shot for the same callid Rollyons Cxiiij Cart Clowt' old xxiij gret bolt' of yron' iij bycornez of yron' j

Will[i]am Com[er]sale To hym' deliu[er]ed by Indenture

First the gret brasyn' gon' w[i]t[h] her' chamb' The Fowler' of Chest[er] w[i]t[h] her' chamb' The litle Edward w[i]t[h] her' chamb' The Messeng' w[i]t[h] her' chamb' j potte gonne of brasse

j potte gonne of yron' CCxl gonne stonez for shot of the same viij Chariett' redy apparellid for the same gonnez gonne powder iij last' xij barell' for þe last eu[er]ly barell' pois' net CC lb' powd' [sic] Crowes of yron' xl

Remanit Cressett' of yron' iij Stele j barell' Candell' C & xij doss' Pavic' [pavises] xviij Lantrannys iij Sawting ladders viij Botys of ledder' iij Pec' of Tymber for a Fleting bregge xlj Fellyng Axes lx

The long Crane w[i]t[h] vj shyves of brasse w[i]t[h] thapparell' The lading Gynne w[i]t[h] the vyce and al other apparell' pelowes of Lede ij Ledyn mallys CCC gret Cuttyng pynsonz iij gret Cuttyng hamers vij gret hok' of yron' w[i]t[h] cheynes vj small' Crowes xv gretTamponnez CCl hegge bill' & hand bill' lx j Trokyll' w[i]t[h] iij whelys j gynne w[i]t[h] iiij pec' callid a stradelyng gynne w[i]t[h] iiij sheves of brasse

To my lord howard m[i]l sheves of Arowes Thom[a]s Philip' CC vj Long bowes DC shef' of Arowes bowstryng' vj gross' Empty chist' lvjti vincent of dou[er] xx long bowes Arowes xxiiij shef' j grosse of bowstring' henry Fryse viij long Bowes xij shef' of Arowis Bowestryng' ij dos' Will[ia]m Smyth' CC shef' of Arowes

54

Two Inventories of the Town and Castle of Calais, and the Castles of Guînes and Hames, Calais Pale, 7 May 1481

Kew National Archives, E 101/198/13
First Inventory of the Town and Castle of Calais, and the Castles of Guînes and Hames, Calais Pale, 7 May 1481

Caleis

In the Warderobe aboue in the vpper Chamb' Crosse bowes of stele Cxlviij Crosse bowes of wode l dowble wyndelasses Cxxxij dowble wynche cord' lxviij payr' Crekys [cranequins] for Crosse bowes xix Cokerys for hand Gonnes xx mares [*sic*, prob. morris pikes] of yron' ij vyces to bend Crossebowes j Arow gyrdelys xij dos' A Bow of Brake [i.e., a device-spanned crossbow] Rolyons Federyd w[i]t[h] papyr' [an unidentified bolt-type] for the same Cxij Casys w[i]t[h] quarell' hedyd C xxiiijti mesures of Tynne for hake Gonnes xl ladyng ladelys of Brasse for hake Gonnes xvij Quarell' Federyd w[i]t[h] wode vnhedyd liiij m[i]l Quarell' Federyd w[i]t[h] wode hedyd xxv m[i]l Quarell' Fedeyred w[i]t[h] gose vnhedyd iij m[i]l DCCC lx Quarell' Fedeyred w[i]t[h] gose hedyd DCCCC xxij Quarell' hedys x m[i]l CCCC Trenche Fyle Dxxxvijti lb' gode Bow stryng' viij grosse In the Low howse by the steyer' Shovelys vnshod Cxij hott' [baskets] xxijti Bokett' of lethyr' xxviijti new shovelys shod w[i]t[h] yron' CC erthyn pott' for vnslekyd lyme m[i]l m[i]l Caltrappes m[i]l D Shyngyll' DCC iiijxx ledyn' mall' [lead mallets] m[i]l xxxiij In the myddell' howse long Bowes m[i]l iiijC iiijxx x Shevys of Arowes m[i]l m[i]l D iiijxx xv sheff' new Arowes vnhedyd D sheff' new Arowes hedyd CCCxl sheff' In the low howse Sulphur j Reynysh' pype long empty chyst' viij Goden dawghes [godendags] w[i]t[h] pik' of yron' ix vij stokkys w[i]t[h] xix shyves of Brasse In the Armery Batell' axes gylt lx Batell' Axes vngylt Clxxij Whyte Byll' callyd Faig' [*sic*, poss. vouges] iiijxx iiij new blak' Bill' Cxix Brigandynes xxiij pair' whyte harnesse complete x payr' Salett' of diu[er]se sort' Cxxti leg harnes ij pair' spere hedys ixC xlj Splynt' xl pair' In the olde Armery hake Gonnes of Brasse w[i]t[h] Sarsonnes visag' [Saracens' faces] xiiij other hake Gonnes of Brasse xvij smale hake Gonnes of Brasse ij hake Gonnes of yron' ij A Rebawdekyn' of brasse w[i]t[h] a trestyll' hand Gonnes of Brasse xv hand Gonnes of yron' xj In the new wolhowse Serpentynes of yron' Redy carted xxiiijti eche w[i]t[h] ij Chamber' new Trestyll' for

Gonnes ij A Bed for a fowler In multons plase A Greate Bumbard of yron' w[i]t[h] her Chamb' called london' w[i]t[h] her Charyet A greate Bumbard of yron' chamberyd of hym selff' [i.e., a bespoke chamber rather than an interchangeable one] w[i]t[h] her Charyet A greate pot Gonne of Brasse w[i]t[h] her Charyet vj greate Bumbardell' of yron' chamberyd of hem selff' j greate Fowler of yron' w[i]t[h] ij Chamber' j pot Gonne of yron' w[i]t[h] her Frame ij smale Fowler' of yron' eche w[i]t[h] ij chamber' stokkyd ij smale Fowler' of Brasse eche w[i]t[h] ij chamber' stokkyd xlj Chamber' of yron' of diu[er]se sort' A new bed for a Serpentyne iij greate Fowler' of yron' eche w[i]t[h] j chamb' carted j Bumbardell' of yron' w[i]t[h] a chamb' of hym selff' carted iij Bumbard' of yron' w[i]t[h] Chamber' of them selff' Redy carted A greate Fowler of yron' w[i]t[h] j Chamb' Redy Carted A Fowler of yron' chambered of hym selff' Redy Carted the long Rede Serpentyne of yron' w[i]t[h] her chamber' Redy Carted iiij Chamberys of yron' for greate Fowler' j long Serpentyn' of yron' chamberyd of hym selff' Redy Carted A greate mandrell' of yron' iiij Keveryd Cart' for sper' [sic, prob. serpentines] ij long Cart' Keveryd w[i]t[h] ledyr w[i]t[h] drawght' of lethyr and the Kyng' [heraldic] Armys vppon' hem vj A Gynne of yron' w[i]t[h] a Trestyll' callyd the worme A nother Gynne callyd the worme w[i]t[h] her trestyll' of tre dowble sawtyng ladder' iij Sengyll' ladderys iiij greate pilowes of lede ij xiiij payr' of new whelys bownde w[i]t[h] yron' iiij payr' log [i.e., wooden] whelys vnshod j payr' of Bastard whelys vnshod vj greate hok' of yron' w[i]t[h] Cheynes lote [or bote?] of lethyr and lethyr shapyn' for ij lot' [bot'?] a fowre fotyd trestyll' w[i]t[h] a vyce for a bow of brake [a device-spanned crossbow] xlj pecys of Tymb' for a Flotyng bryge greate pynsons of yron' of diu[er]se sort' vj payr' greate Kuttyng hamerys xvij a Bycorn' of yron' Bolt' of yron' iiij mattokk' and pykaxes CClxxviij ij Axeltreis of yron' for engynes

Guysnes

spadys and shovelys shod DClviijti long chest' bownde w[i]t[h] yron' xxijti long chest' for Arowes CC hege byll' and hand byll' viij mall' of lede w[i]t[h] pik' of yron' CC iiijxx xviij whereof iiij w[i]t[h]owte helvys Blak' byll' Clxij Blak' byll' w[i]t[h]owte helvys Bowes of Ew [yew] DCCCC iiijxx ij and iij brokyn' Bowes of Elme CCxx Bowstryng' Clx grosse Sperys of Reynysh' Clyst' DCCC xliij vn' delib[er]at' [of which are delivered] CCC Sperys made of Fyrre iiijC iiij Shypp' sperys hedyd xv dos' Shypp' sperys vnhedyd xlviijti dart' for shyppes hedyd xxxij dos' marespik' [morris pike] of Ashe hedyd xvij dos' Shaft' for marespik' made of Fyr vnhedyd xxx dos' d[imid] i stakys for the Felde hedyd w[i]t[h] yron' at both the endys Cxxxvj dos' Croperys of ledyr w[i]t[h] Cheynes of yron' for greate Ordynance lxviij hamurs of tre xxx pair' Crowes of yron' of diu[er]se sort' x Fellyng Axes xxiij stak' w[i]t[h] owte hedys xv dos' new Trapers for horses ix payr' shovelys of yron' xiiij spadys shod w[i]t[h] yron' iij ledyr [of] hungry j hyde d[imid]i pynnes of yron' for Cart' Cxl Shevys of Arowes of viij ynches ix ynches and vij ynches vij m[i]l DCCxlvj sheff' shevys of Arowes to be mendyd m[i]l CCClxxv sheff' shevys of Arowes vnhedyd CCxxxj sheff' Kuttyng Sawes ij hasyll' stavys for pavicys CC short ladyng Gynne of tymb' w[i]t[h] the Apparell' [no no. recorded] new bynder' xl pair' new Axeltreys xxvj a bed for a Serpentyne a Frame of tre for a pot Gonne Serpentynes of Brasse Redy carted xiiij

Serpentynes of yron' w[i]t[h] chamber' of theym' selff' Redy Carted v Serpentynes of
yron' eche w[i]t[h] ij chamber' Redy cartyd iiij pavyces of diu[er]se sort' CCCCxxv
Stele j Barell' Spadys and shovelys shod xij spadys and shovelys vnshod' xvij mattokk'
and pykaxes helvyd xij mattokk' vnhelvyd xlij stouyn' morterys ij Gonstonys of
diu[er]se sort' m[i]l m[i]l m[i]l CC Gonstonys of marbyll' CC iiijxx pavyces xliij
Bolt lokkys iij ledyn weyght' Dl lb' Tamponnes m[i]l D Andefeld' in the smethy j
Wache bell' iij pelett' of lede m[i]l DCCC lxx Sulphur j Reynysch' pype lynde cole
[linden-wood charcoal] j Barell' Salt petyr' ij Oyle Fatt' Salt petyr paired vj barell'
Chest' for long Bowes v empty Fyrkyns j In the Gonpowder towre Gonpowder xj
Barell' Serpentyne powder v halff barell' and a hole barell' pois' CCC lb' Culueryne
powder iij Fyrkyns' Abowte the Wall' and in the Bulwerk' and murderer' Fowler' of
yron' greate and smale xxvj Chamber' of yron' to them lxiij Serpentynes of yron' xvj
Chamberys of yron' to them' xliij Trestyll' Gonnes of yron' ij w[i]t[h] vj Chamber' A
Bumbardell' chamberyd of hymselff pot Gonnes of yron' j Cart Gonnes ix vppon'
iij Cart' w[i]t[h] xxvj Chamberys Cart Gonnes vncartyd' vj w[i]t[h] xiiij chamber'

hammes

wache bell' iij whereof j [in] the gate and one in the chyrche pois' CCC lb' & j brokyn
wynde mill' j Andefeld' in the Smethy j Smethys Belowes j payr' pavyces xj spade' and
shovill' xxxij See Cole j Chaldre pelett' of lede Clti gonne powder v barell' pois' xvC
xx lb' a s[er]pentine of yron' carted w[i]t[h] iij Chambres iij barell' of bombard' powd'
pois' vjC lb' j barell' of s[er]pent' powd' pois' ijC lb' Tamponn' vC powchis w[i]t[h]
cheynes pois' xxvj lb' bowstreng' iiij gross' long bowys xxx xxx sheff' of Arowys of
viij and ix ynchis shovill' and spad' xxiiij marespik' [morris pike] xx vj hakebusshes
of brasse belonging to my lord of Glowcest' w[i]t[h] tokyn of the bore j barell' of
fyne Cole iij Crosbowys of wode w[i]t[h] iij winlan' iij Crosbowys of stele w[i]t[h]
iij winlac'

Kew, National Archives, E 101/198/13
Second inventory of the Town and Castle of Calais, and the Castles of Guînes and Hames, Calais Pale, 7 May 1481

In the olde storehouse xxxvj maresse pyke' xlv pyke axes & mattokk' helvyd xl pike
axes & mattokk' vnhelvyd xlvij hok' for lopys ij barell' for Cole powd' j Reynesshe
pype w[i]t[h] Sulphur and a gret Tubbe pois' m[i]l m[i]l lv lb' d[imid]i lx shovils and
spad' shodm[i]l m[i]l Tork' vij Cressett' of yron' v[n]stokkyd j gret panne for gonne
powd' xlj pavic' for the felde In the store house and before the Con[sta]ble dore
gonne stonys m[i]l m[i]l m[i]l DCC xxti pelett' of Lede vijC d[imid]i pelett' of yron'
iij [sic, recte iijC?] Tamponnys iij m[i]l CC In the Forge

vj fyre hok' of yron' ij smale hok' vnstokkyd j peir' of belowys ij Andeveld' j bycorn'
vij ham[er]s of dyu[er]s sort' vj pair' of Tong' gret & small' j peir' of Tong' w[i]t[h] the
Fyling stok for a lokyer [i.e., locksmith] j water trowgh' In the howse vndir the Rode
Gonstonys of diu[er]se sort' xj m[i]l DCCCxxxiiij pelett' of lede for Sepentynes m[i]l

CCCCxxj pelett' of yron' Cx pelett' of lede for hake Gonnes DCCvij pelett' of lede for Culuerynes m[i]l iiijC l Tamponnes of diu[er]se sort' xiij m[i]l Brymstone vnbrokyn' ij Chest' full' In the Gonpowder howse vnder olde Cales a myll' to make gonpowder w[i]t[h] x pestelys and all' other Apparell' lynde cole powder [linden-wood charcoal] xvj barell' Sulphur powder xxxj barell' j Trowgh' of Tre [wood] w[i]t[h] v stamperys and v swepys of tre to brake in sulphur and saltpet' and other stuff for Gonpowder a morter of brasse w[i]t[h] a pestell' of yron' a Beme of yron' w[i]t[h] ij balanc' of laten' great brasyn' pannes ij Bultyng tonnes ij Tubbes for medelyng of Gonpowder xxiiij Syffes to Syft w[i]t[h] gonpowder vj j swepe w[i]t[h] a medelyng pestell' steryng ladelys of yron' iij At the sowth' west Corn' vppon the wall' Serpentynes of yron' eche w[i]t[h] ij chamber' iij Fowler' of yron' eche w[i]t[h] ij chamber' iij In the sowth' west towr' Gonstonys of diu[er]se sort' Clviij pelett' of lede of diu[er]se sort' l a morter of stone in a blok Gonpowder j barell' d[imid]i Serpentyne powder vij Fyrkyns j trestyll' for a Gonne Crowes of yron' iiij a Fethyr and a Reste of yron' shovelys shod w[i]t[h] yron' iiij iiij leverys and vj hand spekys Rollys of Tymber iij ladyng ladelys of brasse vij and ij stamperys A laddyr' ij Fowleres of yron' in the bothom of the to[we]r w[i]t[h] iij chamber' j Ramme of tymb' to dryve in Tampo[n]nes Tamponnes of diu[er]se sort' m[i]l m[i]l lxx In the Brokyn Warde at the West ende A Serpentyne of yron' w[i]t[h] ij chamber' cartyd A Fowler of yron' w[i]t[h] ij Chamberys carted In the Gonpowder towr' next Bolen gate Gonpowder xxiij barell' & j Fyrdekyn' empty half barell' to bere in gonpowder iiij j Trowgh' of Tre to bete in gonpowder a stouen' morter brokyn' a swepe w[i]t[h] a stamper In the Warde betwene the Gonpowder towres a Bumbardell' w[i]t[h] a chamb' of hym selff [i.e., a bespoke chamber rather than an interchangeable one] v shot of stone for the same In the Gonpowder towr' ayenst Joh[a]n Totwothes new howse Gonpowder xxv Barell' empty hand barell' iij Rammes for Tamponnes iij stavys to Ram in Gonpowder iiij Pestell' of Tymb' ij bolsterys of tre for Gonnes vij mallys of tymb' v Weg' of tymb' iiijxx shyves of tymb' iiij leverys and hand spek' viij Tamponnes of diu[er]se sort' m[i]l m[i]l Cl By the Bushe steyer A Serpentyne of Brasse vppon a trestyll' with' a chamb' of hym selff In the Warde by West develyns towre A Serpentyne of Brasse vppon' a Trestyll' chamberyd of hym selff A Fowler of yron' stokkyd w[i]t[h] ij chamber' In the Warde betwene develyns Towre and mylk gate iij Fowler' of yron' stokkyd ech w[i]t[h] ij Chamber' In the howse vndyr mylk gate A Trestyll' for a Gonne A Ramme for Tamponnes hand mall' of tymb' ij Gonpowder j Fyrkyn' Gonstonys of diu[er]se sort' iiijxx xvj Tamponnes C pelett' of lede xxviij Weg' of Tymb' l greate bolt' of yron' ij hopys of yron' j In the Brokyn' Warde greate Gonstones vij Serpentynes of Brasse Redy Carted iij In the Towre be West Lantern gate A Serpentyne of yron' stokkyd w[i]t[h] a chamb' pelett' of lede iiij Tamponnes vj In the Litull' Towre by est the lantern Gate A Sperpentyne of yron' w[i]t[h] ij Chambr' stokkyd pelett' of lede iiij Gonstones iiij Tamponnes xvij Gonpowder j Fyrdekyn' bounde w[i]t[h] yron' In the Towr' ayenst Boket strete j Fowler of yron' w[i]t[h] ij Chamber' stokkyd In the Bothum of Beachamp towr' A Serpentyne of yron' w[i]t[h] j Chamber stokkyd Gonstonys of diu[er]se sort' CCC pelett' of lede of diu[er]se sort' xxix Tamponnes of diu[er]se sort' iiijC Roll' of Tre vij mall' of wode ij shovelys ij leverys and hand spek' vij weg' of wude lv Fetherys of yron' for gonnes ij Fyllyng stavys ij In [the] Beachampe Bulkwerke in the North towre of the same iiij Fowler' of yron' stokkyd eche w[i]t[h] ij Chambr'gonstonys of diu[er]se sort' xlj Koveryng' of wode for the same ij A Rolle and a blok j Serpentyne of yron' w[i]t[h] ij Chambr' A Coveryng and x shot of stone for the same A Sepentyne of yron' w[i]t[h] ij Chamber' and a Koveryng and xv shot of stone for the same A Fowler of yron' w[i]t[h] a chamber and a Koveryng and vij shot of stone for the same j Fowler of yron' w[i]t[h] ij Chamber j Koveryng and x shotte of stone for the same j Fowler of yron' w[i]t[h] iiij Chamber' a Koveryng & xvj shot of stone A greate Fowler of yron' w[i]t[h] ij Chamber' In the Postern' Bulwerk Fowler' of yron' ix eche w[i]t[h] ij Chamber' and j w[i]t[h] iiij Chamber' Gonstones of di[uer]se sort' Cxxxij Tamponnes C hand spekys of wode xxiiijti A Botyll' a malle and a Rolle of Wode In Bolengate Bulwerk Fowlerys of yron' stokkyd vij w[i]t[h] x Chamber' Serpentynes of yron' iiij eche w[i]t[h] ij chamber' Koveryng for Gonnes iiij Gonstones lxx Tamponnes xxiiijti

The Castell' of Cales Syr Joh[a]n donne lieutenant

In the wache howse towr' A Serpentyne of yron' w[i]t[h] a chamb' stokkyd A Fowler of yron' w[i]t[h] A Chamb' stokkyd In the Gate Towr' A Serpentyne of yron' w[i]t[h] ij chamberys stokkyd A Trestyll' for A Gonne A wache belle In the Nursery A Fowler of Brasse w[i]t[h] ij Chamber' stokkyd A Trestyll' for a Gonne A Serpentyne of yron' w[i]t[h] a chamb' stokkyd In the Tower vnder the wache towre A new serpentyne of yron' w[i]t[h] a Chamb' In the Posteren' Bulwerk new Serpentynes of yron' eche w[i]t[h] ij chamber' iiij A Serpentyne of Brase w[i]t[h] a chamb' of hym selff Redy Carted In the dungeon' j peyre of hangyng stokk' bownde w[i]t[h] yron' A wache bell' hangyng In the store howse j Fowler of Brasse w[i]t[h] ij Chamber' of brasse stokkyd Gonstonys of diu[er]se sort' xxx pelett' of lede xviij Tamponnes C In the Arthery [i.e., Archery/Artillery] long Bowes xx Shevys of Arowes iiijxx viij quarell' Federyd w[i]t[h] wode and hedyd iij m[i]l DC quarell' hed' m[i]l DCC Chest' for quarell' hed' j Sperys vnhedyd xj mall' of lede vj

Rysebank Towr' anno xxjmo R' E' iijti Aboue on' the ledys A Serpentyne of yron' w[i]t[h] iij Chamber' stondyng vppon' a Trestyll' A wache belle In the landyr howse and preson' howse A Fowler w[i]t[h] ij Chamber' A Gonne w[i]t[h] ij Chamber' A payr' of stokk' In the Bothum of the dyke A Serpentyne of Brasse chamberyd of hym selff Redy Carted w[i]t[h] the kyng' [heraldic] Armes A Serpentyne of yron' w[i]t[h] ij Chamber' and a Rest of yron' A greate Fowler w[i]t[h] ij Chamber' of yron' A Serpentyne w[i]t[h] ij Chamber' of yron' In the middell' Chamb' hake Gonnes of Brasse iij w[i]t[h] iij stamper' of yron' In the Arthery long Bowes xij Shevys of Arowes xxvj in mall' of lede x quarell' lxxij and iij Casys w[i]t[h] new quarell' A Crosbow of wode w[i]t[h] a wyndelasse Caltreppys DCCC

The Castell' of Guynes Anno xxj E' iijti Syr Rauff hastyng' lieutenant

In the Arthery Long bowes CCxlij Shevys of Arowes DCxlv Bow Stryng' x grosse iij dos' Crossebowes of stele xxv Crossbowes of wode xvj Crankynnes j wyndelasses xxvij Trenchefyle Cxiiij lb' Quarell' v m[i]l Cxlv quarell' hedys ix m[i]l CCC iiijxx Caltrappys xij m[i]l Sper' vnhedyd l Spere hedys l ledyn' mall' C hake Gonnes of yron' vj hake Gonnes of Brasse vj hand Culuerynes xxxijj smale Culu[er]ynes of yron' v whereof iij stokkyd and ij vnstokkyd Cokerys for hand gonnes xix mold' of brasse iij a Flayle w[i]t[h] a balle and cheyn' of yron' Tylores for Crosbowes v In the Store howse Restys of yron' iiij Cressett' stokkyd xij Cressett' vnstokkyd xij Tork' to them m[i]l m[i]l CC In the Chapell' dyu[er]se plat' & iij wache bell' In the Store howse Gonstonys [no no. recorded] a Chambr' of yron'

The Castell of hammes James Blount lieutenant vijo die may Anno xxjmo R' E' iiijto

Gonnes of yron' and Brasse xiiij Chamberys of yron' to them' xxxiij hake Gonnes of brasse v w[i]t[h] iij stoppyng yrons Cart Gonnes of yron' ij Redy Carted w[i]t[h] ij chamber' pot Gonnes of brasse j hand Gonnes of brasse xij Gonstonys of diu[er]se sort' m[i]l DCCCClti Tamponnes for Gonnes m[i]l lti Salt petyr j barell' pois' [blank] long Bowes Cxxxiij Bow stryng' vij grosse shevys of Arowes CCCxij Crosse bowes of stele j Crosse bowes of wode ij wyndelasses to them' ij Quarell' Federyd and hedyd m[i]l DC Quarell' Federyd vnhedyd v m[i]l DC Quarell' hedys Dxlti Caltrappes iiij m[i]l DCC Sperys vnhedyd xx Spere hedys xij laden' mall' xxxvj Cressett' v mattokkys and pykaxes vij Trenchefyle j barell'

55

Unlocated Document from the Registers of the Dukes of Milan, printed in W. Boeheim, 'Werke Mailänder Waffenschmiede in den kaiserlichen Sammlungen', *Jahrbuch der Kunsthistorischen Sammlungen des Allerhöchsten Kaiserhauses* 9 (1889), pp. 375–418 (at pp. 390–1)

Letter from Jacomino Ayroldo, Armourer to Louis XI of France, to the Duke of Milan, undated but written during the King's reign (1461–83)

Charles VII granted 'Jaquemin hairolde marchant natif de la ville de milan' lettres de naturalité in February 1450 for the 'good and agreeable services which the said supplicant has given Us in the past for the sale of harness, We wishing it to be brought into Our said realm' ('des bons et aggreables seruices q' led' suppl' nous a faiz le temps passe oud' fait de marchandise de harnois voulans Icelui attraire en n[ost]re d' Roy[au]me').[17] *In this letter the armourer states that he is 'a little old and tired for riding, and a little infirm' ('uno poco vecchiarello et stracho per il cavalcare, et uno poco infermo').*

Supplicatio Jaconini [*sic*] Ayroldi armorery et nunty [*sic*] Serenissimi Regis Francorum. Enendendo el Senerissimo Re de Franzia fare et fabricare alcune gentile et belle armature per la persona sua et deli altri baroni, signori et scuderi stano ad la corte sua et non havendo magistri che li para debiano supplire a la voluntà de la Sua

---

[17]   Paris, Archives nationales, JJ//180, fol. 50r.

Regale mayestate et a quella factione et maynere che luy e li suoy voriano, madava de la celsitudine vostra Jacobino Ayroldo, armorero suo, con lettere sigillate et segnate de propria mano del prefato Re, pregando affectuosamente et caramente la prefata Signoria Vostra et per sumo piacere: La si degnasse madare con esso Jacomino [*sic*] duo deci compagni instucti di fare armature de la sua mayestate con li loro istrumenti apti a tale lavorerio offerendo molto ben meritarli et facta la opera remandarli: et come esso Jacobino de la mente sua regale era informata. Et ha presentate tale lettere del prefato Re ad la vostra Excellentissima consorte. La quale le ha remandate al vostro consiglio secreto che non li fa altra provvisione ad la reschesta de la sua Mayestate benche siano trovati li compagni essendo contenta la Signoria Vostra. Et questo crede esso Jacomino restate sollo per livore et invidia de alcuni armoreri, che credono volere tenire tuto el guadagno per se dicendo che seria dano ad la citade de Milano a mandarli via; che non e vero et si madasse ben el prefato Re le mesure a Milano per se et per li suoy non vendandose le loro persone ne intandando le maynere ne que ne come non si suppleria ad la voluntade Regale ne de li suoy baroni et seria grande disturbio et fatiche a mandarle inanze et inderieto et facilmente essendo facte le bisogneria desfare non piacendoli et essendo di la quilli compagni richiesti con li loro usedegli de grado in grado si potra vedere et intendere quello habieno a fare et facta la opera retornariano come alias fecino quilli fureno madati al glorioso dalphino che complito el lavore retornareno a Millano. Et quantunche ne le parte de la et Franzia siano molti armoreri. Non e viso al prefato Re et suoy baroni debiano suplire al suo talento et pero haveva scripto ad la Signoria Vostra sperando indubie, che non solamente in questo ma in mazore cuose li dovesse compiacere.

Onde esso Jacobino, armorero et messo del prefato Re, trovandosi pur uno poco vecchiarello et stracho per il cavalcare, et uno poco infermo manda el presente portatore de la Signoria Vostra con esse lettere che aperse la prefata Madona overo esso consiglio pregando la vostra benigna signoria la si degna per sue lettere essere contenta de mandare dal prefato Re essi compagni XV [*sic*] o al mancho octo con li istrumenti per satisfare a questo Regale desiderio et suoy baroni.

The supplication of Jacomino Ayroldo, armourer, and emissary of the Most Serene King of the French

The Most Serene King of France, intending to have some fine and beautiful armours made and crafted for His own person and for the other nobles, knights, and squires at His Court and having no masters who can provide them to His Royal Majesty's will and to such making and manner as He and His nobles wish, has sent to Your Highness, Jacomino Ayroldo, His armourer, with letters sealed and signed with the said King's Own hand, praying affectionately and dearly that it be greatly pleasing to Your said Lordship that You deign to send with this Jacomino twelve companions who are instructed to make armour for His Majesty with their suitable tools and offering to reward them well and, having done the work, to send them back: and that this Jacomino was informed of His Royal mind [intention]. And [Jacomino] has presented the said King's letters for Your most excellent consideration and has forwarded them to Your secret council so that it shall give no other

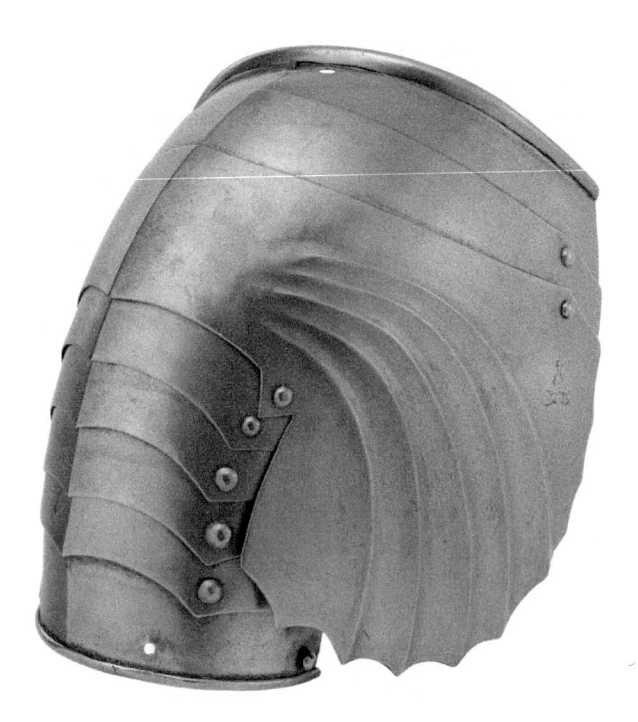

Figure 20. Pauldron, made by a Milanese armourer working in Lyon, c. 1490
(Glasgow Museums, R. L. Scott bequest, E.1939.65.0.[2]).

instruction in response to His Majesty's request other than, with Your Lordship's agreement, the companions shall be found. And Jacomino believes that they have not left [i.e., the companions have remained '*restate*' in Milan] solely because some armourers, out of spite and envy, believing he wishes to keep all the profits for himself, are saying that it will be detrimental to the City of Milan to send them away, which is not true, and if the aforesaid King were to send His own and His courtiers' measurements to Milan, they would not be seeing their person nor have any understanding of the manners (i.e., be able to observe the body and its movements), in any way whatsoever [lit. 'nor what nor how']. This would not fulfil the royal wish nor those of His nobles and it would be a great inconvenience and trouble to send them [the armours] back and forth, and while easy to make, the armour would then have to be unmade if they did not please them [i.e., the King and his nobles]. Instead, being there [in France] as requested, those companions, with their tools, step by step could see and understand what they need to do, and the work being done they will return, as [*inter alia*] did those [armourers] who were sent to the Glorious Dauphin, who returned to Milan when the work was completed. And although there are many armourers in those parts and in France, the aforesaid King and His nobles have preferred not to use their talent, and therefore He [the King] has written to Your Lordship truly hoping that not only in this but in many things you will satisfy him.

Therefore, this Jacomino, armourer, and envoy of the said King, finding himself a little old and tired for riding, and a little infirm, has sent the present messenger to Your Lordship with these letters that the said Madonna [Duchess] or Her council opened, supplicating that Your benign Lordship shall deign by His letters to be content to send to the aforesaid King these 15 [*sic*] – or at least eight – companions, with their tools to satisfy this regal desire and that of His nobles.

56

Lille, Bibliothèque municipale, Fonds Godefroy, Ms Godefroy 22, *Dominici Mancini, de occupatione regni Anglie per Riccardum tercium*, pp. 28–9

Domenico Mancini's Description of the Fighting Men and Hunting Women of England, 1483

Domenico Mancini was a Roman scholar and chronicler, probably an Augustinian monk, active in the scholarly circles of Paris. He was in England during the tumultuous events of April to July 1483 that saw Richard III seize the throne. He finished his account – written for Angelo Cato, Archbishop of Vienne – on 1 December of that same year.

Admonet me res ipsa que agitur: vt de brita[n]noru' militum armatura pauca refera' Nullus fere est sine galea: Nullus sine arcu et sagictis Arcus vero et sagitte solidiores ac longiores su[n]t q[uam] cetere gentes vtantur: q[ue]madmodu' et ispi corpore robustiores: ferreas vid[ea]nt' h[abe]re manus et brachia Non minoris Jacture eoru' su[n]t arcus q[uam] n[ost]re sint Babliste [*sic, recte* balliste] Vnicuiq[ue] preterea ad latus pendet ensis etsi no' minus longus: grauis t[ame]n ac solidus Ensi semper Junctus est ferreus vmbo: hec enim precipua studia illius gentis: vt passim per vicos: festis diebus Juniores ceter' vmbonibus obtrisis gladiis creptita[n]tibus vel loco gladi-or[um] solidioribus baculis Vbj vero adultj sunt: in campis cu' arcubus et sagittis. Nec ip[s]e quide' mulieres in venando huiusmodj armor[um] sunt ignare In pectore et reliqua parte corporis nil habent ferrj pro munime[n]to preterq[uam] nobiliores: quj toracibus vtuntur et catapultis [*sic, recte* cataphractis[18]] Vulgus vero militum tunicas habet aptiores infra inguen demissas stupa siue alia mollj materia referctas Ictus sagictaru' et gladior[um] tanto melius sustinere eas dicunt: q[ua]nto molliores sunt Propterea estate minus graues q[uam] ferru' et hyeme vtiliores: huiusmodj igitur armatura euocatj milites vener[u]nt munitj: et preterea equites non q[uod] ex equo consueuer[i]nt pugnare: sed quia illis vtantur: vt portentur ad locu' pugne vt ibj sint

---

[18] In his edition, Armstrong very plausibly suggests *cataphractis*. See *The Usurpation of Richard the Third: Dominicus Mancinus ad Angelum Catonem de Occupatione Regni Anglie per Riccardum Tercium Libellus*, ed. and trans. C. A. J. Armstrong (London, 1936), p. 98.

recentiores neq[ue] fessi labore vie: ideo quibuscu[m]q[ue] equis insident: etia' dorsu-
ariis: Vbj ad locu' pugne ventu' fuerit o[mne]s relictis equis [preterquam] equo marte
pugnant vt nullj sit spes fuge Sed hiis statis

With these goings on I am minded to say a little of the arms of the soldiers of
Britannia. Few are without a helmet: none are without bow and arrows. Truly, the
bow and arrows are stronger and longer than those used by other nations: because
of this they have robust bodies – it seems as though they have arms and hands of
iron. They shoot their bows no less far as our crossbows. Furthermore, each has a
sword slung at the hip and if it is no less long (than ours) nevertheless it is as heavy
and strong. The sword is always paired with an iron buckler: for this race has such
a particular enthusiasm for it that everywhere the youths go through the streets
on feast days with others shattering bucklers with clashing swords or, instead of
swords, strong staves.

   Truly, as soon as they are adults they go into the fields with bows and arrows.
Nor are the women when hunting ignorant of such weapons. On the chest and
the rest of the body none have iron (defences) for protection, save the nobles who
have cuirasses and *cataphractis* (i.e., prob. complete harness). Truly, the common
soldiers have suitable tunics extending below the groin stuffed with tow or other
soft material. The blows of arrows and swords are much better endured, they say,
when it is softer. For this reason, it is less heavy than iron (armour) in summer and
more useful in winter. It was in this type of armour that the soldiers who had come
were protected as well as horsemen, who are accustomed to fight without the horse,
but they use them to carry them to the place of the fight so that they are refreshed
and not worn out by the journey: therefore, they ride any horse – even a packhorse.
When they have arrived at the place of the fight they leave their horses – (unless)
they fight with a war horse – so that none consider flight but stand (together).

57

Kew, National Archives, E 101/198/13

Inventory of the Castle of Guînes, Calais Pale, 13 August 1483

In the Arthery [i.e., Archery/Artillery] Sheves of Arowes D iiijxx ix sheff' long Bowes
CC xxxij Crosbowes of stele xxj Crosbowes of stele vnteleryd iiij Crosbowes of
wude xiiij Crosbowes of wude vnteleryd j Crankyns j wyndelasses to them' xxiiijti
Bow stryng' xij grosse hand Culuerynes of yron' xxxij w[i]t[h] ther stampers hake
go[n]nes of yron' ij Coker' to them xix mall' of lede [lead mallets] C Tiler helt' v
Quarell' Fedryd w[i]t[h] wude and hedyd' iij m[i]l CC Quarell' hed' ix m[i]l CCC
Cultrappes xij m[i]l Trenchfyle Cxiiij lb' mold' of brasse iij Flayles of yron' j Blak
bill' iiij iij Barell' w[i]t[h] the seid stuff' [in a different hand at the bottom of the fol.]
Garb' sagitt' [sheaves of arrows: no. not recorded] [back to original hand] In the new
Bulwerk Beneth' j Serpentyne w[i]t[h] iiij Chamber' & j powche stokkyd j Serpentyne

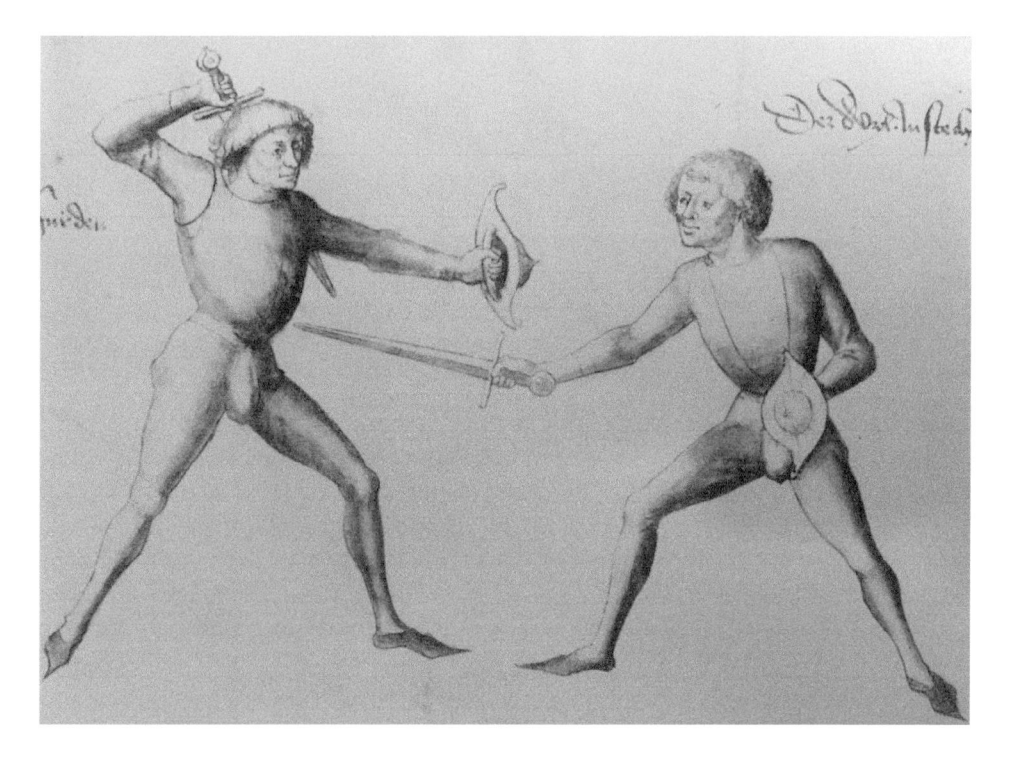

Figure 21. Illustration from Hans Talhoffer's fight manual, German, 1467.

Figure 22. Fencing buckler, Italian (poss. Milanese), c. 1500–10
(Glasgow Museums, R. L. Scott bequest, E.1939.65.ph).

Figure 23. Arming sword, second half of the fifteenth century
(Glasgow Museums, A.1964.9.b).

w[i]t[h] iij Chamber' & j powche stokkyd j Serpent' w[i]t[h] iij Chamber' j powche
stokkyd j greate Fowler w[i]t[h] ij chamber' j powche stokkyd aboue [the new
bulwark] j long serpent' w[i]t[h] iij chamber' w[i]t[h] a powche stokkyd ij Trestyll'
gonnes w[i]t[h] vj chamb[er]es w[i]t[h] powches In the new murderer vnder the kepe
iiij Serpentynes eche w[i]t[h] iij Chamber' w[i]t[h] powches and chaynes stokkyd j
pyntell' of yron' w[i]t[h] a bolt By the steyer at the new Bulwerk j Fowler of yron'
w[i]t[h] a chamb' and j powche stokkyd By the Arthery vppon' the wall' j Fowler
w[i]t[h] j chamb' vppon' a trestyll' j small' Serpentyne w[i]t[h] iij chamber' vppon' a
Trestyll' j Small s[er]pent' in the kepe w[i]t[h] iij chamb[er]es j Trestyll gon' vppon'
the west syde w[i]t[h] ij chamber' j Fowler vppon' a trestyll' w[i]t[h] iij chamber' In
the Chamb' warde j Serpent' w[i]t[h] iij Chamber' Redy Trestylled j Fowler w[i]t[h]
iij Chamber' Redy stokkyd j Fowler w[i]t[h] iij Chamber' Redy Trestylled [in the
second hand at the bottom of the fol.] Serpent' xj cu' xxxiij camr' de ferr' foulers vj
cu' xiiij camer' ferr' Trestill' gunn' iij cu' viij camer' ferr' [back to original hand] In
the dore by Chamb[er]ward steyer j Bumbardell' of yron' a greate Serpent' w[i]t[h]
ij Chamber' stokkyd Betwyxt the yate how[se] and the Fane Tower vppon' the wall'
ij Fowler' eche w[i]t[h] iij Chamber' w[i]t[h] ther powches trestylled a Serpent' of
yron' w[i]t[h] iij chamber' Trestylled Betwyxt the Fane Tower and the New Towre iij
Fowler' eche w[i]t[h] iij Chamber' Trestylled In The Chapell' warde j Fowler w[i]t[h]
ij chamber' Trestylled j Fowler w[i]t[h] iij Chamber' Trestylled In the New garder'
j great Fowler w[i]t[h] ij chamber' Redy stokkyd Be Fore the wache dore j great
Serpent' w[i]t[h] ij chamber' Redy stokkyd Anoþ[er] Serpent' w[i]t[h] iij chamber'
Redy stokkyd By the Forge j Serpent' w[i]t[h] iij chamber' Redy stokkyd and in the
Forge' j serpent' w[i]t[h] ij chamber' Redy stokkyd By the Tavern' j great Fowler
w[i]t[h] ij Chamber' vppon' a sled j great Fowler w[i]t[h] one chamber vnstokkyd A
pot gon' of yron' [in the second hand] Bomb[ar]d' of Iron j sine camer' S[er]p[en]t'
de ferro vj cu' xv camer' Foulers de ferro x cu' xxij camer' potgonnes de ferr' j [back
to original hand] In the Olde Bulwerk Beneth' j Fowler w[i]t[h] iij chamber' Redy
stokked j Serpent' w[i]t[h] iij chamber' Redy stokkyd j Fowler w[i]t[h] ij chamber'
Redy stokked j greate Fowler w[i]t[h] ij chamber' Redy Stokked j Serpentyne w[i]t[h]
iij chamber' Redy Stokked j lytull' Serpent' w[i]t[h] iij chamber' Redy stokkyd Aboue
[the old bulwark] j long Serpent' w[i]t[h] iij chamber' Redy stokkyd j Fowler w[i]t[h]
ij chamber' Redy stokkyd j great' Fowler w[i]t[h] ij chamber' Redy stokkyd In the

Braye betwene the olde Bulwerk and þe yate howse j Serpentyne w[i]t[h] iij Chamber’
Redy stokkyd j small’ Serpent’ w[i]t[h] a chamb’ stokked j small’ Serpent’ w[i]t[h]
ij chamber’ stokked In the murderer by the bray ij smale Serpent’ eche w[i]t[h] iij
chamber’ stokked iij hake bushes yron’ vj hake gon’ of brasse In the porter’ loge j
greate Fowler w[i]t[h] iiij chamber’ Redy stokkyd w[i]t[h] a powche By the herse
iij Serpent’ w[i]t[h] vij chamber’ Redy stokkyd By the warde howse j Serpentyn’
w[i]t[h] A chamb’ stokkyd Betwene the gat’ j long Serpent’ w[i]t[h] ij chamber’ Redy
stokkyd j Serpentyne w[i]t[h] iij chamber’ Stokkyd iij smale Trestyll’ gonnes eche
w[i]t[h] ij chamber’ [second hand] Foulers vj cu’ xv camer’ Serp[en]t’ de ferro xv
cu’ xxxvij camer’ hakebuss’ de Ere vj Trestillgunn’ iij cu’ vj camer’ de ferr’ [original
hand] In the litull’ Bastort’ [bastion] j long Serpent’ w[i]t[h] iij chamber’ stokkyd j
Fowler w[i]t[h] iij chamber’ stokked j litull’ Serpent’ w[i]t[h] j chamb’ stokkyd In
the Gonpowder Towre v barell’ of gonpowder of olde stuff’ Serpent’ powder d[imid]i
barell’ pois’ Cxxxj lb’ Culueryne powder iij Fyrkyns C iiijxx vij lb’ vij barell’ whereof
one of Bumbard powder and vj of Serpentyne powder pois’ net m[i]l ixC iiijxx ix lb’
In the Store howse Rest’ of yron’ for gonnes ij and j in the Forge Cole powder ij barell’
pavic’ [pavises] xliij viij in tholde bulwerk pavic’ for lopes lj hok’ of yron’ for the same
xlvijti marespik’ [morris pikes] helvyd xlti p[...] [pickaxes] and mattokk’ helved xxxij
Sulphur j Reynesch pype pois’ ij m[i]l lv d[imid]i lb’ Cressett’ vnstaued xij Cressett’
staved xij Tork’ for thayme m[i]l m[i]l CC Bolt lokk’ j Spad’ and shovelys shod xlij
Spad’ and shovelys vnshod xij ledyn’ weight’ DCl lb’ vnslekyd lyme ij pipes Bukk’ to
lade water iij Erthyn pott’ DCCC [second hand] Serpent’ de ferro ij cu’ iiij camer’
Foulers de ferro j cu’ iiij camer’ [original hand] In the New Arthery aboue the Seler
Sper’ olde and new lxiiij Spere hed’ l Quarell’ Federyd w[i]t[h] wode vnhedyd m[i]l
m[i]l C whyte bill’ xiij In the mille howse and vppon’ the wall’ gonstones of diu[er]se
sort’ m[i]l iiijC l in the store howse and be fore the Constabelys dore m[i]l m[i]l CCC
morterstones to stamp in gonpowder ij In the Fane to[we]r Tamponnes of diu[er]se
[sort?] m[i]l l pelett’ of lede m[i]l CCCxxxti pelett’ of yron’ iij wache bell’ iij stele
xxxvj lb’ empty Chest’ for arawes xvj xv Barell’ serpent’ [powder] pois’ iij m[i]l DC
iiijxx ij lb’ [worth] Cliij li’ viij s’ iiij d’ ij barell’ d[imid]i hakebush’ p[owde]r pois’ net
Dxxxiiij lb’ [worth] xxiiij li’ ix s’ vj d’ iij Fyrkyns towche p[owde]r pois’ net C iiijxx vij
lb’ [worth] ix li’ vij s’ v Barell’ Bumbard p[owde]r pois’ net m[i]l CCxxv lb’ [worth]
xlvij li’ x s’ S[um]ma xxiij barell’ j Fyrkyn pois’ v m[i]l DC xxxij lb’ Arg’ [sic] [total]
CCxxxiiij li’ xiiij s’ x d’ The whiche stuff and habiliment’ of warre so valued was
deliuered to my lorde mountJoye by Indenture beryng date the xxth daye of August
A[nn]o p[ri]mo R’ Ric’ tercij [1483]

58

Kew, National Archives, E 404/78/33

Letter from Richard III to the Treasurer and Chamberlains of the Exchequer regarding the Payment of Foreign Merchants, 6 February 1484

we of late haue bought of oon Gillam de Bretayne m[er]chaunt of Bretayne and Lewes de Grymaldes m[er]chant of Jene (Genoa) Clxviij harneys complete for fyve m[ar]k' the harneys so for vs bought at our Towne of Sandewiche by our s[er]uant Robert lilborne whiche herneys were delyu[er]ed into our Towre of London by the handes of our trusty s[er]uant Joh[a]n Stockes the so[m]me of whiche herneys in alle amounteth Dlx li' whereof we haue paied and contented vnto the said Gillam CCxx li' and so restith due vnto the said Lewes de Grymaldes CCCxl li' whereof he hath not p[er]ceiued of vs any paiement [orders payment to be made]

59

Household Accounts of Louis, Duke of Orléans, 26 February 1484–1 September 1485

London, British Library, Additional Charter 2645

[27 February 1484]

En la p[rese]nce de moy guill[aum]e de villebresme sec[re]taire de mons[eigneu]r le duc dorleans et de Milan etc loys de pons escuier s[eigneu]r de moruac conseill[ie]r & chambeilan de mond' s[eigneu]r le duc A confesse auoir Receu de maistre mace guernadon aussi conseill[ie]r & t[re]sorier g[e]n[er]al dud' s[eigneu]r la so[m]me de huit liures cinq solz tourn' pour Restitucion de p[ar]eille so[m]me p[ar] lui baillee p[ar] lordennan' de madame la duchesse po[u]r acheter vng harnois de Juoxte [*sic*] q' bertran du part auoit engaige a bourges lequel lui auoit este prest p[ar] madame la duchesse de laquelle so[m]me de viij l v s t' Il sest tenu pour content & bien paie [etc.] Tesmoing mon seing manuel cy mis [signed] Villebresme

> In the presence of me, Guillaume de Villebresme, secretary to my Lord the Duke of Orléans and of Milan etc., Louis de Pons, squire, Seigneur du Moruac, councillor and chamberlain of my said Lord the Duke confesses to have received from Master Mace Guernadon, also councillor and treasurer-general of the said Lord, the sum of 8 *livres* 5 *sous tournois* for restitution of the same sum paid by him on the order of my Lady the Duchess to buy a jousting harness that Bertran du Part had pledged at Bourges which he had taken by my Lady the Duchess the sum of 8 *l.* 5 *s. t.* He is obliged to be content and well paid [etc.] Witnessed, my signature hereon [signed] Villebresme

London, British Library, Additional Charter 2655

[6 July 1484]

Nous francois de cugnac escuier s' de Joy et Janot de casault escuiers descuierie de mons[eingneu]r le duc dorleans de Milan etc Certiffions a tous a qui este app[er]tient vne Il est deu destienne painnaye La somme de six escuz pour auoir fair dorer les solerez du vne harnois de Jambe de mon s[eigneu]r Et a[u]ss' po[u]r au' fait dorer son arest de sa vielle curasse a la mode despaigne pour lentree du Roy a paris et ce p[ar] m[ar]che fait p[ar] nous a lad' so[m]me de six escuz Tesmoing noz Seings manuelz cy mis [signed] De cugnac [and] Casault

> We, François de Cugnac, squire, Seigneur de Joy, and Janot de Casault, squires of the *écuyerie* of my Lord the Duke of Orléans, Milan etc., certify to all those to whom it may concern that the sum of 6 *écus* is owed to Estienne Painnaye for having gilded the sabatons of my Lord the Duke's legharness. And also, for having gilded the (lance) rest of his old cuirass in the Spanish fashion for the entry of the King into Paris. And this by the mark made by us the said sum of 6 *écus*. Witnessed, our signatures hereon [signed] Du Cugnac [and] Casault

London, British Library, Additional Charter 2657

[4 August 1484]

En la p[rese]nce de moy guill[aum]e callipr[e]s seruete' de mons[eigneu]r le duc dorleans de Milan etc Estienne painnaye A confesse auoir eu Receu de Jaques hurault conseill[ie]r tresorier argentier R[eceueu]r g[e]n[er]al des finan' de mon d' s[eigneu]r La so[m]me de quarant deux deniers t' qui dout luy estoit Cest ass' pour vng demy chanfrin a grant Rondelle glavaille po[u]r la Jouste xxx s t' Pour deux parie de gans senstrez glavaill' quant mon d' s[eigneu]r Jousta contre mess[ir]e glaude [i.e., Claude] de vaudray vij s iiij d t[ournoi]s Pour auoir fait vng viz au grant gardebraz le Jour quant mon d' s[eigneu]r Jousta alencontre dud' mess[ir]e glaude v s t' p[ar]cels mont' ensemb[l]em[en]t la d' so[m]me de xlij s iiij d t[ournoi]s de laq[ue]lle le d' painnaye sest tenu [etc.] Tesmoing mon Seing manuel cy mis [signed] Callipr'

> In the presence of me, Guillaume Callipres, *serviteur* of my Lord the Duke of Orléans, Milan etc., Estienne Painnaye has confessed to have received from Jacques Hurault councillor, treasurer, *argentier*, receiver-general of the finances of my said Lord [the Duke], the sum of 42 *deniers tournois* which were owed him. That being for a demi-shaffron with a large spiked rondel for the joust 30 *s. t.*, for two pairs of spiked (prob. knuckle-gadelings) left[-hand] gauntlets when my said Lord jousted against Sir Claude de Vaudray 8 *s. 4 d. t.*, for having made a vice/screw on the gardebras (i.e., pauldron) on the day that my said Lord jousted against the said Sir Claude 5 *s. t.* altogether the said sum amounting to 42 *s. 3 d. t.* which the said [Estienne] Painnaye is obliged [etc.] Witnessed, my signature hereon [signed] Callipr'

Figure 24. Detail of a painting by the Master of Moulins, French, c. 1500
(Glasgow Museums, 203).

Glasgow, Glasgow Museums, R. L. Scott Library, MS E.1939.65.1174, fol. 8r

[16 September 1484]

Pierre le liassier dit orleans herault darmes de mons[eigneu]r le duc dorleans Confesse
au' eu et Receu de Noble homme Sire Jaques hurault tresorier de mon d' s[eigneu]r
le duc dorl[ean]s la so[m]me de quara[n]te solz tourn[ois] que led' herault a paiee a
vng paintre qui a paint vng escu ouquel estoient pains dun teste les armes de mon d'
s[eigneu]r le duc dorl[ean]s et de laut' teste plus[ieur]s l[ett]res a son deuise po[u]r
le pas de mess[i]re claude de vaudray desquelz quarante solz tourn' led' de liassier se
tient po[u]r bien content & en quicte le d' mons[eigneu]r le duc son d' tresorier &
to[us] aut[re]s promet' &c oblig' &c p[ar] &c [signed] Eprestre [signed] Dautais

> Pierre de Laissier, called Orléans Herald-at-Arms of my Lord the Duke of Orléans,
> confesses to have had and received from the nobleman Sir Jacques Hurault, treasurer
> of my said Lord the Duke of Orléans, the sum of 40 *sous tournois* that the said herald
> had paid to a painter who had painted a shield which was painted with one head of
> the [heraldic] arms of my said Lord the Duke of Orléans and the other head with
> several letters of his device for Sir Claude de Vaudray's *pas* [*d'armes*]. The which 40
> *s. t.* the said [Pierre] de Laissier is obliged as well content and quitclaimed of my
> said lord the duke, his said treasurer, and all others [signed] Eprestre [and] Dautais

London, British Library, Additional Charter 2663

[14 April 1485]

Je francois de giuerlay escuier s[eigneu]r de la Riuiere p[re]mier escuier descuierie de
mon s[eigneu]r de duc dorl[ean]s de milan etc Certiffie a tous a qui Je app[er]tient
Que Jaques hurault conseill[ie]r tresorier argentier et Receueur g[e]n[er]al d[e]s finan'
de mon d' s[eigneu]r A paie & baille contant A phelipot de hutes armurier dem' a
paris La so[m]me de six vingts deux liures huit sols tourn' qui dont luy estoit po[u]r les
p[arce]lles qui se[n]suiue[n]t Cest ass' pour vng grant gardebraz po[u]r f[air]e armes et
po[u]r les Ressors po[u]r f[air]e tumber lagard xviij l x iiij s t' Po[u]r vng armet a deux
bauiers lune grant et lautre petite xviij l x iiij s t' Po[u]r vng viziere p[ar] luy f[aic]t et
vne grant bauie' a f[air]e armes xj l xviij s t' Po[u]r vng viziere a groin de lit part et vne
baui' x l iiij s t' Po[u]r vne viziere en manie' de frontain lxviij s t' Po[u]r au' fait vne
main de fer pour mond' s[eigneu]r xiij l xij s t[ournoi]s po[u]r vne segrete xxxiiij s t'
Po[u]r vne grant tasste lxviij s t pour vne cuirasse sans maille xliij l xiiij s t Po[u]r au'
fait vng vis de cuirasse viij l x s t Po[u]r auoir fait dessus lad' cuirasse vng plastron a
tout la grant lame xiij l xij s t' Tesmoing mon seing manuel cy mis [signed] F guierlay

> I, François de Giuerlay, squire, Seigneur de La Rivière, premier squire of the *écuyerie*
> of my Lord the Duke of Orléans, Milan etc., certify to all whom it may concern
> that Jacques Hurault, councillor, treasurer, *argentier*, and receiver-general of the
> finances of my said Lord [the Duke], has paid and granted content to Philipot de
> Hutes, armourer of Paris, the sum of 122 *livres* 8 *sous tournois* which he was owed

for the following parcels. That is: for a gardebras (pauldron) for feats of arms and for the springs to make the guard (i.e., pauldron reinforce) fall 18 *l.* 4 *s. t.*, for an armet with two bevors one large and the other small 18 *l.* 4 *s. t.*, for a visor made by him and a great bevor for feats of arms 11 *l.* 8 *s. t.*, for a visor with a snout on the weak part and one bevor 10 *l.* 4 *s. t.*, for a visor in the shape of a forehead 68 *s. t.*, for having made a manifer for my said Lord 13 *l.* 12 *s. t.*, for a secret[19] 33 *s. t.*, for a large tasset 68 *s. t.*, for a cuirass without mail 43 *l.* 14 *s. t.*, for having made a vice/ screw for the cuirass 8 *l.* 10 *s. t.*, for having made [to place] upon the said cuirass a plastron (reinforcing breastplate) complete with large lames 13 *l.* 2 *s. t.* Witnessed, my signature hereon [signed] F Guierlay

London, British Library, Additional Charter 2668

[1 September 1485]

En la p[rese]nce de moy Jehan cotreau secrete' de mons[eigneu]r Le duc dorleans de milan etc Janot de casault escuier descuierie de mond' s[eigneu]r A confesse au' eu Receu de Jaques hurault conseill[ie]r tresorier argentier et R[eceueu]r g[e]n[er]al des finan' dicelui s[eigneu]r La so[m]me de dix liures dix solz t' po[u]r le Rembourser de p[ar]eille se' q' la baill' po[u]r cloier le harnois de guerre de mond' s[eigneu]r Tesmoing mon seing manuel cy mis [signed] J Cotereau

> In the presence of me, Jehan Cotereau, secretary of my Lord the Duke of Orléans, Milan etc., Janot de Casault, squire of my said Lord's *écuyerie*, confesses to have received from Jacques Hurault, councillor, treasurer, *argentier*, and receiver-general of the finances of this Lord, the sum of 10 *livres* 10 *sous tournois* for reimbursement of the same granted to him for nailing (i.e., riveting) my said Lord's war harness. Witnessed, my signature hereon [signed] J. Cotereau

Glasgow, Glasgow Museums, R. L. Scott Library, MS E.1939.65.1174, fol. 9r

[24 April 1485]

En la p[rese]nce de moy Jehan cotereau secretaire de mons[eigneu]r le duc dorl[ean]s de milan &c philipot soier a confesse auoir eu et Receu de Jaques hurault conseill[ie]r tresorier argentier et Re[c]e[ueu]r g[e]n[er]al des finances de mond' s[eigneu]r La somme de Cent solz tourn' pour six Roquetz six grappes et six contrarondelles quil a baill' pour le s[er]uice de mond' s[eigneu]r aux Joustes a Rouen Tesmoing mon seing manuel cy mis [signed] J cotereau

> In the presence of me, Jehan Cotereau, secretary of my Lord the Duke of Orléans, Milan etc., Philipot, silk-worker, has confessed to have had and received from Jacques Hurault, councillor, treasurer, *argentier*, and receiver-general of my said

---

[19] An, as yet, unidentified piece of jousting equipment. See R. Moffat, 'The Medieval Tournament: Chivalry, Heraldry and Reality. An Edition and Analysis of Three Fifteenth-Century Tournament Manuscripts' (Ph.D. thesis, University of Leeds, 2010), pp. 38–9.

Lord's finances, the sum of 100 *sous tournois* for six coronals, six grappers, and six 'contrarondelles'[20] granted to him for the use of my said Lord at the jousts at Rouen. Witnessed, my signature hereon [signed] J. Cotereau

Glasgow, Glasgow Museums, R. L. Scott Library, MS E.1939.65.1174, fol. 13r

[2 May 1485]

En la p[rese]nce de moy guillaume callipel secretaire de mons[eigneu]r le duc dorleans de milan &c Raoulin sochon m[ar]chant demourant a Rouen A confesse auoir eu et Receu de Jaques hurault conseill[ie]r tresorier argentier et Receue[u]r g[e]n[er]al des finances de mo[n]d' s[eigneu]r La somme de Cent dix sept liures cinq solz tournois Cest ass[auoi]r iiij^xx iiij l' t' pour xxiiij aulnes damas blanc pris et achapte de luy pour faire vne houssuere au cheual de Jouste de mond' s[eigneu]r et pour faire treize hoquetons a treize gentilz ho[m]mes qui ont s[er]uy mond' s[eigneu]r a la Jouste au pris de lxx s' t' laune xxiij s' iiij d' t' pour vng tiers damas Rouge pour faire vne coeffe a mectre soubz le heaulme de mond' s[eigneu]r xxxij l' j s' viij d' t' pour vne aulne de[m]ie et vng tiers daulne drap dor pour faire deux grans soulez sur la d' housseure de mond[i]t s[eigneu]r au pris de xvij l' x s' t' laune Lesquell' parties mont' ensemblement la d' somme de Cxvij l' v s' t' [signed] Callipel

> In the presence of me, Guillaume Callipel, secretary of my Lord the Duke of Orléans, Milan etc., Raoulin Sochon, merchant of Rouen, has confessed to have had and received from Jacques Hurault, councillor, treasurer, *argentier*, and receiver-general of my said Lord's finances, the sum of 117 *livres* 5 *sous tournois*. That is: 84 *l. t.* for 24 ells of white damask taken and bought from him to make a housing (i.e., trapper) for my said Lord's jousting horse, and for making 13 aketons for 13 gentlemen who served my said Lord at the joust at the cost of 70 *s. t.* an ell, 23 *s. 4 d. t.* for a third [of an ell] of red damask to make a coif to place under my said Lord's helm, 32 *l.* 1 *s.* 8 *d. t.* for a half-ell and one third of an ell of cloth of gold to make two great suns (to be sewn) on my said Lord's said housing worth 17 *l.* 10 *s. t.* the ell, the which parties together amount to the sum of 117 *l.* 5 *s. t.* [signed] Callipel

Glasgow, Glasgow Museums, R. L. Scott Library, MS E.1939.65.1174, fol. 12r

[27 May 1485]

En la p[rese]nce de moy [Guillaume Callipel] secretaire de mons[eigneu]r le duc dorl[ean]s de milan &c estienne pannaye A confesse au' eu & Receu de Jaques hurault conseill' tresorier argentier & R[eceueu]r g[e]n[er]al des finan' de mond' s[eigneu]r la so[m]me de soixante huit solz t' laquelle led' s[eigneu]r luy a ordonnee estre baill'

---

20 An, as yet, unidentified lance fitting. See Moffat, 'Medieval Tournament', pp. 41–5.

po[u]r aller de la ville de Rouen a p[ar]is q[ue]iri le harnois de Jouste de mond' s[eigneu]r les laches & aut[re]s choses po[u]r s[er]uir mond' s[eigneu]r a la Jouste aud' Rouen de laq[ue]lle so[m]me de lxviij s' le d' estienne pannaye sest tenu [etc.] [signed] Callipel

> In the presence of me [Guillaume Callipel], secretary of my Lord the Duke of Orléans, Milan etc., Estienne Pannaye has confessed to have had and received from Jacques Hurault, councillor, treasurer, *argentier*, and receiver-general of my said Lord, the sum of 68 *sous tournois* which the said Lord ordered to be granted to him for going from the town of Rouen to Paris to seek out my said Lord's jousting harness, the straps, and other things to serve my said Lord at the joust at the said [town] of Rouen. The which sum of 68 *s.* the said Estienne Pannay is obliged [etc.] [signed] Callipel

60

Kew, National Archives, E 154/2/4

Inventory of the Goods of William Catesby, City of London, 10 December 1484

> *Unless otherwise stated, all goods are at Warwick's Inn.*

an Armyng doblet of white fustian /blac chalkid\[21] a pair' of Brigandynes of blewe & tawny saten' a pair' of Brigandynes cou[er]ed w[i]t[h] clothe of gold ij salet' garnisshed (i.e., fitted with straps and linings) ij pair' of gusset' ij Aprons of mayle & ij standard' of mayll' (mail collars) a pair' of Bumbard' gardes and canons[22] ij pair' of gauntelet' j Bukler & a Bowe at Woborn' j bukler þat Marche hath xiiij wepon' billes wherof xiij at War' In' & j at Woborn' xiij billes of my lord Ferres [i.e., Ferrers] gift a grete shaft w[i]t[h] a brode Arowe hed

61

Kew, National Archives, E 101/198/13

Inventory of the Castle of Guînes, Calais Pale, 18 February 1485

Gonnes vppon the Wallys j Fowler' w[i]t[h] a Chamb[er] j Fowler' w[i]t[h] a Chamb' j Fowler' w[i]t[h] iij Chamb' j litle s[er]pentyne w[i]t[h] iij chamb' j litle s[er]pent' w[i]t[h] iij chamb' ij Fowler' w[i]t[h] vj chamb' j Fowler' w[i]t[h] iij Ch' j Fowler' w[i]t[h] iij [Chambers] j s[er]pent' w[i]t[h] iij Chamb' j Fowler' w[i]t[h] iij chamb' j

---

21 This has been added in a later hand.
22 Components of plate shoulder- and arm-defences. See the illustrated glossary under *Bumbards*.

Figure 25. Stained glass panel, English, fifteenth century
(Glasgow Museums, Burrell Collection, 45.145).

s[er]pent' w[i]t[h] iij Chamb' j Fowler' w[i]t[h] iij chamb' j Fowler' w[i]t[h] ij Chamb'
j Fowler' w[i]t[h] iij chamb' j s[er]pent' w[i]t[h] iij chamb' j s[er]pent' w[i]t[h] iij
chamb' Benethe in the place j litle s[er]pent' w[i]t[h] iij chamb' j gret' Fowler' w[i]t[h]
ij chamb' j s[er]pent' vnstokkd w[i]t[h] ij chamb' j bombardell' w[i]t[h] ij chamb' j pot
gonne j gret' Fowler' w[i]t[h] a chamb' j long' s[er]pent' w[i]t[h] ij chamb' on' a slede j
bombardell' of yron' w[i]t[h] j chamb[e]r of him selff' [i.e., a bespoke chamber rather
than an interchangeable one] j stone mort[er] for gonne powd' before þe chapell'
Betwene the gat' j long s[er]pentyn' w[i]t[h] ij Chamb' vppon a slede j litle s[er]pent'
w[i]t[h] a Chamb' j litle s[er]pent' w[i]t[h] a Chamb' In the litle basto[u]rt' [bastion] j
s[er]pentyn' w[i]t[h] ij chamb' j litle s[er]pent' w[i]t[h] ij chamb' j Fowler' w[i]t[h] iij
Chamb' In the gret basto[u]rt' j litle s[er]pentyne w[i]t[h] iij Chamb'
In the porters logge j Fowler' w[i]t[h] iij Chamb' Betwene the hers and' þe Gate j litle
s[er]pentyne w[i]t[h] iij Chamb' j litle s[er]pent' w[i]t[h] ij Chamb' j nother w[i]t[h] ij
Chamb' j hakebushe of yron' w[i]t[h] ij chamber' In the litle store howse in þe fawsbray
j Fowler' w[i]t[h] a Chamb' j s[er]pent' w[i]t[h] iij chamb' iij hakebusshez of yron'

w[i]t[h] vj Chamb' In the Fals bray j s[er]pent' w[i]t[h] ij Chamb' j s[er]pent' w[i]t[h] iij Chamb' In thold bulwerk j Fowler' w[i]t[h] iij chamb' j litle s[er]pent' w[i]t[h] iij chamb' j Fowler' w[i]t[h] ij chamb' j Fowler' w[i]t[h] ij chamb' j s[er]pent' w[i]t[h] iij Chamb' j nother' s[er]pent' w[i]t[h] iij chamb' j long s[er]pent' w[i]t[h] iij chamb' j Fowler' w[i]t[h] ij Chamb' j Fowler' w[i]t[h] ij Chamb' In the Kepe j litle fowler' w[i]t[h] iij chamb' In the new blok howse j s[er]pent' w[i]t[h] iij chamb' j s[er]pent' w[i]t[h] iij Chamb' j nother' w[i]t[h] iij Chamb' j other' w[i]t[h] iij chamb' In the new bulwark j s[er]pent' w[i]t[h] iij Chamb' j s[er]pent' w[i]t[h] iij Chamb' j s[er]pent' w[i]t[h] ij Chamb' j Fowler' w[i]t[h] ij Chamb' j long s[er]pent' w[i]t[h] iij chamb' j Trestill' gonne w[i]t[h] iij chamb' j other trestle gonne w[i]t[h] iij chamb' brokyn' j stone mort' for gonne powd' S[um]ma of the s[er]pentinez xxxiijti S[um]ma of the Fowler' xxiijti S[um]ma of þe Bombardell' ij And j potte gon' all' thyes of yron' S[um]ma [of] all' the Chamb[er]es Clvj hande gonnes xxxij w[i]t[h] their' stamp[er]s of yron' hackebusshe of yron' iiij j hakebusshe w[i]t[h] a chamb' of yron' vj hakebusshez of brasse S[um]ma to[ta]l of all' the gonnes gret and smalle Ciiij Clvti Chambers Ou[er] the gate howse now in [the] new Artery [artillery] iiijxx iiij of new ledyn' mall' [lead mallets] iiijxx xiij old ledyn' mall' xvij Crosbowys of stele tillerd [i.e., with stocks] ij stele bowys vntillerd xiij Crosbowys of wode tillerd xviij wynlac' [windlass] cordyd ij wynlac' w[i]t[h]out hok' j Crosbow of wode vntillerd iij mowld' of brasse xix Cokers [poss. covers] for þe hande gonnes j flayle of yron' m[i]l m[i]l CCC Quarell' hedyd m[i]l m[i]l Quarell' new vnhedyd in ij Chest' j barrel' and x lb' of Trenchefile [a type of crossbow cord] gude iiij lb' of Trenchefyle Fawty m[i]l m[i]l C d[imid]i quarell' vnhedid lxvij sperys hedyd iij sperys vnhedid ix gross' d[imid]i of bowstryng' gude CC vij long bowys gode xviij brokyn' bowys Fawty vjC xlijij shevys of Arowys In the old Artery [artillery] v Tyllers for Crosbowys xj m[i]l DC Caltrappys viij m[i]l ixC of quarell' hed' In the gonne powd' To[we]r xxij barell' and j Ferkyn' of gonne powd' pois' [weighing] v m[i]l iijC lb' j barell' of Sulphur pois' CCl lb' half a ferkyn' of gonne powd' in the gonn' To[we]r pois' xxx [lb'] In the old store howse xxxvj marespik' [morris pikes] xlvti pycaxes and mattok' helvid [i.e., with handles] xl pycosses and mattokk' vnhelvid xlvij hok' for lopys ij barell' for Cole powd' j Reynysshe pipe for sulphur and a gret Tubbe poiss' m[i]l m[i]l lv lb' d[imid]i lx shovill' and spad' shod j gret pan' for gonne powd' xlj pavus' [pavises] for the feld gonne stonys in the store' ho[use] & before the Constable dore m[i]l m[i]l m[i]l DCC xxti pelett' of lede DCC & d[imid]i pelett' of yron' iij Tamponnys m[i]l m[i]l m[i]l CC In the Forge vj fyre hok' of yron' for fire ij smale hok' vnstokkyd j peyr of belowys ij Andeveld' j bycorne vij ham[er]s of diu[er]s sort' vj peyr of Tong' gret and small' j peyr of Tong' w[i]t[h] the filing' stok' for a lokyer [locksmith] j water' Trowgh' [On] the vijth daye of June the ijde yere of Kyng' Richard the iijde The copie of this boke was deliu[er]ed vnto s[i]r Jamys Tyrell' Knyght lieutenant of the Castell' of Guy[...] by me William Rosse vitteler of Cales &c' Tho [sic] beyng present Adrian Wh[...] Comptroller' of Cales forseid [On] the last day of August A[nn]o do[mi]ni m[i]l CCCC lxxxv [...] vnto Richard pile In the name of S[i]r Jamys Tyrell' lieutenant of the Castell' of Guysnes j barell' of salt petre poiss' net CC xiiij lb' It' a Chald' of luk' Cole [Luik/Liège] deliu[er]ed the last day of Feu[e]r' A[nn]o iijo h' vijme Vnto Thom[a]s Rasshe gonn[er] for and in the name of sir Jamys Tyrell' Knyght lieut' of the Castell' of guysnes j gret serpentine of brasse redy cartyd and an axeltre & ij shod whelys w[i]t[h] a lymon [cartshaft] to the same val' xxx li' St' The said gonne to be redy comyng at my lord' plesure

62

Kew National Archives, E 101/198/13

Inventory of the Castle of Hames, Calais Pale, 17 July 1485, and Record of New Equipment provided 20 August–10 September 1485

betwene the To[we]r of seint gartrude and the Chapell' j serpentine w[i]t[h] ij Chamber' which' must be new stokkyd ij Serpentines eche w[i]t[h] ij Chamber' vppon' ij c[...] [prob. carts] j Fowler w[i]t[h] ij Chamb' which' must be new stokkyd vppon the wardrobe To[we]r j s[er]pentine w[i]t[h] ij Chamb' which' must be new stokkyd and new Trestillid vnder the mille To[we]r

ij smale Fowlers eche w[i]t[h] ij Chamber' ou[er] the gate howse ij smale Fowlers eche w[i]t[h] ij Chamb' to be new stokkyd In the East murdrer' of þe basto[u]rt [i.e., bastion] ij smale Folwers eche w[i]t[h] ij Chamb' In the west murdrer' of the basto[u]rt j smale Fowler w[i]t[h] iiij Chamb' j serpentine of yron' w[i]t[h] ij Chamb' which must be new stokkyd Ou[er] the same murderer' j s[er]pentine of brasse w[i]t[h] a Chamb' which' must be new stokkyd and trestillid In the murdrer' before the Sluse j smale Fowler w[i]t[h] ij Chamb' In the South murdrer' j smale Fowler w[i]t[h] v Chamb' A yenst the Cawsy j gret Serpentine w[i]t[h] ij Chamber' which lakkyth a powche before the storehowse j serpentine of yron' w[i]t[h] iiij Chamb' j pot gonne of brasse In the store howse

j gret Fowler w[i]t[h] ij Chambers hake gonnes of brasse xij wherof som' must be new stokkid and som' be crokid v hake gonnes of yron' w[i]t[h] v stamp[er]s wherof j brokyn' j smale s[er]pentine of brasse w[i]t[h] a Chamb' vj hand gonnes of brasse xij long bowys lxvij shef' of Arowys iiij Crosbowys of wode wherof j brokyn' and the Remanent vnstrynged j barell' & d[imid]i of s[er]pentine powd' and d[imid]i barell' of bombard' powd' iiij half barell' bounde w[i]t[h] yron' to bere gonne powd' yn' vij sperys iiij Cressett' of yron' gonne stonys of diu[er]s sort' m[i]l CCC lx pelett' of lede xij spad' & shovill' j Andveld' j bycorne & a peyr' of belowys In the Countyng howse j barell' and j Tubbe w[i]t[h] brymstone <j barell' w[i]t[h] Sulphur'> [scored out] <Quarell' m[i]l CC p[er] vet' Rem' [old remain]> <Sperys vnhedded vij p[er] vet' Rem'> pavises iiij p[er] vet' Rem' <lxxviij long bowes> <iij sheves of arowes p[er] vet' Rem'> Caltrappes of iron' m[i]l ixC lxiiij j chest' w[i]t[h] CCCxxxviij quarell' hed' quarell' hedes vnfed[er]d' iiij m[i]l CCC <Tampons for gonnys m[i]l C>

Newe stuffe deliu[er]ed vnto S[ir] Thomas a wortley knyght' lieutenant of the Castell' of hammes the xxv day of August' iiijxx long bowys iiijxx shevys of Arowys iiij gross' of bowstring' iij hakbusshes of brasse j yron' ladill' to cast pelett' vj hakebusshes of yron' xl new ledyn' mallys xxxti old ledyn' mallys j pece of lede pois' DCl lb' for pelett' deliu[er]ed the xxt[h] day of August A grete Fowler new bounden w[i]t[h] her chamb' xx Sperys hedyd j barell' of bombardine powd' pois' net CC lb' ij barell' of s[er]pentine powder pois' net CCCC lb' j Ferkyn' of hakbusshe powd' pois' net xxxvj lb' deliu[er]ed to henry Wyot the xxvj day of August vj Crosbowys of stele w[i]t[h] their Tyllers vj wynlac' to theym' w[i]t[h] their cord' deliu[er]ed to William Becham' s[er]uant [of] S[ir] Thomas a wortley the xxxti day of August xijC of Tamponnys of diu[er]s sort'

Receyvid from hammys the ix day of Septemb[e]r j Crosbow of stele brokyn' j Crosbow of stele w[i]t[h] a tyller brokyn The xth day of Septemb[e]r deliu[er]ed for the seid Crosbowys ij other Crosbowys of stele

63

New York, Pierpont Morgan Library, MS M775, fol. 3r–fol. 4v and fol. 122v–fol. 123r

Two Extracts from a MS made for Sir John Astley, before 1486

Sir John performed feats of arms before European royalty in the third and fourth decades of the century and was a successful soldier who was created Knight of the Garter in 1461. He died in 1486.

To crie a Justus [sic] of Pees

We herrowdys of Armis beryng scheldis of deuijs [i.e., heraldic devices] here we yeue in knowlache vn to all' Gentill' men of name and of armus [sic, i.e., of repute in feats of arms] That ther ben vj Gentilmen of name & of armus that for the gret desire and worschippe that the sayde vj Gentilmen hath taken vp pon them to be þe iij day of May nex comyng be fore þe hy & myghtty redowttyd ladys & Gentyll' wymmen in thys hey & most honorabull' Court And in theyre p[re]sens þe sayde vj Gentilmen there to a pere at ix of þe belle be fore noone and to Juste a yens all' comers w[i]t[h] oute on þe sayd day vn to vj of þe belle at after noon And then þe a vise of þe sayde ladys & Gentill' wymmen to yeue vn to þe best Juster w[i]t[h] oute A Diamunde of xl li' And vn to the nexte þe best Just' a rube of xx li' And vn to þe thyrde well' Just' a sausser of x li' And on þe sayde day there beyng offecers of armis schuyng thayre mesure of thayre speris garnyst That ys Cornall' wamplate & grapers all' of a syse that the schall' Juste w[i]t[h] and that þe sayde Comers may take þe lengthe of þe sayde speris w[i]t[h] the a vise of þe sayde offecers of armys that schall' be in defferant vn to all' parteys on þe sayde day

The comyng in to the felde

The vj Gentilmen most com in to þe felde vn helmyd and theyre helm' borne be fore tham & thayre seruant' on horsbake beryng eyther of tham a spere garniste þ[a]t is the sayde vj speris þe wheche þe sayde seruantis schall' ride be fore them in to þe felde & as þe sayde vj Gentilmen ben com be fore þe ladyys & Gentilwi[m]me' Then schall' be sent an harawde of arm' up vn to the ladys & Gentill' wummen sayyng in this wise Hey & myghtti redowtyd & ryght worschypfull' ladys & Gentylwymmen these vj Gentill' men ben come in to yowre presens and reco[m]maundit all' vn to yowr goode grace in as lowli wyse as they can be sechyng yow for to gyffe vn to iij the best Justers w[i]t[h] owte a Diamownd & a Rube & a sausser vn to them that þe thenk best can deserue hit

Thenne this message is doon then þe iij Gentill' men goyth vn to þe tellws [*sic*, i.e., tilt] and do on theyr helm' And when the harrawdis cri a lostell' a lostell' then schall' all' þe vj Gentill men w[i]t[h] in vn helme them be fore the sayde ladyys and make theyre abeisans and go hom vn to ther loggyng' & chaunge them

Abiliment for the Just' of the pees

A helme well' stuffyd w[i]t[h] a Crest of hys de vijs [heraldic device] A peyre of platus [*sic*, i.e., pair of plates] and xxx Vyders A hanscement for the Bode w[i][t]h sleuis A botton w[i]t[h] a tresse in þe platis A schelde couerid w[i]t[h] his deuijs A Rerebrace w[i]t[h] a rolle of ledyr well stuffid A maynfere with a ring A rerebrasce a moton [i.e., polder-mitton] A vambrase and a gaynpayne & ij brickett'

And ij dosyn tress' and vj vamplat' And xij Grapers and xij Cornallis & xl Speris And a Armerer w[i]t[h] a hamor and pynsons And naylys w[i]t[h] a byckorne

A Goode Cowrscer and row schode w[i]t[h] a softe bytte and a gret halter for þe rayne of the brydyll' A Sadyll' well stuffud and a peyre of Jambus [*sic*, poss. jambers] and iij dowbyll' Gyrthis w[i]t[h] dowbill' bokollus and a dowbill' sengull' w[i]t[h] dowbill' bokullus and a rayne of ledir hungre teyyd from the horse hede vn to the gyrthys be twen þe forther bowse [i.e., boss] of the horsce for reuassyng [i.e., to prevent being forced back on impact with an opponent's lance] A Rennyng paytrell' A Croper of leder hongre A Trappar for the Courser And ij seruantis on horsebake well' be sayne And vj seruantis on fote all' in a sute

How a man schall' be armyd at his ese when he schal fighte on foote

He schal haue noo schirte up on him but a dowblete of Fustean lynyd with satene cutte full' of hoolis the dowblete muste by strongeli bou[n]de' there the poyntis muste be sette aboute the greet of the arme and the b ste [*sic*] before and behynde and the gussetis of mayle muste be sowid vn to the dowbelet in the bought [*sic*] of the arme and vndir the arme the armynge poyntis muste by made of fyne twyne suche as men make stryngis for crossebowes and they muste be trussid small' and poyntid as poyntis Also they muste be wexid with cordeweneris coode and than they woll'

Figure 26. Miniature from Sir John Astley's MS, English, before 1486
(New York, Pierpont Morgan Library, MS M775, fol. 122v).

neythir recche nor breke Also a payr' hosyn' of stamyn sengill' [i.e., a single layer of woven cloth] and a peyre of shorte bulwerkis of thynne blanket to put aboute his kneys for chawfynge of his lighernes [sic] Also a payre of shone of thikke cordewene and they muste be frette with smal whipcorde thre knottis vp on a corde and thre coordis muste be faste sowid vn to the hele of the shoo and fyne cordis in the myddill' of the soole of the same shoo and that ther be betwene the frettis of the heele and the frettis of the myddill' of the shoo the space of thre fyngris

Firste ye muste sette on Sabatones and tye [t]hem vp on the shoo with smale poyntis that wol [not] brake And then griffus & then Quisses & þe[n] the breche of mayle And the[n] tonletis And the brest And þe vambras and þe[n] rerebras and then glouys And then hange his daggere vpon his right side And then his shorte swerde vpon the lyfte side in a rounde rynge all' nakid to pulle it oute lightli And then putte his [heraldic] cote [armour] vpon his bak And then his basinet py[n]nid vp on two gret staplis before the breste with a dowbill' bukill' behynde vp on the bak for to make the basinet sitte iuste And then his longe swerde in his hande And then his pensill' (pennant) in his hande peyntid of seynt George or of oure lady to blesse him with as he goeth towarde the felde and in the felde

The day that the Pelaunt and the defendaunt shall' fighte what they shal haue w[i]t[h] [t]hem in to the felde

[A] tente muste by pight [*sic*] in the felde Also a cheyre a basyn' vj loues of breed ij galones of wyne a messe (food course) of mete flesshe or fisshe a borde and a peyre of trestelis to sette his mete and drynke on a borde clothe a knyf for to kutte his mete a cuppe to drynke of a glas with a drynke made Also a dosen tresses of armynge poyntis Also an hamyr and pynsones and a bicorne Also smale nayles a dosen' Also a longe swerde shorte swerde and dagger Also a kerchif to hele the viser of his basinet Also a pensill' to bere in his hande of his avowrye

64

Kew, National Archives, E 101/198/13

Inventory of Calais Castle, 30 March 1486

in the Bastewarte [bastion] j Rede [i.e., red] Serpentyne of yron' chamberyd of hym selff' [i.e., a bespoke chamber rather than an interchangeable one] j Serpentyne of yron' w[i]t[h] ij chamber' iiij Serptenynes of Brasse w[i]t[h]owte chamber' A Fowler of brasse w[i]t[h] iij chamber' of brasse vppon the toppe of the dongeon' j Sepentyne of Brasse chamberyd of hym selff' In the watche howse j Fowler of yron' w[i]t[h] j chamb' j Serpentyne of yron' w[i]t[h] ij chamb' Vnder the watche howse j Septenyne of yron' w[i]t[h] ij chamber' In the p[ri]son howse j Fowler of Brasse w[i]t[h] ij chamber' of brasse In the ende of the Norsery j Fowler of yron' w[i]t[h] on' chamb' In the chapell' towre j Serpentyne of yron' w[i]t[h] ij chamber' gaffull' of yron' in diu[er]s' plac' xiiij [at the bottom of the fol. in a different hand] Pagin' [i.e., the sum of this page] Serpent' de ferro v Camer' de ferr' p[ro] eisde' viij Serpent' de Ere v Foulers de Ere ij Camer' Ere p[ro] eisde' v Fowlers de ferro ij Camer' pro eisd' ij Gaffull' de ferr' p[ro] dict' gunnis xiiij [back to original hand] In the Brut Towre j Serpentyne of yron' w[i]t[h] ij chamber' Vnderneth' the same j Serpentyne of yron' w[i]t[h] ij chamber' Gonpowder j barell' pois' [weighing] CC lb' Gonstones of diu[er]se sort' Clvijti pelett' of lede of diu[er]se sort' Clij Tamponnes CCxxx ladyng ladelys iij v[n]d' [Lat. *unde*: of which] ij brokyn In the Armery hake Gonnes of Brasse vj Crosbowes of Stele viij whereof j brokyn wyndelasses iiij Gyrdelys to bend' w[i]t[h] ij pelett' of lede for hake Gonnes Cxxxij In the hartery [*sic*, i.e., Artillery] Long bowes xlix shevys of harowes Clxxij quarrel' m[i]l DCC mall' of lede [lead mallets] iiijxx xiij wherof iiij brokyn' Spere' hedyd xx bowe stryng' j gross' & d[imid]i [half] [at the bottom of the fol. in a different hand] Pagin' Serpent de ferro ij Camer' pro eisdem iiij Pulu[er]e gunnor[um] j barell' CC lb' Lapid' gunnor[um] Clvij Pellett' de pl[u]mbo Clij & xij pro hakebuss' pond' Cxx [lb'] Tampons CCxxx Lading ladill' iij vn' ij def[r]act' Hakgunn' de ere vj Balist' de calibe viij vn' j defract' wyndlac' iiij Bending girdall' ij

Arc' manual' xlix Garb' sag' Clxxij Quarell' m[i]l CCC Mall' de plu[m]bo iiijxx xiij vn' iiij def[r]act' Capit' lanc' xx Cord' pro Arc' manual' j g[ro]ss' d[imid]i

65

Now-Lost Original Document from the Archives municipales de Douai, printed in E. J. Soil de Moriamé, 'Armes et armuriers tournaisiens. Heaumiers, haubregonneurs, forbisseurs, couteliers. Contribution à l'histoire des métiers d'art et à l'histoire militaire de Tournai de XIIIe au XVIIIe siècle', *Bulletin de l'Académie royale d'archéologie de Belgique*, unnumbered (1913), pp. 36–154 (at p. 107)

Will of Bauduin du Pryez, Douai, 1487

aux compaignons archiers dont je suiz connestable ma journade perlisié, Jean de le motte dit Vertjus me [*sic*] cotte d'achier et une secrette d'achier et avec ce me cotte renardière

> to the Company of Archers of which I was *connétable* my *journade* (body garment) decorated with pearls, Jean de le Motte, called 'Vertjus', a coat of steel (mail) and one steel (mail) secret (a mail shirt borne beneath civilian clothing) and with this my *cotte renardière* (fox-hunters' coat)

66

Kew, National Archives, E 101/198/13

Inventory of the Town of Calais and Castle of Guînes, Calais Pale, 22 August 1487

Tamponn' p[ro] gonn' ix m[i]l CCC iiijxx xvij Cures complet' de millen' iiij Salett' cu' visores xxj bicokett' de millen' xxix Salett' de diu[er]s' sort' xxxiij Standard' de maill' lxxij Brigandin' viij pair' Billett' [*sic*] D lanc' sine capit' Clxvj pulu[er]e Sulphur' viu' iiijxx xiij lb' Sulphur' viu' xiiij m[i]l CC xlv lb'pulu[er]e Carbon' de linde ijb[us] [*sic*] pulu[er]e carbon' saliciu' CCCxxx lb' Arcub[us] manual' iijC lxij garb' sagitt' m[i]l CC xxxvj Balist' iij Balist' de Calib' xix dowble winch' lxxiij pulleis de Ere p[ro] winch' balist' tendend' xxij Cer' de ferr' calib' mixt' p[ro] tellur' balist' viij dowble winch' cord' iiijxx x par' Stiroppes de Ferr' p[ro] balist' vj Capit' quarell' p[ro] balist' xiiij m[i]l DCCCC quarell' p[ro] balist' pennat' cu' capit' vj m[i]l DC iiijxx vj Quarell' p[ro] balist' pennat' de ligno sine Capit' xv m[i]l Clxx quarell' p[ro]

balist' pennat' de lign' cum capit' viij m[i]l DCCCClxxij plat' de Ferr' et Calib' mixt'
p[ro] Brigandin' Dviij marespik' cu' capit' de Ferr' vj Godendaughes cu' pik' de Ferr'
ix Shaft' de ligno p[ro] marespik' Cxxvj Shaft' de lign' de asshe p[ro] bill' & Axes lxxij
Shaft' de lign' de hasill' xxiiij hott' xx Rest' de Ferr' p[ro] gonn' iiij martell' de Ferr'
j maundrell' de Ferr' ij Crowes de Ferr' iiij Oll' luteis p[ro] cals' Imponend' CCCl
Caltrappes de Ferr' m[i]l m[i]l m[i]l DCCCl dowble winch' p[ro] balist' tendend' j
Filo p[ro] cord' balist' voc' trenchefile CCCxxxv lb' pavic' depict' iij pavic' long' xxx
Shingl' CCCCxij morter' de Ere j cu' ijb[u]s pestell' de Ferr' Stokk' long' ligat' cu'
ferr' j par' picossis j mattokk' vj Stater' de Ferr' cu' ijb[us] balanc' j cu' ix pond' de
plumb' quol[ibe]t pond' iiijxx x lb' Stater' p[ar]u' de Ferr' cu' ijb[us] balanc' j Tong'
de Ferr' vj vn' v p[ro] Fabr' Aunderon' de Ferr' v vn' iij p[ro] plumbat' mall' de plumb'
ligat' cu' daggar' [sic, underlined] Ferr' sine daggar' CCxxv mall' de plumb' ligat' cu'
Ferr' m[i]l CClj Capit' de plumb' p[ro] mall' xlv pynnes de Ferr' p[ro] gonn' ij vn' j
pond' CCCxl lb' et j pond' Cxl lb' Axeltreys de Ferr' p[ro] gun' ij vn' j pond' DCC
iiijxx xj lb' & j pond' Cxx lb' Camer' de Ferr' p[ro] gonn' ij pond' iiijxx viij lb' Camer'
de Ferr' p[ro] gonn' de diu[er]s' sort' ij pond' Int' se Ciiij lb' Cistern' de plumb' iiij
Furnac' vj vn' j defract' Camer' gross' de Ferr' p[ro] gonn' j Aundfeld' j Scal' long' voc'
Standard' j pulleis de Ere xvj vn' x defract' ponderant' Inter se Cl lb' Campan' p[ro]
vigil' vj vn' ij defract' Squyrt' de laton' ix molendin' ventritic' iiij

 lapid' voc' Grineston j patell' de Ere gross' iij patell' p[ro] effut' plumb' j Tubb'
gross' p[ro] taratantarizac' sal[is]pet' sulphur' viu' & carb' saliciu' j morter' stones
gross' ad Infradend' sal[is]petr' sulphur' viu' & Carbon' saliciu' j Trowghes de ligno
ad infragend' sal[is]petr' sulphur' viu' & carb' saliciu' j magn' Capit' de Ra[m]mes
iij Trokill' p[ro] cariag' gonn' ligat' cum ferr' j cu' ijb[us] Rot' pip' vac' iij gonn' de
Ferr' p[ro] lapid' Cj vn' j vocat' seint powle j voc' le Crowne & iiij gross' Fowlers
quol[ibe]t cu' duab[us] Camer' & j Fowler' cu' ijb[us] Camer' pond' Inter se Cxij lb'
xj quol[ibe]t cu' duab[us] Camer' liiij quol[ibe]t cum duab[us] Camer' vn' xiiij vocat'
Fowler' empt' in anno xijo pond' Inter se v m[i]l DCC vij lb' xiij cum vna Camer'
ac xj sine Camer' ac j pond' iii[i]l CCC xxiiij lb' similir' empt' in A[nn]o xijo et iiij
gonn' gross' de Ferr' p[ro] lapid' vn' j defract' et <j> pond' m[i]l DCCCC xxxiiij lb'
gonn' de Ferr' p[ro] lapid' vocat' glowcestr' gross' Fowler' j cu' ijb[us] Camer' gonn'
long' de Ferr' vocat' serpentines vj vn' iij cu' duabus Camer' & j cu' duab[us] Camber'
pond' Inter se DCCClviij lb' j cum vn' Camer' pond' Dxxix lb' ac j pond' CCxxx lb'
gonn' de Ferr' p[ro] pelett' iij gonn' de Ferr' voc' Culu[er]ynes v gonn' de Ferr' voc'
handgonnes xxv vn' vj de Reman' Compot' Joh[ann]is Thirske gonn' de Ferr' voc'
hake gonn' xv gonn' de Ere p[ro] lapid' xj vn' ij quol[ibe]t cum duab[us] Camer' ij vn'
j serpentine poderan' Inter se DCC lb' j cu' vn' Camer' et j vocat' dame Anable gonn'
de Ere p[ro] pelett' j gonn' de Er' voc' handgon' lxxiijj vn' xij de Reman' Compot'
Joh[ann]is Thirske lapid' gonn' maior[um] assise xvj

 lapid' gonn' de diu[er]s' sort' xvj m[i]l CCxix Cist' long' p[ro] Arc' manual' iiij
Glevys de Ferr' voc' bill' xxiiij Carbon' de lynde iij quart' iiijb[us] Salett' vocat' Skull'
ij Batell' Axes xv Targ' coop[er]t' cu' correo vij molendin' ad molendinand' Sulphur'
Sal[is]petr' et al' stuffur' p[ro] pulu[er]e gonn' j Bolis de Ferr' voc' gonnestones de

Ferr' Cvj Instrument' de Ferr' voc' le vyce j Swepys cu' ix stamper' et ix capit' p[ro] eids[e]m n[u]l' Ferr' veter' C lb'

the Castell' of Guysnes

Gonn' de Ferr' p[ro] lapid' voc' Fowler' de diu[er]s' sort' xij vn' j cu' duab[us] Camer' pond' CC xxiij lb' j cu' duab[us] Camer' pond' CCCxl lb' j cu' vna Camer' pond' CCCxxxvj lb' j cu' trib[us] Camer' pond' Dlx lb' & j cu' duab[us] Camer' pond' CCCCl lb' j cu' trib[us] Camer' pond' CCCClx lb' j cu' trib[us] Camer' pond' CCCCx lb' j cu' trib[us] Camer' pond' C iiijxx lb' j cu' trib[us] Camer' pond' m[i]l DC lb' j cu' duab[us] Camer' pond' m[i]l DCCCC lb' j cu' duab[us] Camer' pond' DC lb' j cu' duab[us] Camer' pond' m[i]l C lb' ac j cu' duab[us] Camer' pond' m[i]l m[i]l m[i]l C lb' gonn' de Ferr' voc' potgonn' j pond' m[i]l m[i]l lb' Camer' de Ferr' p[ro] vn' Fowler' de staur' Reg' iij pond' cu' ligat' dict' Fowler' CCxlviij lb' huiusmodi Camer' de Ferr' p[ro] vn' Fowler' de staur' R' j pond' cu' ligat' dict' Fowler' ac Rep[ar]ac' duar[um] Camer' de staur' R' p[ro] eod[e]m Fowler' CCxlij lb' hui[us]mo' Camer' de Ferr' p[ro] vn' Fowler' de staur' R' vj pond' cu' ligat' dict' Fowler' CCCCiiij lb' hui[us]modi Camer' de Ferr' p[ro] vn' Fowler' de staur' R' iiij pond' cu' ligat' dict' Fowler' C iiijxx xj lb' Ferr' op[er]at' tam sup[er] ligat' et fortificat' ix Camer' p[er]tin' sept' Fowler' de staur' R' vna cum ligat' eor[un]d[e]m pond' In toto m[i]l DClxxviij lb' Camer' fact' p[ro] duab[us] tristell' gonnes de staur' R' iij pond' cum ligat' dict' gonn' C iiijxx xiiij lb' gonn' de Ferr' in trib[us] Carect' ix cu' xxvj Camer' eisd[e]m p[er]tin' pond' cu' ligat' dict' gonn' m[i]l m[i]l CCCC lb' Rot' ligat' cum Ferr' p[er]tin' eisd[e]m trib[us] carect' vj pond' cu' ligat' eor[un]d[e]m DC lb' gonn' de Ferr' voc' serpentinez xij vn' j cu' iijb[us] Camer' pond' cu' ligat' eiusd[e]m CC iiijxx iij lb' j cu' trib[us] […] hui[us]modi Camer' de Ferr' p[ro] vn' fowler' de staur' R' iij pond' cu' ligat' dict' Fowler' Clxxix lb' Camer' pond' cu' ligat' eiusd[e]m CCCxxv lb' ij cu' vj camer' pond' CCC iiijxx v lb' ij cu' vj Camer' pond' CC lb' j cu' vn' Camer' pond' CC iiijxx lb' j cu' trib[us] Camer' pond' m[i]l m[i]l m[i]l m[i]l CC lb' j cu' duab[us] Camer' pond' m[i]l m[i]l C lb' j cu' duab[us] Camer' pond' m[i]l CCCC lb' j cu' trib[us] Camer' pond' DCCl lb' ac j cu' duab[us] Camer' pond' DCCl lb' gonn' de Ferr' vocat' handgonn' xxxij cu' lez stopping yronz & powchez pro eisd[e]m wynchez p[ro] balist' tendend' xxvij Camer' de Ferr' p[ro] vn' Serpentin' de staur' R' j pond' cu' ligat' eiusd[e]m Cxij lb' gonn' de Ferr' voc' soket Culu[er]ynez vj Balist' de Calibe xxxvj Balist' xx Quarell' p[ro] balist' cum capit' de diu[er]s' sort' m[i]l m[i]l m[i]l DCCCC capit' quarell' p[ro] balist' viij m[i]l DCCCC Caltrappes de Ferr' de diu[er]s' sort' xij m[i]l lapid' gonn' p[ro] magn' Fowler' CC iiijxx xij lapid' gonn' p[ro] p[ar]u' Fowler' m[i]l Cxij picossijs de Ferr' de diu[er]s' sort' absq[ue] helvys x Cressett' de Ferr' xxiiij vn' xij cu' shaft' et xij sine shaft' Tork' in eisd[e]m comburend' m[i]l m[i]l CC Morter' marmor' p[ro] pulu[er]e gonn' Imbi triturand' j magn' Gonn' de Ferr' p[ro] carect' vj cu' xxiij camer' pond' m[i]l DC lb' Gonn' de Ferr' voc' Culu[er]ynes ij vn' j cu' camer' et j sine Camer' mold' de Ere p[ro] pelett' Imbi Fabricand' iij lapid' marmor' p[ro] lez mag' Serpentin' iiijxx xix lapid' marmor' p[ro] lez p[ar]u' s[er]pent' CC pelett' de Ferr' p[ro] lez magn' s[er]pentin' ij pond' xx lb'

Reman' stuari de p[ro]mi' Wil[he]lmi Rosse cu' CClxxiij li' x s' st' Arc' manual'
v Garb' Sagitt' pennat' de swan' iij Singl' p[ro] Sagitt' ix duod' Balist' xxix Balist'
de Calibe iiijxx xvij dowble winch' p[ro] balist' tendend' liij par' Cord' p[ro] Arc'
manual' xx gross' Quarell' p[ro] balist' pennat' de ligno sine Capit' xxxvij m[i]l
molendin' p[ro] fact' pulu[er]is gonn' j lanc' voc' demy launcez sine capit' Cxx lanc'
fact' de Renysshe clist' sine capit' n[u]l' Stak' p[ro] Campo cu' capit' de ferr' m[i]l
D Bokett' de Correo l Gonn' long' de Ferr' voc' serpentinez j cu' vn' Camer' pond'
Inter se m[i]l DCCC lb' gonn' de Ere voc' serpent' pond' Inter se vj m[i]l CC xxj
lb' xviij Gonn' de Ere voc' hake gonnez pond' Inter se CCC iiijxx xiiij lb' xvj Gonn'
de Ere voc' hake gonn' cu' Saresonnez visag' viij Carect' p[ro] p[re]dict' Serpent' xv
Rot' ligat' cu' Ferr' p[ro] cariag' ordinac' xxx par' lyme' p[ro] p[re]dict' Carect' lvj
pulu[er]e gonn' CCCC iiijxx xiij lb' pavic' fact' de Popler' CCC Gonn' de Ferr' voc'
Fowlers pond' Inter se m[i]l m[i]l xij lb' viij Capit' de Ferr' p[ro] quarell' xix m[i]l
demy barell' ligat' cu' ferr' xij Firkyns ligat' cu' Ferr' xx Filo p[ro] Cord' balist' voc'
trenchefile CC lb' Plumbo p[ro] pelett' iij Fader' Capit p[ro] Sagitt' viij m[i]l Curesse
complete de millen' n[u]l' Caltrappes de Ferr' xxiiij m[i]l Tamponn' p[ro] gonn' iiij
m[i]l Crek' p[ro] balist' tendend' xx Cokers p[ro] hand gonnez xx Sulphur viu' m[i]l
m[i]l m[i]l lb' Campan' pro vigilac' de ha[m]mes j Casez p[ro] quarell' CCxxxiiij Oll'
lut' p[ro] Calc' Imponend' m[i]l DC lanc' voc' Shipsperys C iiijxx xvj dart' p[ro]
Shippez CCCl Batell' axes xl Pavic' depict' CCxxv

tampions for guns: 9,397, complete cuirasses of Milan (make): four, sallets with
visors: 21, bicokets of Milan (make): 29, sallets of divers sorts: 33, mail standards: 72,
brigandines: eight pairs, bills: 500, lances lacking heads: 167, quick sulphur powder:
93lb, quick sulphur: 14,245lb, linden-wood charcoal powder: two [prob. barrels],
willow-charcoal powder: 130lb, hand-bows (i.e., longbows): 362, sheaves of arrows:
1,236, crossbows: three, crossbows of steel: 19, double winches: 73, brass pulleys
for winches for spanning crossbows: 22, mixed iron and steel locks for crossbow
tillers: eight, double winchcords: 90 pairs, iron stirrups for crossbows: six, crossbow
quarrel-heads: 14,900, fletched crossbow quarrels with heads: 6,686, crossbow
quarrels fletched with wood lacking heads: 15,170, crossbow quarrels fletched with
wood with heads: 8,972, mixed plates of iron and steel for brigandines: 508, morris
pikes with iron heads: six, godendags with iron spikes: nine, wooden shafts for
morris pikes: 126, ash-wood shafts for bills and axes: 72, hazel-wood shafts: 24,
baskets: 20, iron rests for guns: four, iron hammers: one, iron mandrels: two, iron
crows: four, clay pots for storing lime: 350, iron caltraps: 3,850, double winches
for spanning crossbows: one, thread for crossbow-strings called trenchfile: 335lb,
painted pavises: three, long pavises: 30, shingles: 412, brass mortars: one – with two
iron pestles, long iron-bound stocks: one pair, pickaxes: one, mattocks: six, iron
scales with two balance-pans: one with nine lead weights which weigh 90lb, iron
scales with two balance-pans: one, iron tongs: six – one of which is for smithing,
iron andirons: five – three of which are for plumbing, iron-bound lead mallets
without daggers (i.e., spikes): 225, iron-bound lead mallets: 1,251, lead mallet-
heads: 45, iron pins for guns: two – one of which weighs 340lb and one weighs

140lb, iron axletrees for guns: two – one weighs 791lb and one weighs 120lb, iron gun-chambers: two weighing 88lb, iron gun-chambers of divers sorts: two weighing 104lb between them, lead cisterns: four, kilns: six – one of which is broken, large iron gun-chambers: one, anvils: one, long ladders called standard: one, brass pulleys: 16 – 10 of which are broken weighing 150lb between them, watchbells: six – two of which are broken, latten syringes: nine, windmills: three, stones called grindstones: one, large brass pans: three, pans for pouring lead: one, large tubs for sieving saltpetre, quick sulphur, and willow-charcoal: one, wooden troughs for mixing saltpetre, quick sulphur, and willow-charcoal: one, large ram-heads: three, iron-bound rollers for gun-carriages: one with two wheels, iron guns for (shooting) stones: 101 – one of which is called Saint Paul, one called The Crown, and four large fowlers each with two chambers, one fowler with two chambers weighing 112lb between them, 11 of them (i.e., the 101 iron guns) with two chambers, 54 of them with two chambers 12 of which are called fowlers bought in the 12th (regnal) year weighing 5,707lb between them, 13 with one chamber, and 11 lacking chambers, and one weighing 1,324lb likewise bought in the 12th year, and four large iron guns for stones one of which is broken and [they] weigh 1,934lb, iron guns for stones called Gloucester's Great Fowler: one with two chambers, long iron guns called serpen- tines: six – three of which have two chambers, one with two chambers weighing 858lb between them, one with one chamber weighing 529lb, and one weighing 230lb, iron guns for pellets: three, iron guns called culverins: five, iron guns called handguns: 25 – six of which are of the remain of the account of John Thirsk, iron guns called hookguns: 15 brass guns for stones: six – two with two chambers two with one, one serpentine weighing 700lb between them, one with one chamber, and one called Dame Anabelle, brass guns for pellets: one, brass guns called handguns: 74 – 12 from the remain account of John Thirsk, gunstones of large measure: 16, gunstones of divers sorts: 16,219, long chests for hand-bows (longbows): four, iron glaives called bills: 24, linden-wood charcoal: three quarters of four?, sallets called skulls: two, battle axes: 15, targes covered in leather: seven, mills for milling sulphur, saltpetre, and other stuff for gunpowder: one, iron balls called iron gunstones: 106, iron tools called the vice: one, sweepers with nine stampers and nine heads for the same: none, old iron: 100lb

Castle of Guînes

iron guns for stones called fowlers of divers sorts: 12 [*sic, recte* 13] – one with two chambers weighing 223lb, one with two chambers weighing 340lb, one with one chamber weighing 336lb, one with three chambers weighing 560lb, one with two chambers weighing 450lb, one with three chambers weighing 460lb, one with three chambers weighing 460lb, one with three chambers weighing 410lb, one with three chambers weighing 180lb, one with three chambers weighing 1,600lb, one with two chambers weighing 1,900lb, one with two chambers weighing 600lb, one with two chambers weighing 1,100lb, and one with two chambers weighing 3,100lb, iron guns called pot guns: one weighing 2,000lb, iron chambers for one fowler of the King's store: three weighing 268lb with the fowler's (iron) bindings, the same kind of iron chambers for one fowler of the King's store: one weighing 240lb with the fowler's bindings and the repair of two chambers of the King's store for these fowlers, the same kind of iron chambers for one fowler of the King's store: six weighing 404lb with the fowler's bindings, the same kind of iron chambers for one fowler of the King's store: three weighing 191lb with the fowler's bindings, iron for working both on bindings and fortifications: nine chambers suitable for seven fowlers of the King's store weighing in total 1,678lb with their bindings, chambers made for two trestle guns of the King's store weighing 194lb with the guns' bindings, iron guns in three carriages: nine with 27 chambers for them weighing 1,500lb with the guns' bindings, iron-bound wheels for these carriages: six weighing 600lb with their bindings, iron guns called serpentines: 13 – one with three chambers weighing 283lb with their bindings, one with three […], the same kind of iron chambers for one fowler of the King's store: three weighing 179lb with the fowler's bindings, chambers weighing 325lb with their bindings: two with six chambers weighing 385lb, two with six chambers weighing 200lb, one with one chamber weighing 280lb, one with three chambers weighing 4,200lb, one with two chambers weighing 1,100lb, one with two chambers weighing 1,400lb, one with three chambers weighing 750lb, and one with two chambers weighing 750lb, iron guns called handguns: 32 with their stopping irons and pouches, winches for spanning crossbows: 27, iron chambers for one serpentine of the King's store: one weighing 112lb with its bindings, iron guns called socket culverins: 6, steel crossbows: 36, crossbows: 20, crossbow quarrels with heads of divers sorts: 3,900, crossbow-quarrel heads: 8,900, iron caltraps of divers sorts: 12,000, gunstones for large fowlers: 292, gunstones for small fowlers: 1,113, iron pickaxes of divers sorts without handles: 10, iron cressets: 24 – 12 with shafts and 12 lacking shafts, torches for lighting them: 2,200, marble mortars for grinding gunpowder: one large (one), iron guns for carriages: 6 with 23 chambers weighing 1,600lb, iron guns called culverins: two – one with chamber and one lacking a chamber, brass moulds for making pellets: 3, marble stones for the large serpentines: 99, marble stones for the small serpentines: 200, iron pellets for the large serpentines: two weighing 20lb

There remains in store as attested by William Rosse with £273 10s: hand-bows (longbows): five, sheaves of arrows fletched with swan: three, archers' belts: 9 dozen, crossbows: 29, steel crossbows: 97, double winches for spanning crossbows: 53 pairs, strings for hand-bows: 20 gross, crossbow quarrels fletched with wood lacking heads: 37,000, mills for making gunpowder: one, lances called demylances lacking heads: 120, lances made of Rhinish 'clist'[23] lacking heads: none, iron-headed stakes for the field (of battle): 1,500, leather buckets: 50, long iron guns called serpentines: one with one chamber weighing 1,800lb between them [*sic*], brass guns called serpentines weighing 6,221lb between them: 18, brass guns called hookguns weighing 394lb between them: 16, brass guns called hookguns with Saracens' faces: 8, carriages for the serpentines: 15, iron-bound wheels for the carriage of ordnance:

---

23 This is currently unidentified.

30 pairs, lymons (cartshafts) for the carriages: 56, gunpowder: 493lb, pavises made of poplar: 30, iron guns called fowlers weighing 2,012lb between them: 8, iron quarrel-heads: 19,000, iron-bound half barrels: 12, iron-bound firkins: 20, thread for crossbow-strings called trenchfile: 200lb, lead for pellets: three fardels, arrow-heads: 8,000, complete cuirasses of Milan (make): none, iron caltraps: 24,000, tampions for guns: 4,000, cranequins for spanning crossbows: 20, cokers for handguns: 20, quick sulphur: 3,000lb, watchbell of Hames (Castle): one, cases for quarrels: 234, clay pots for storing lime: 1,600, lances called ship spears: 196, darts for ships: 350, battleaxes: 40, painted pavises: 225

67

Edinburgh, National Records of Scotland, NAS, PA2, vol. 5, fol. 150r

Act of the Parliament of Scotland, passed at Edinburgh, 18 May 1491

ITem It is Statute & ordanit that Ilke s[chi]ref Stewart or baliʒe of þe Realme ger wapynschawing' be maid foure ty[m]mes in þe ʒere i[n] all plac' Convenient w[i]t[h]in his bailʒery In this wise That Ilke ge[n]tilma' hafand ten pund' worth of land or mare be sufficiently harnest & Anarmit w[i]t[h] bassanat Sellat quhyte hat [i.e., white (polished-steel) hat] gorgeat or peissane hale leg harnes Swerd spere & dager And ge[n]tilme' haffand less extent of land' or vnlandit sall be Armit at thare gudely power eftre the sicht and discretioun' of the s[chi]reff balʒeis and sic personis as oure sou[er]ane lord sall depute [com]miss[ioner]is thareto And honest ʒemen hafand sufficient power þat lik' to be men' of Armes sall be harnest sufficiently eftre the discretioun' of the said s[chi]reff or [com]miss[ioner]is and all vthir ʒemen of the Realme betuix sexten' and sexty sall haf sufficient bowis & schaiff Swerd buklare knyff spere or gud ax in sted of the bow And that all burges & Induellar' of borrowis [burghs] of the Realme in lik man' be anarmit & harnest and mak wapynschawing' as said Is four ty[m]mes in þe ʒere and that the ald[er]man and bailʒeis apon' the quilk' þe chaum[er]lane or his deput' sall knaw and execut the said thing' And þat all men' of the Realme to burgh' and to land' Sp[irit]uale me[n]nis s[er]ua[n]d' and temp[er]ale be wele pruvait of the said harnes and wapy[n]nis be the fest of midsom' nixt to cu' quhilk sall be the day of thare wapy[n]schawing – vndre the pains folowand' þ[a]t Is to say of Ilke gentilma' þat defaltis at the first wapi[n]schaw' xl s' & þe secund defalt vþ[er] xl s' and the thrid defalt x li' And als' me[i]kle als oft ty[m]mes as he defalt' thareaft' x li' And of Ilke bowman at þe first falt x s' at the secund x s' & at þe thrid xl s' And sa furth' als oft of ty[m]mes as he beis fundin falt' thareft' xl s' and þ[er] eft' þe faculte of þ[er] land' and gud' that eu[er]e man' be furnist & bodin In his body with quhite harnes brekanetynis or gude Jakk' with splent' & gluff' of plait & Complet harnes wele horsit Corespondent to þ[er] land' & gud' be the discretioun' of the s[chi]ref Co[m]miss[ione]r' or officiare forsaid And atto[u]r' [in addition] that In na place of the realme be vsit fut bawis gouff or vther' sic vnproffitable sport' bot for [com]moun' gude & defence of the realme vndre þe pane of xl s' to be Rasit be the s[chir]ef & bailȝeis forsaid of Ilke p[ar]ochoun' [parish] Ilk ȝere quhare It beis fundin þat bow mark' be no[ch]t maid na schvting hantit [practiced] as said Is

68

Kew, National Archives, E 36/15, fol. 33v

The Remain of the Tower of London, 1492

This document is very fragmentary.

Gonnes

Bumbardell' of brasse with their' Apareill' eich Carted Apon' iiij wheles iren' bound' & shotyng CClxxiij lb' iren' & lx li' poudre ij Curtowes of brasse with their Apareill' eich Apon' ij wheles iren' bouden' shotyng C lb' iren' & xl lb' poudre ij demy [...] [prob. curtowes] of brasse [...] [prob. serpentines] of iren' Apon' ij wheles iren' bouden' & shotyng xl lb' iren' & xxvj lb' poudre vij Serpentynes of brasse with' their' Apareill' eu[er]y of them carted Apon' ij wheles iren' bounden' & shotyng vj lb' iren' & vj lb' poudre vij Faucons of brasse for the feld' eu[er]y of them carted Apon' ij wheles iren' bound' & shotyng j lb' d[imid]i lede & j lb' d' poudre xlvj hakbusses of iren' xliij Shot of iren' for bumbardell' C [...] Curtowes DCCCxx demy Curtowes m[i]l DCC iiijxx Curtowes & demy Serpen[...] DC iiijxx Serpentynes Clxxj Shot of iren' for b[ombar]dell' lxx [...] Cur[towes] [...] demy Curtowes [...] Cxxxiij Shott' of led[...] m[i]l m[i]l [...] Gonne poudre xx last d[imid]i Speyres l[...]xiij Shipspeyres lxx marespik' [morris pikes] C iiijxx Stak' for the feld [...] v m[i]l DCCl bowes vij m[i]l vj bowstryng' lxx gross' in barell' Arrow[...] of [...] ynches vnfeder[...] iij m[i]l DC shef' lyu[er]ey [...]rows CCCCl shef' billes xlvj halberd' of the fincs[...] yng [poss. finest makyng] Clxxiij hegge bill' [...] Cxxxij Garde [*sic*] quarell' [prob. garbs of crossbow quarrels] [...] Casys [...] [various woodworking tools] Anfeld' iij Bellowes vj pair' pynsons of sundrie sort' xviij pair' [...] hand hamurs xxxiij For hand hamurs ij Globe [globe-headed] hamurs x Shoying hamurs x For hamurs xxj hakhamurs iiij Small' hamurs iiij Fyles iiij bicornes ij Tong' for smyths viij pair' herthstaves vij washers vj Towirens iiij Gryndestones iij vices of iren' iiij wynches for gryndestones iij Salp[...] [saltpetre] in stour' bareld' xlix m[i]l DC lb' Cole poudre in barel' xiij m[i]l CCCC lb' brymston' in stour' bareld' xj m[i]l CCC lb' Speyre hed' [...] CCC hed' for [...] Iren' d[imid]i tonne doubles of plate for charging ladell' xxxiiij pec' Sengle plat' for chargyng ladell' l pec' Tallow ij m[i]l lb' Calveskynnes for burryng of speres xxxv skynnes [...] wheles vnshod' for grate ordnaun' ij pair' wheles shod' for [...] iij par' Lymo[n]s [cartshafts] for grate ordnaun[...] xj pair' [...] hurters [axle parts] xxv Tract' for ordnaun' garnished [clamps, locks, and nails of various sort] [...] pec' of broken' gonnes of brasse xxxij

69

Kew, National Archives, E 101/198/13

Inventory of the Defences of Calais, 10 September 1493

In the wache howse ij gonnes stokkyd w[i]t[h] ij chamber' j gon' of brasse stokkyd w[i]t[h] owte a chamb' iiij mall' of lede In the south' to[we]r & in the chamb' ovyr yt j Serpentyne w[i]t[h] ij chamber' In the greate hall' & in the greate chamb' j Gon' of yron' w[i]t[h] a chamb' j gon' of brasse w[i]t[h] ij chamber' j laddre of xiiij Reng' In the towre vnder the wachehowse

j Fowler w[i]t[h] a chamb' [in the] bakhowse iij gonstonys [at the bottom of the fol. in a different hand] S[um]ma pag' [sum of the page] Gunn' de ferr' iij cu' iijb[us] camer' Gunn' de Ere ij cu' ijb[us] camer' mall' de plu[m]bo iiij Serpente' de ferro j cu' ijb[us] camer' Foulers de ferro j cu' camer' lapid' gunnor[um] iij [back to original hand] In the Arthery [i.e., Archery/Artillery] j Almery closyd w[i]t[h] xix long bowes iiijxx viij shevys of Arowes xj sperys vnhedyd iij pavic' whereof' ij pey[n]ted m[i]l m[i]l m[i]l DC quarell' hedyd Federyd w[i]t[h] wode m[i]l DCC quarell' hed' & a cofur for the same In the Est towre j Fowler of yron' w[i]t[h] ij chamber' In the gate howse towre j trestyll' for a gon' j laddyr w[i]t[h] vj stavys j wache bell' In the Armery ij Formys to skore vppon' harnesse j olde laddyr ij great Almeryes In the sowth' towre j Rest of yron' for a gon' In the Bastowrte (i.e., bastion) j Fowler of yron' w[i]t[h] j chamb' liij gonstonys ij Gunnez of brasse w[i]t[h] vj chamber' j trestyll' for a gon' j serpentyne of yron' w[i]t[h] a chambyr [in different hand] S[um]ma pag' viz de Longbowes xix Arowes iiijxx viij sheif' pavic' iij vnde ij depict'

quarell' iij m[i]l DC cu' capit' & penn' de ligno Foulers ij cu' iijb[us] camer' quarell' hed' m[i]l DCC in j cist' de ligno Campan' pro vig[il]is j Rest' de ferr' p[ro] gunn' j lapid' gunnor[um] liij Gunn' de Ere ij cu' vj camer' Serpent' j cu' j camer' lanc' sine capit' xj [original hand] In the dungon' and to[w]r of the same j peyre of hanging stokk' j wache bell' brokyn j lytull' wache bell' xxviij Gonstonys j laddyr and ij Rest' of yron' for Gonnes In the Storehowse next [to] the Chapell'

ix Chambers' of yron' iij Chamber' of brasse j bolt of yron' xliiij Gunstonys and l Tamponnes w[i]t[h] owte the bakhowse dore j greate morter of Stone On the lede alone next [to] the Arthery Gonpowdyr CC lb' [different hand] [summa] pag' videl[ice]t de Campan' pro vigil' ij defract' lapid' gu[n]nor[um] lxxij Rest' de ferro p[ro] gunn' ij Camer' de ferr' p[ro] gu[n]n' ix Camera de Ere p[ro] gu[n]n' iij Bolt' de ferro j Tampon' p[ro] gu[n]n' l Stock' j par' hanging morter' de lapid' j magn' Pulu' gunn' CC lb' [original hand] Towre of Rysebank In the porter' loge j pulley of brasse ij gontrestell' of the Stapull' (Staple of Calais) ij Fyrdekyns of Gonpowder whereof oone weyeth' xlviij lb' iij hakegonnes w[i]t[h] iij stamper' to them' lx shot of lede for the same viij dos' bowstreng' xxj shot of lede for a serpentyne lx shot of stone for the same lx shot of stone for the Gon' in the hall' xxv shot of stone for the Gon' in the lardyr' lx shot of stone for the Gon' in the p[ri]son' howse xxxiij shot of stone of diu[er]se sort'

Cl Tamponnes ij Cart gonnes w[i]t[h] v chamber' & ij Cart' l shot' of Gunstonys l
tampo[n]nes [different hand] S[um]ma pag' v[i]z de pulleis' de Ere j
Trestill' ij pulu' gu[n]nor[um] ij Fyrdekyns Cord' pro Arc' man' viij dos' pellott' iiijxx j
   Lapid' gu[n]nor[um] CC iiijxx viij Tampons p[ro] gu[n]n' CC Gunn' de ferr' voc'
Cart' gunn' ij hake gunn' iij cu' iijb[us] stamp[er]s

70

P. Monte, *Exercitiorum atque artis militaris collectanea in tris libros distincta*, book 2 (Milan, 1509), ch. 128

Pietro Monte's Expert Opinion on Iron and Steel for Armour, between 1495 and 1497

Monte was an Iberian fightmaster based in Milan in the second half of the fifteenth century. Although his work was not published until 1509, in this extract he refers to both Duke Sigismund of Austria (1427–97) and the Italian War of 1494–5. Baldesare Castiligoni – who had studied in Milan from 1494 – claimed that Monte had been tutor to the condottiere Galeazzo da Sanseverino (b. c. 1458–60, d. 1525) who is also mentioned in this passage.

Et si quisqua' vult arma leuia ac tuta: agere oportet oiuo ferru' siue calibe' optimum
assumere.

   Inspruco germanie ciuitate optima' ferrum: & calibs inuenitur. Ideo illic magistri
dant ad experiendum arma cu' balistis: & vulgariter dicitur q[uod] talis temperies
causetur p[ro]pter vna' aqua' per loca illa tra[n]seunte'. Sed in rei veritate cum
quacunq[ue] aqua frigida tempera[n]t: & visa bonitate illius ferri aliqui experiri
voluerunt ad faciendum thorace' resistentem sclopetis: que species bombardar[um]
paruula est: & ispas compertu': Nihilomin' oportet ponere cultra' bombicea' &
tela' nimium sutam super thorace. Du[m]q[ue] madesit fortior redditur· licet talis
armatura grauis sic secundum quod alemani deferre solent: non autem secundum
quod itali aut galli: & hec armatura per omnes partes fortis esse debet.

   Nunc vero in italia fere adeo bona arma fiunt sicut & inspruco: Qua[m]qua' ars
nuper ex germania ortum habuerit: & postq[uam] de natura bona & optime appurata
fuerint mauis secretum consistit in contunde[n]do nimiu' arma quando iam frigida
sunt: & quod forte temperamen prebeant: tamen quod non rumpantur: sed maneant
tanq[ue] aliquod ferru' sagitte teli: & horum similium: que neq[ue] rumpuntur:
neq[ue] duplicantur.

   In tempore quo ego co[m]ponebam hoc opus dux Sigismundus de austria:
Galeacius de sancto seuerino: & Claudius de voldre natione burgu[n]dius nimiu'
in inquirendis diuersis generibus armorum negociabant': ante ipsos vero fere omnes
armigeri vno & eodem modo armabantur prefertim de armis indutiuis: hi tres illustres
viri multa noua arma inuenerunt ta' pedestribus: quam equestribus attinentia: & non
tantu' diuersa i[m]mo vtilima.

Et q[ue] parum post galli ingressi sunt Italia' ad debellandum regnum Neapolis: & ducatum Mediolani ad hanc debellationem plures germani: & hyspani concurrerent: taliter quod iam in diebus istis arma diuersa fiunt: atq[ue] optima: prius enim arma defensibilia inspruco facta ta[n]tum fortissima erant ca[n]temperationis [*sic*]: & q[ue] p[er]cutieba[n]t ipsam nimium super frigium dum ia' forma' cepera[n]t: nunc vero hoc & illud in pluribus locis scitur. Inue[n]to res tamen istius bonitatis dux Sigismundus fuit primus: & secundus Galeacius de sancto seuerino.

And whosoever wants to have light and secure armour, to bear himself, must acquire the best iron and steel.

The best iron and steel is to be found in the German City of Innsbruck. The masters there test the cuirasses with crossbows and it is commonly said that the cause of such temper is on account of a type of water that passes through that place. But the truth of the matter is that they temper with any kind of cold water; and having seen the quality of this iron, in order to test it, some wanted to make a cuirass proof against the *scoppiette* which is a type of small bombard, this was then revealed (i.e., proved to be the case). Nevertheless, it is necessary to fit padded cotton and extremely well-sewn linen over the cuirass: whilst it is damp it gives it more strength: although such heavy armour is of the sort the Germans are wont to bear but not that of the Italians or French – and this armour must be strong in all parts.

It is true that in Italy now armours are made that are as good as those of Innsbruck, although the technique has of late originated in Germany. After it was discovered that it was the good natural properties and the best preparation it was the worst-kept secret that it turned out to be the thorough hammering of the armours when they were cold that would give them such good temper that they would not break but endure to the same extent of a spearhead, arrow, or suchlike, to neither break nor bend.

At the time I was composing this work, Duke Sigismund of Austria, Galeazzo da Sanseverino, and Claude de Vaudray, of the Burgundian nation, busied themselves exceedingly with the discovery of divers (types) sorts of armour. It is true that, before these, almost all men-at-arms were armed with the same type of armour. These three illustrious men invented many new types of armour both for (fighting) on foot and from horseback, not only divers but, moreover, useful.

Not long after, Italy was invaded by the French in the war of the Kingdom of Naples and the Duchy of Milan. Many Germans and Spaniards were drawn into this war to the extent that – these days – divers armours are made. Whereas before the best defensive armours were made strongest in Innsbruck by tempering and by thoroughly hammering them whilst cold once they had already been shaped, in truth it is now the case that this (technique) is known in many places. Duke Sigismund was the first to discover this good property and the second was Galeazzo da Sanseverino.

Figure 27. Woodcut of the allegorical 'White King' (*Weisskunig*) visiting his armour workshop at Innsbruck. The book was written by Maximilian I and his courtiers. The text (p. 98) refers specifically to the Innsbruck master-armourers Kaspar Rieder and Konrad Seusenhofer, both in this Emperor's service.

71

Unlocated Original Document printed in E. Forestié, 'Un mobilier seigneurial du XVe siècle. Le Château de Montbeton en 1496', *Bulletin archéologique et historique de la Société archéologique de Tarn-et-Garonne* 22 (1895), pp. 17–57 (at pp. 47–9)

Inventory of the Château of Montbeton, County of Quercy, 1496 (Extract)

una pessa d'artilharia rompuda, apelada fauco una autra pessa [apelada] arcubuta a crochet una pessa d'artilharia [apelada] ung petart una colobrina, arma rompuda de metalh quatre autras pessas apeladas acabuta, tres am crochet, et una sens crochet de fer ung paves de buy ung patoc de porta viures; a Roussilhou

> one broken artillery-piece called 'falcon', another piece called an arquebus with rest, one artillery-piece called a 'petard', one culverin – with broken fittings – of metal (i.e., alloy), four other pieces called arquebuses – three with iron rests and one without, one wooden pavise, one 'patoc' (prob. quiver) for carrying crossbow bolts; at Roussilhou (prob. Castell Rosselló, near Perpignan)

72

Brescia, Archivio di Stato, Archivio Gambara

Accounts of the Gambara Family, Brescia, 26 April 1499–13 October 1504

[26 April 1499] p[ar] coracine 25 barberi 25 12 celadinj 25 dare p[ro] il Co. J[acop]o Piero di [name illegible] [22 January 1500] p[ar] coracine 25 barberi 25 12 celadine 25 p[ar] il Co. J[acop]o Pet[r]o […] It[em] p[ar] co[ra]zini sin falda aprizo Ant[oni]o malinzo Ad xj oct' p[ro] guponi 4 celade 4 barbozi 4 dar[e] a m[ae]s[tro] Lucio cu[m] di[u]no p[ar]o d[i] brazalettj […] It[em] p[ro] vna celada ala franciza cu[m] vno barbozo de maya 12 [?] vno p[ar]o d[i] gau[n]ti p[ar] m[ae]s[tro] Lucio […] It[em] p[ar] vno gupo' d[i] piastre p[ar] m[ae]s[tro] Julio malinzo [2 June 1503] p[ro] vno corscato cu[m] vno p[ar]o spalarole brazale 12 barbozo dar[e] a g[i]org[i]o Albaneso [2 January 1504] p[ar] coracine 50 & 50 celadine & 50 barbotte i[n]tegrat' & xij coracine i[n]tegrate xij celatj dun copa spegatj cu[m] li chiodi de ottone & barbotte xij spegade […] [24 May 1504] p[ar] corazine ij i[n]tergrade coop[er]te de cordoeno cellatj 2 spezate da bal[iste]ro & ij barbottj spezatj & pectoralj d[i] Tuttj dare p[er] il Co Z[oan]o maraniscotto i[n] […] [13 October 1504] p[ar] coracine 26 dun dozena adonise celladine 26 & barbottj 26 & coracine 12 i[n]tegratj & cellatj 12 spizatj & barbotte 12 spezati dar[e] al cont' […]

[26 April 1499] 25 pairs of little cuirasses (i.e., brigandines), 25 bevors, 12 small sallets 25 [prob. florins] given by Count Jacopo Piero di [name illegible] [22 January 1500] 25 pairs of small cuirasses (brigandines), 25 bevors, 12 *fl.*, 25 small sallets [...] one pair of little cuirasses (brigandines) without a fauld taken by Antonio Malinzo on 11 October [...] for 4 sallets, four *barbozzi* (mail chin and neck defences) given to Master Lucio along with one pair of small arm defences [...] for one French-style sallet with one mail *barbozzo* 12 *fl.*, one pair of gauntlets by Master Lucio [...] one pair of jupons of plates (i.e., pair of plates) by Master Julio Malinzo [2 June 1503] for one corset with one pair of spaulders, 12 arm defences, one *barbozzo* given to Giorgio Albaneso [2 January 1504] 50 pairs of small cuirasses (brigandines) and 50 small sallets complete with 50 *barbozzi*, and 12 complete small cuirasses (brigandines), 12 sallets with a broken skull (helmet bowl) with latten nails and 12 broken *barbozzi* [24 May 1504] two complete pairs of small cuirasses (brigandines) covered with cordwain, two sallets broken by a crossbow, and two broken *barbozzi* and breastplates all given by Count Zoan Maraniscotto [13 October 1504] 26 pairs of small cuirasses (brigandines), 26 small sallets and 26 *barbozzi*, and 12 complete small cuirasses (brigandines), and 12 broken sallets and 12 broken *barbozzi* given to count [...]

73

Paris, Bibliothèque nationale de France, MS fr. 22335, fol. 113r–fol. 119r

Inventory of the Château of Amboise, 23 September 1499

vne dague enmanchee de licorns la poignee de cristalin no[m]me la dague saint charlcmaigne vne espee enmanchee de fer garnie en façon de clef no[m]me lespee de lancelot du lac et dit on quelle est fee vne espee darmes garnie de fouet blanc et au po[m]meau a vne n[ost]re dame dun coste et vng souleil de lautre no[m]mee lespee de la victoire vne espee darmes la poigne garnie de fouet blanc et au po[m]meau vne n[ost]re dame dun coste et vng souleil de lautre no[m]me lespee du Roy charles vije appellee la bien amee vne autre espee darmes la poignee de fouet blanc et au po[m]meau y a vne n[ost]re dame dun coste Et de lautre coste vng souleil nommee lespee du Roy qui fonda saint denis vne espee darmes la poignee couuerte de fouet blanc et au po[m]meau a vne n[ost]re dame dun coste et vng saint michel de lautre no[m]mee lespee du Roy de france qui fist armes contre vng gean a paris et le conquist Lespee aux armes du pape caliste Le fourreau garny dargent dore et vng chapeau de veloux cramoisy garny et semeiees de perles que le Roy que dieu pardonnit fist mectre en son armeurey vne espee darmes la poignee de fouet blanc ou po[m]meau dun coste a vne n[ost]re dame et de lautre coste vng sainct michel Et fut a Jehan de breze Lequel en couppa le poing a vng ho[m]me darmes auecques le canon et le gantelet vne espee la poignee de fouet blanc au po[m]meau vne n[ost]re dame dun coste et saint michel

de lautre nommee lespee du Roy descosse qui fut fort hardy la quelle fut donnee Au
feu Roy loys quant Il espousa ma dame La daulphine Vne espee La poingnee de fouet
blanc Le pommeau long dun coste vne n[ost]re dame a lautre coste vng saint martin
no[m]me la bonne espee du Roy loys quil auoit a la conqueste quil fist premier sur les
suysses no[m]mee estresuze vne espee la poignee de fouet blanc vng po[m]meau long
en facon de ceur esmaille blanc et Rouge no[m]me lespee du Roy charles sexte quil
portoit sur son courset vne espee la poignee de fouet blanc le po[m]meau en facon
dun cueur ou Il y a quatre lozenges deux dun coste et deux de lautre no[m]me lespee
ph[i]l[ipp]e le bel vne espee garnie de fouet blanc la poignee sans esmail nommee
lespee du Roy Jehan vng cousteau en facon de semeterie no[m]me le cousteau
saint pierre de luxembourg vne espee le foureau blanc la poignee garnie de boys au
po[m]meau vne n[ost]re dame dun coste et vng saint martin de lautre nommee lespee
de pape quil enuoya au Roy loys vne espee garnie de cuir Rouge a long po[m]meau
nommee lespee du gean qui fut conquis par vng Roy de france en lisle n[ost]re dame a
paris vne espee longue Rabatue a creusetz pendans qui fut au conte de vistambert vne
espee la poignee de cuir Rouge no[m]me lespee qui soit trouuee en vng fondement
de bouleuart de la porte neuf de tours et fut trouue au pies vne teste dont la teste
tenoit cinq ou six seaulx de ane vne dague a Rouelle de boys enboestee en vng estuy
de cuir que feu Roy loys faisoit touiours porter quant et luy vne hache a vne main qui
fut au Roy saint loys vne autre hache a deux mains autresfoiz esmaillez de fleurs de
lix qui fut aud' Roy saint loys vne hache a deux mains qui estoit a vng Roy de france
qui conquist le gean en lisle n[ost]re dame a p[ar]is vne hache en facon de coignee le
manche long no[m]me la hache du grant turc vne hache ouuree nomme la hache du
Roy clouys premier Roy [chrest]ian vne hache a trois pometes de dyamant nommee
la hache de messire bertrand du clusquin vne hache couuerte toute de fer no[m]me
la hache que vng Roy de france conquesta sur vng payan a paris qui fut trouue au
louure a paris vne hache a deux mains en facon de fleurs de litz nommee la hache
dun allemant q[ui] fist tant darmes a nuz vne espee darmes le fourreau de veloux
noir qui fut aud' feu Roy charles huitiesme laquelle Il auoit a larson de sa selle a la
Journee du fo[u]rnauue vne autre espee le fourreu de veloux noir q[ui] led' feu Roy
charles huit[iesm]e auoit en sa main a lad' Journee de fo[u]rnauue vng fer de lance
court a trois grans queries trenchans [le] harnoys de la pucelle garny de gardebraz
dune paire dy mytons & dun abillement de teste ou Il y a vng gorgery de maille le
bort dore le dedans g[ar]ny de satin cramoisy double de mesme vne brigandine de
taillebot couuerte de veloux noir tout vse et sa sallade noire couuerte dun houlx de
broderie fait sur veloux noir tout vse vnes vielles brigandines longues couuertes dun
viel drap dor Rouge le hault fait en facon de cuirasse et le bas en le[m]mes dassier et
vng bort de sade ferme a boucle au coste gauche vne autre vielle brigandine affise sur
veloux noir vielle & vsee le hault du deuant en facon de cuirasse et le demourant de
le[m]mes enuiron quinze ou seize sallades & bassinetz a la mode antique sans sauoir
ne declairer a qui Ilz ont seruy

one unicorn-horn-hilted dagger – the grip of crystal – called 'The Dagger of Saint
Charlemagne', one iron-hilted sword fitted in the manner of a key called 'The

Sword of Lancelot of the Lake' and it is said to be enchanted, one arming sword – (the grip) fitted with white (leather) binding and on one side of the pommel an (image of) Our Lady and a sun on the other – called 'The Sword of Victory', one other arming sword – the grip fitted with white-leather binding and Our Lady on one side of the pommel and a sun on the other – called 'The Sword of King Charles VII called the Well Beloved', one other arming sword – the grip white-leather bound and Our Lady on one side of the pommel and a sun on the other – called 'The Sword of the King who founded Saint-Denis', one arming sword – the grip covered with white-leather binding and Our Lady on one side of the pommel and Saint Michael on the other – called 'The Sword of the King of France who fought a Giant and defeated it', the sword with the (heraldic) arms of Pope Calixtus – the scabbard garnished with silver gilt and a chapeau (hat) of crimson velvet garnished and strewn with pearls that the King – whom God absolve – caused to be placed in his armoury, an arming sword – the grip white-leather-bound, Our Lady on one side of the pommel and Saint Michael on the other – and it belonged to Jehan de Brézé who broke the hilt on a man-at-arms with the 'canon' [*sic*, cannon?] and the gauntlet, one sword – the grip white-leather-bound – Our Lady on one side of the pommel and Saint Michael on the other, called the 'Sword of the King of Scotland who was Very Bold' which was given to the late King Louis when he married my Lady (Margaret) the Dauphine, one sword with white-leather-bound grip – the pommel long with Our Lady on one side and Saint Martin on the other – called 'The Fine Sword of King Louis which He wielded at His First Defeating the Swiss, called "Judgement"', one sword with white-leather-bound grip – one long, white- and red-enamelled heart-shaped pommel – called 'The Sword of King Charles VII which He carried on His Corset', one sword with white-leather-bound grip – the pommel heart-shaped, on which there are four lozenges on one side and two on the other – called 'The Sword of Philip the Fair'

one sword fitted with white-leather grip without enamel called 'The Sword of King John', one knife in the shape of a cemetery [*sic*] called 'The Knife of Saint Pierre of Luxembourg', one sword – the grip white-leather-bound fitted with wood, Our Lady on one side of the pommel and Saint Michael on the other – called 'The Sword which the Pope sent to King Louis', one sword fitted with red-leather (grip) with a long pommel called 'The Sword of the Giant who was defeated by a King of France on the Île de Notre Dame of Paris', one rebated longsword with hanging crucible which belonged to the Count of Furstenberg, one sword – the grip red-leather-bound – called 'The Sword which was found in a Foundation of the Boulevard of the New Port (gate) of Tours' and a head was found at the feet and the head held five or six ass-saddles (or seals?), a dagger with a wooden rondel secured in a leather trousse which the late King Louis always carried about His Person, one one-handed axe which belonged to King Saint Louis, one two-handed axe which was once enamelled with fleur-de-lys which belonged to the said King Saint Louis, one two-handed axe which belonged to a King of France who defeated the giant on the Île de Notre Dame of Paris, one hatchet-shaped axe with a long haft called 'The Axe of the Grand Turk', one ornate axe called 'The Axe of King Clovis the

Figure 28. Sword-hilt, c. 1460 (Glasgow Museums, Burrell Collection, 2.83).

First Christian King', one axe with three little pommels of diamond (i.e., spherical finials) called 'The Axe of Sir Bertrand du Guesclin', one axe – completely covered in iron – called 'The Axe with which a King of France defeated a Pagan at Paris' which was found in the Louvre at Paris, one two-handed, fleur-de-lys-shaped axe called 'The Axe of a German who fought Naked (i.e., without armour)', one arming sword – the scabbard of black velvet – which belonged to the late King Charles VIII which hung from his saddlebow at the Battle of Fornovo, one other sword – the scabbard of black velvet – which the said late King Charles VIII brandished in his hand at the said Battle of Fornovo, one short lancehead with three large sharpened edges, the harness of The Maid (of Orléans, i.e., Joan of Arc) fitted with pauldrons, a pair of mittens (poss. mitten gauntlets?), and a head defence which has a mail gorget – the edge gilded and the inside lined with matching crimson satin, one of (Lord) Talbot's brigandines covered with completely-worn-out black velvet and his black sallet (i.e., black from the hammer) with a completely-worn-out covering of embroidered black velvet, one (pair of) old, long brigandines covered with red cloth-of-gold – the upper (part) made in the manner of a cuirass and the lower made of steel lames and an edge of straps that buckle up on the left-hand side, one other old brigandine (the lames) affixed on old, worn out black velvet – the upper (part of) the front made in the manner of a cuirass and the remainder of lames, around 15 or 16 old-fashioned sallets and basinets without knowledge or (anything) saying by whom they were used

74

Oxford, Balliol College Library, MS 354, p. 218 and p. 470

Three Recipes from Richard Hill's Commonplace Book, completed in 1536, but undoubtedly earlier

> *Richard Hill (active 1508–36) was a London merchant. Although his Commonplace Book was completed in 1536, it contains copies of older works such as the 'Confessio amantis' of the poet John Gower (d. 1408).*

an olye for harnes

Take a peny worth of oyle of net[es] fete [neatsfoot] & þe fatt[e] of a peny worth of a loyne of mot[o]n & the[n] mynse þe fatt[e] & melt it i[n] a pa[n]ne whe[n] it is melt put þ[er]to þe qua[n]tite of half a walnot of polen [polish] wax & claryfye it & whe[n] it is claryfied put þe oyle of net[es] fett[e] þ[er]to & store them[e] to geder & c[etera]

an oyntment for harnes

Take þe mou[n]tenau[n]ce of a walnot mor[e] of wax tha[n] of Rosen[e] & melt the[m] to geder & take þe freshe grese of a swyne & ob[olus] [halfpenny] worth of woll[e] oyle first melt þe grese & put þe oyle þ[er]to to hit [i.e., until it] be Fried & tha[n] put wex & Rosen[e] þ[er]to & let it be still[e] & c[etera]

The Craft to skowre mayle harnes

Take yo[u]r mayle & put it in an armerers barell[e] & put þ[er]to a good qua[n]tite of oyle & torne it in þe barell[e] ij owres w[i]t[h]out restyng and tha[n] put þ[er] to a good qua[n]tite of stale pisse and torne it an owre all[e] to geder w[i]t[h] owt restyng and tha[n] take som[e] bran[e] & put [it] þ[er]to & torne it a lytill[e] while and tha[n] tak[e] it owt and Rownse it well[e] i[n] a canvas made þ[er]for[e] w[i]t[h] dry sawe duste or bran[e] tyll[e] þe moyst[ur] be of & tha[n] it will[e] be bryght and so ye may kepe it in þe same barell[e] yf ye lay dry bran[e] ynowgh betwen[e] eu[er]y pece & so let it lye

Part III

Illustrated Glossary

B

Bard (**7**, **36**)

armour for a warhorse constructed of large, solid plates. Of steel (**7**). Of cuir bouilli (**36**). The word's origin lies in the Ital. for packsaddle: *barda*. Both of our examples have links to men from that peninsula.

Biquoquet (**10**, **50**, **66**)

a type of helmet, *possibly* in the shape of the type sported by Robin Hood.[1]

Bombard, also spelt *Bumbard* (**47**, **53**, **54**, **61**, **70**)

probably from the Lat. *bombus*: a humming noise, this is one of the earliest names for a gunpowder weapon.[2] By this half of the century it refers to the largest member of the cannon family. Pietro Monte (**70**) uses it to mean a handheld gun.

Bombardelle, also spelt *Bumbardelle* (**53**, **61**, **68**)

a smaller version of the bombard.[3]

Bonnet, steel (**30**, **52**)

presumably an open-faced helmet in the shape of this civilian headwear.

Bumbards (**29**, **60**)

Eaves and Norman, drawing on evidence from late-sixteenth- and early-seventeenth-century working documents from the Armoury at the Tower of London, reveal that 'bombardes' are 'integral spaulders to protect the shoulders' as a component of low-cost armours known as Almain corslets.[4] The 'pair' of Bumbard' gardes and

---

[1] See the detailed discussion in the illustrated glossary of Moffat, *Medieval Arms and Armour: A Sourcebook. Volume II.*

[2] *The Oxford English Dictionary*, ed. J. Simpson (Oxford, 2004), online edn.

[3] H. L. Blackmore, *The Armouries of the Tower of London, 1: Ordnance* (London, 1976), p. 200; D. Spencer, *Royal and Urban Gunpowder Weapons in Late Medieval England* (Woodbridge, 2019), pp. 234–5. For the elasticity of this name in the first half of the century see Moffat, *Medieval Arms and Armour: A Sourcebook. Volume II*, p. 197.

[4] I. Eaves and A. V. B. Norman, *Arms and Armour in the Collection of Her Majesty the Queen: European Armour* (London, 2016), p. 196.

Figure 29. Horse bard, by Pier Innocenzo da Faerno,
Milanese, c. 1450 (Wien Museum 127151).

canons' (**60**), as the above authors' work informs us, are spaulders, couters, and the tubular arm-defences known as the upper- and lower-cannons of the vambrace. The use of these arm-defence terms – discounted due to them being sixteenth-century vocabulary in my first sourcebook[5] – can now be confidently employed from the 1460s.

C

Culverin (**10, 27, 50, 52, 66**)

a gunpowder weapon. The editors of the *Oxford English Dictionary* state that the name derives from 'Latin *colubrīnus* of the nature of a snake'.[6] This serpent-like form has led authorities such as Blackmore to conclude that it was a 'type of gun which was long in proportion to its bore'.[7] Spencer – in a detailed study of English royal accounts – concludes that they 'varied in size, with the smaller models resembling handguns'.[8]

Curtowe (**53, 68**)

a gun of the cannon family with a short ('curt') barrel.[9]

F

Falcon (**68, 71**)

Spencer categorises it as a 'small type of gun which was primarily used on the battle-field'.[10] Evidently it was of the same family as the serpentine. The editors of the *Oxford English Dictionary* provide an excerpt from a Scottish nobleman's letter to Henry VII of 1496. He lists at Edinburgh Castle ten 'falconis or litill serpentinis'.[11] See also *Culverin, Fowler*, and *Serpentine*.

---

5   Moffat, *Medieval Arms and Armour: A Sourcebook. Volume I*, p. xxxiii and p. 289.
6   *Oxford English Dictionary*, ed. Simpson.
7   Blackmore, *Armouries of the Tower of London, 1: Ordnance*, p. 224.
8   Spencer, *Royal and Urban Gunpowder Weapons*, p. 237. One of the reviewers has kindly pointed out that the culverins in these sources are almost certainly 'the small fifteenth-century guns – probably handheld, mounted on rests, or mounted on walls – and not the large late-sixteenth-century culverins that were primarily naval weapons'. Indeed, in doc. **54** there are listed 'hand Culuerynes'.
9   *Oxford English Dictionary*, ed. Simpson, under 'curtal'.
10   Spencer, *Royal and Urban Gunpowder Weapons*, pp. 242–3.
11   *Oxford English Dictionary*, ed. Simpson, citing *Original Letters, Illustrative of English History*, ed. H. Ellis, vol. 1 (London, 1824), p. 31.

Fowler (**47**, **49**, **53**, **54**, **57**, **61**, **62**, **64**, **66**, **69**)

lit. one who shoots fowl. A breech-loading gunpowder weapon of varying size. Spencer, in his extensive study, records its use from 1415 stating it to be:

> the single most popular type of gun recorded in English accounts in the fifteenth century. These weapons varied considerably in size [...] [they were] used in small numbers on royal ships in the first half of the fifteenth century, but appear to have been most effective in offensive and defensive siege warfare.[12]

See also *Falcon, Culverin,* and *Serpentine.*

G

Godendag (**54**, **66**)

Dutch for 'good day': a wooden club with metal spikes.

H

Hakebusshe (**45**, **54**, **57**, **61**, **62**, **64**)

a handgun with a downward-projecting lug on the underside of the barrel which acts to prevent recoil when hooked over a parapet. It is a name employed in several West Germanic languages and means 'hook gun'. Why English speakers use this name in these sources is not entirely clear, in this author's opinion. There is almost certainly no difference between this weapon and the hookgun (or 'hake gonne').[13] See also *Hookgun.*

Halberd (**45**, **68**)

a staff weapon fitted with a head consisting of a combined axe-blade, top thrust-ing-spike, and (often) a dorsal fluke. It is a compound noun originating in the German for shaft and broad-bladed axe.[14] The chronicler Jean Molinet (1435–1507)

---

12   Spencer, *Royal and Urban Gunpowder Weapons*, pp. 243–5.
13   C. Blair, 'Early Firearms', *Pollard's History of Firearms*, ed. C. Blair (New York, 1983), pp. 25–32 (at p. 29). I am grateful to one of the reviewers for their assistance with defining this term.
14   *Oxford English Dictionary*, ed. Simpson.

Figure 30. Handgun, c. 1500 (Glasgow Museums, A.1977.14.b).

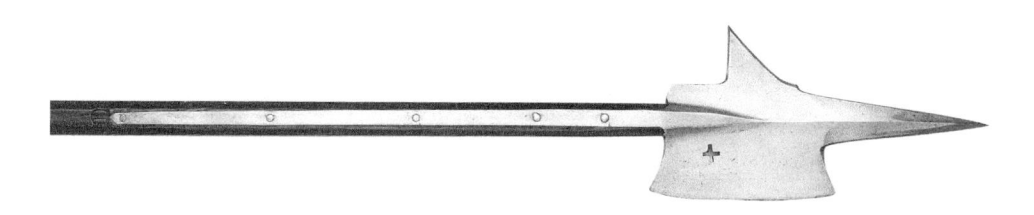

Figure 31. Halberd, Swiss, 1470–90 (Royal Armouries, VII.1497).

records the slaying of both Charles the Bold, duke of Burgundy at Nancy in 1477 and Richard III at Bosworth by men armed with the 'hallebarde'.[15]

Hookgun, also spelt *Hake gonne* (**45, 54, 57, 62, 64, 66, 69**)

a handgun with a downward-projecting lug on the underside of the barrel which acts to prevent recoil when hooked over a parapet. See also *Hakebusshe*.

Hounskull (**13, 30, 52**)

a mail head and neck defence of currently unknown form.[16]

Huvette (**13**)

a type of helmet, probably of the skullcap or chapel de fer type. Its name possibly derives from the diminutive of *huve*, a type of ladies' coif.

---

15 *Chroniques de Jean Molinet*, ed. J.-A. Buchon, vol. 1 (Paris, 1827), p. 234 and p. 409. I am extremely grateful to the reviewer for sharing these references.
16 See Moffat, *Medieval Arms and Armour: A Sourcebook. Volume I*, p. 226.

L

Langue de boeuf (ox-tongue) (**13, 15, 27**)

a long-bladed staff weapon, the shape of the blade giving it its name.

M

Morrispike (**45, 54, 57, 61, 66, 68**)

a staff weapon of some sort. The appellation 'morris' is Eng. for Moorish which suggests it is of a type of foreign origin.

P

Partisan (**37, 52**)

a staff weapon fitted with a tapering, triangular-shaped blade, often with additional points either side of the base. The name originates in the Fr. for an implacable adherent to one party; a reflection of frequent factional violence and its association with personal bodyguards armed therewith. In both Fr. and Ital. it is a feminine-gendered noun, almost certainly to differentiate the weapon from its (most commonly) male wielder.

Pisan (**1, 3, 17**)

pronounced *peas Anne*, a close-fitting mail collar named after the city of Pisa.

Plançon (**13, 30**)

according to Blair it is 'a club used in Flanders from the late thirteenth century to the early fourteenth'.[17]

---

[17] C. Blair, *European and American Arms, c. 1100–1850* (London, 1962), p. 29.

Figure 32. Partisan, Italian, late-fifteenth century
(New York, Metropolitan Museum, 14.25.209).

Pot gun (**53, 61**)

'A large gun that was probably used as a mortar'.[18]

S

Secret (**7, 65**)

a mail defence borne beneath civilian clothing.

Serpentine (**25, 45, 54, 61, 62, 66, 68**)

a gun that is long relative to its calibre (not unlike the culverin) and varies considerably in size.[19] Spencer charts its use from the 1440s in France to the 1490s and beyond in England, notably on royal ships.[20] See also *Culverin*, *Fowler*, and *Falcon*.

T

Tassets (**17, 26, 59**)

a pair of (often) spade-shaped plates that offer protection to the upper thigh, buckled to straps riveted to the paunce of plate (or fauld) (see Figure 1 and Figure 10).[21] The name derives from Fr. *tasche* or *tasse*: a purse or pouch hanging from the belt. Initially borne as a single pair, a smaller, supplementary pair might be affixed to offer more protection. This explains the meaning of the old cuirass lacking 'ij hynd tasse & j fore tasse' (**17**).

---

18 Spencer, *Royal and Urban Gunpowder Weapons*, p. xvi.
19 Blackmore, *The Armouries of the Tower of London, 1: Ordnance*, p. 242.
20 Spencer, *Royal and Urban Gunpowder Weapons*, pp. 252–6.
21 For the paunce of plate, see its entry in the illustrated glossary of Moffat, *Medieval Arms and Armour: A Sourcebook. Volume II.*

There might also be included in this setup a plate to protect the rump – now known by its seventeenth-century name as the *culet*.[22] The diminutive – tasset – is the form now used in modern scholarship.[23]

Tonlet (**22, 23, 63**)

a hooped skirt of articulating lames. The name is a diminutive of the Fr. word for tun (i.e., cask), the shape of the lames aping the wooden hoops. In modern scholarship tonlet is exclusively reserved for the extensive flaring skirt developed for prearranged foot combats from the outset of the sixteenth century.[24] A fine example is the so-called 'Tonlet armour' of Henry VIII crafted for his foot combat with swords at the Field of Cloth of Gold in 1520 (Royal Armouries, II.7). This armour, according to Viscount Dillon, 'has been called the tonlet, or, as in the Tower inventories it is written, the trundlet suit'.[25] The Viscount is likely alluding to the ledger of the receipts, issues, and returns from the Office of the Ordnance at the Tower of London from 1675 to 1679.

How the tonlet in our sources differs from the paunce of plate is not entirely clear.[26] The survival of three examples in our sources is slim evidence on which to base any detailed interpretation. It may well just be a synonym – especially in Fr. (**23**). On the other hand, there is a temptation to view the other two in a different light. One is a passing comment on armour for fighting on foot (**22**) whereas another (**63**) deals specifically with single combat on foot. It is possible, therefore, that the difference lies in its size and length. Capwell has charted the dramatic increase of the length of cuirass-skirts in the fifteenth century precipitated by the need for better protection and mobility when fighting on foot in a military context.[27] There is another reference that lends weight to this interpretation. An armourer accounting for the harness in his keeping in 1515 that had belonged to James IV, records 'thre pair of tumbletis for fute'.[28]

W

Waster (**19**)

a training sword, the blade's edges 'wasted' (i.e., rebated, blunted) for safety.

---

22 C. Blair, *European Armour, circa 1066 to circa 1700* (London, 1958), p. 80.
23 For their introduction in Europe, see Blair, *European Armour*, p. 81. For a detailed study of their introduction in Italy and England in the 1420s, see T. Capwell, *Armour of the English Knight, 1400–1450* (London, 2015), pp. 132–3, and development in England thereafter, pp. 221–7.
24 Blair, *European Armour*, p. 56 and p. 164.
25 Viscount Dillon, 'Notes on Armour in the Tower', *The Antiquary* 29 (1894), pp. 25–9 (at p. 26).
26 For the paunce of plate, see its entry in the illustrated glossary of Moffat, *Medieval Arms and Armour: A Sourcebook. Volume II.*
27 Capwell, *Armour of the English Knight, 1400–1450*, pp. 125–30 and pp. 221–4.
28 *Acts of the Lords of Council in Public Affairs, 1501–54*, ed. R. Kerr Hannay (Edinburgh, 1932), p. 59.

Bibliography

Unpublished Primary Sources

Brescia, Archivio di Stato, Archivio Gambara

Brussels, Archives de l'État en Belgique/Rijksarchief in België, Chambre de comptes 46397

Dorchester, Dorset History Centre, DC-BTB/FG

Durham Cathedral Archives, Accounts of the Sacrists and Hostillers of Durham Priory

Edinburgh, National Records of Scotland, NAS, PA2

Glasgow Museums, R. L. Scott Library, MS E.1939.65.341, E.1939.65.1144

Glasgow University Library, MS Hunter 252 (U.4.10)

Kew, National Archives: C 66, C 81, E 36, E 101, E 122, E 154, E 159, E 403, E 404, E 405

Leeds, Royal Armouries Library, RAR.0241; I.241

Lincoln, Lincolnshire Archives, DIOC/REG/19

London Metropolitan Archives, London Letter-Book K, Plea and Memoranda Roll A80

London, British Library, Additional MS 27445, MS Cotton Vespasian F. VII

London, Society of Antiquaries of London Library, MS SAL/MS/211

Mantua, Archivio di Stato di Mantova, Archivio Gonzaga, busta 2422

Marseille, Archives départementales des Bouches-du-Rhône, B 2479

New York, Pierpont Morgan Library, MS M775

Nottingham, Nottinghamshire Archives, CA1

Paris, Archives nationales, Chartrier de Thouars 1AP/1669, JJ//195, KK//328

Paris, Bibliothèque nationale de France, MSS fr. 192, 2692, 2695, 5873, 16830, 22335

Southampton Archives, SC 5/4/7–11

Tours, Archives départementales d'Indre et Loire, 3E1/1

Tours, Archives municipales, CC 39, CC 40

Published Primary Sources

Armstrong, C. A. J., ed. and trans., *The Usurpation of Richard the Third: Dominicus Mancinus ad Angelum Catonem de Occupatione Regni Anglie per Riccardum Tercium Libellus* (London, 1936)

Arnould, E. J., ed., *Le Livre de Seyntz Medicines: The Devotional Treatise of Henry of Lancaster* (Oxford, 1940)

Buchon, J. A. C., ed., Olivier de La Marche, *Mémoire sur la maison de Bourgogne* (Paris, 1836)

— ed., *Chroniques de Jean Molinet*, vol. 1 (Paris, 1827)

Carson, A., ed. and trans. with intro. and historical notes, Domenico Mancini, *De occupatione regni Anglie* (Horstead, Sussex, 2021)

Davis, N., ed., *Paston Letters and Papers of the Fifteenth Century*, vol. 2 (Oxford, 1976)

Forestié, E., 'Un mobilier seigneurial du XVe siècle. Le Château de Montbeton en 1496', *Bulletin archéologique et historique de la Société archéologique de Tarn-et-Garonne* 22 (1895), 17–57

Gairdner, J., ed., *The Paston Letters, A.D. 1422–1509*, vol. 3 (London, 1904)

Given-Wilson, C., and others, eds, *The Parliament Rolls of Medieval England, 1275–1504*, digital edn (Leicester, 2005)

Hergsell, G., ed., *Talhoffers Fechtbuch aus dem Jahre 1467* (Prague, 1887)

Jones, P. E., ed., *Calendar of Plea and Memoranda Rolls of the City of London, 1458–82* (1961)

Kerr Hannay, R., ed., *Acts of the Lords of Council in Public Affairs, 1501–54* (Edinburgh, 1932)

Maximilian I, and others, *Der Weisskunig: Eine Erzehlung von den thaten Kaiser Maximilian* (Vienna, 1775)

Merlet, L., *Registres et minutes des notaires du comté de Dunois (1369 à 1676)* (Chartres, 1886)

Mollat, M., ed., *Journal du Procureur Dauvet*, vol. 2 (Paris, 1953)

Monte, P., *Exercitiorum atque artis militaris collectanea in tris libros distincta* (Milan, 1509)

Quatrebarbes, T. de, ed., *Œuvres complètes du Roi René*, vol. 1 (Paris, 1845)

Varin, P., ed., *Archives législatives de la Ville de Reims* (Paris, 1844)

Reference Works

Du Cange, C. du Fresne, sieur, and others, eds, *Glossarium mediæ et infimæ latinatis* (Niort, 1883–7), online edn

Gamber, O., and others, *Glossarium armorum: Arma defensiva* (Graz, 1972)

Gay, V., *Glossaire archéologique du Moyen Âge et de la Renaissance*, 2 vols (Paris, 1887–1928)

Godefroy, F., *Dictionnaire de l'ancienne langue française*, 10 vols (Paris, 1881–1902)

Latham, R. E., and others, eds, *Dictionary of Medieval Latin from British Sources* (London, 1975–), online edn

Lewis, R. E., and others, eds, *Middle English Dictionary* (Ann Arbor, MI, 1952–2001), in *Middle English Compendium*, ed. F. McSparran and others (Ann Arbor, MI, 2000–18), online edn

Martin, R., and others, eds, *Dictionnaire du moyen français* (Nancy, 1998–), online edn

Moffat, R., *Medieval Arms and Armour: A Sourcebook. Volume I: The Fourteenth Century* (Woodbridge, 2022)

— *Medieval Arms and Armour: A Sourcebook. Volume II: 1400–1450* (Woodbridge, 2024)

Owen-Crocker, G., E. Coatsworth and M. Hayward, eds, *The Encyclopedia of Medieval Dress and Textiles of the British Isles, c. 450–1450* (Leiden, 2012)

Simpson, J., ed., *The Oxford English Dictionary* (Oxford, 2004), online edn

Stone, L. W., and W. Rothwell, eds, *The Anglo-Norman Dictionary* (London, 1977–92), online edn

Books and Articles

Beuing, R. and Augustyn, W., eds, *Schilde des Spätmittelalters und der Frühen Neuzeit* (Passau, 2019)

Blackmore, H. L., *The Armouries of the Tower of London, 1:* Ordnance (London, 1976)

Blair, C., *European Armour, circa 1066 to circa 1700* (London, 1958)

— *European and American Arms, c. 1100–1850* (London, 1962)

— 'Early Firearms', *Pollard's History of Firearms*, ed. C. Blair (New York, 1983), pp. 25–32

Blore, E., *Monumental Remains of Noble and Eminent Persons, Comprising the Sepulchral Antiquities of Great Britain* (London, 1826)

Boeheim, W., 'Werke Mailänder Waffenschmiede in den kaiserlichen Sammlungen', *Jahrbuch der Kunsthistorischen Sammlungen des Allerhöchsten Kaiserhauses* 9 (1889), 375–418

Capwell, T., *Armour of the English Knight, 1400–1450* (London, 2015)

— *Armour of the English Knight, 1450–1500* (London, 2021)

Dillon, Viscount, 'A Letter of Sir Henry Lee, 1590, on the Trail of Iron for Armour', *Archaeologia* 51 (1888), 167–72

— 'Notes on Armour in the Tower', *The Antiquary* 29 (1894), 25–9

Eaves, I., and A. V. B. Norman, *Arms and Armour in the Collection of Her Majesty the Queen: European Armour* (London, 2016)

Eco, U., *The Name of the Rose*, trans. W. Weaver (London, 1983)

Fossati, F., 'Per il commercio delle armature e i Missaglia', *Archivio Storico Lombardo*, 6th Ser., 59 (1932), 279–97

Gelli, J., and G. Moretti, *Gli armaroli milanesi. I Missaglia e la loro casa* (Milan, 1903)

Grummitt, D., 'The Defence of Calais and the Development of Gunpowder Weaponry in England in the Late Fifteenth Century', *War in History* 7 (2000), 253–72

— *The Calais Garrison: War and Military Service in England, 1436–1558* (Woodbridge, 2008)

Hope, T. E., *Lexical Borrowing in Romance Languages: A Critical Study of Italianisms in French and Gallicisms in Italian from 1100 to 1900*, 2 vols (Oxford, 1971)

Jones, R. W., *A Cultural History of the Medieval Sword: Power, Piety and Play* (Woodbridge, 2023)

Motta, E., 'Armaiuoli milanesi nel periodo Visconteo-Sforzesco', *Archivio Storico Lombardo*, 5th Ser., 41 (1914), 187–232Schmidt, H., *The Medieval and Renaissance Buckler* (Bregenz, 2022)

Smith, R. D., and K. DeVries, *The Artillery of the Dukes of Burgundy, 1363–1477* (Woodbridge, 2005)

Soil de Moriamé, E. J., 'Armes et armuriers tournaisiens. Heaumiers, haubregonneurs, forbisseurs, couteliers. Contribution à l'histoire des métiers d'art et à l'histoire militaire de Tournai de XIIIe au XVIIIe siècle', *Bulletin de l'Académie royale d'archéologie de Belgique*, unnumbered (1913), 36–154

Spencer, D., *Royal and Urban Gunpowder Weapons in Late Medieval England* (Woodbridge, 2019)

Stothard, C. A., *The Monumental Effigies of Great Britain* (London, 1876)

Sturgeon, J., *Text and Image in René d'Anjou's* Livre des Tournois: *Constructing Authority and Identity in Fifteenth-Century Court Culture* (Woodbridge, 2022)

Zanoboni, M. P., *Artigiani, imprenditori, mercanti: organizzazione del lavoro e conflitti sociali nella Milano sforzesca (1450–76)* (Florence, 1996)

Theses and Dissertations

Moffat, R., 'The Medieval Tournament: Chivalry, Heraldry and Reality. An Edition and Analysis of Three Fifteenth-Century Tournament Manuscripts' (Ph.D. thesis, University of Leeds, 2010)

Tzouriadis, I.-E., 'The Typology and Use of Staff Weapons in Western Europe, c. 1400–c. 1550' (Ph.D. thesis, University of Leeds, 2017)

Wiedemer, J. E., 'Arms and Armor in England, 1450–1470: Their Cost and Distribution' (Ph.D. dissertation, University of Pennsylvania, 1967)

Index

Armour and Weapons

I.

The Artillery of the Dukes of Burgundy, 1363–1477
Robert Douglas Smith and Kelly DeVries

II.

'The Furie of the Ordnance': Artillery in the English Civil Wars
Stephen Bull

III.

Jousting in Medieval and Renaissance Iberia
Noel Fallows

IV.

The Art of Swordsmanship *by Hans Lecküchner*
translated by Jeffrey L. Forgeng

V.

The Book of Horsemanship *by Duarte I of Portugal*
translated by Jeffrey L. Forgeng

VI.

Pietro Monte's Collectanea: *The Arms, Armour and Fighting Techniques
of a Fifteenth-Century Soldier*
translated by Jeffrey L. Forgeng

VII.

The Medieval Military Engineer: From the Roman Empire to the Sixteenth Century
Peter Purton

VIII.

Royal and Urban Gunpowder Weapons in Late Medieval England
Dan Spencer

IX.

The Sword: Form and Thought
edited by Lisa Deutscher, Mirjam Kaiser and Sixt Wetzler

X.

Medieval Arms and Armour: A Sourcebook. Volume I: The Fourteenth Century
Ralph Moffat

XI.
A Cultural History of the Medieval Sword: Power, Piety and Play
Robert W. Jones

XII.
The Thun-Hohenstein Album: Cultures of Remembrance in a Paper Armory
Chassica Kirchhoff

XIII.
Medieval Arms and Armour: A Sourcebook. Volume II: 1400–1450
Ralph Moffat

Printed in the United States
by Baker & Taylor Publisher Services